LARGE-SCALE ENERGY PROJECTS: ASSESSMENT OF REGIONAL CONSEQUENCES

An International Comparison of Experiences with Models and Methods

Studies in Regional Science and Urban Economics

Series Editors

ÅKE E. ANDERSSON
WALTER ISARD
PETER NIJKAMP

Volume 12

NORTH-HOLLAND – AMSTERDAM • NEW YORK • OXFORD

Large-Scale Energy Projects: Assessment of Regional Consequences

An International Comparison of Experiences
with Models and Methods

Editors

T. R. LAKSHMANAN
B. JOHANSSON

International Institute for
Applied Systems Analysis,
Laxenburg, Austria

1985

NORTH-HOLLAND – AMSTERDAM ● NEW YORK ● OXFORD

©INTERNATIONAL INSTITUTE FOR APPLIED SYSTEMS ANALYSIS, 1985

ISBN: 0 444 87724 X

Publisher:
ELSEVIER SCIENCE PUBLISHERS B.V.
P.O. Box 1991
1000 BZ Amsterdam
The Netherlands

Sole distributors for the U.S.A. and Canada:
ELSEVIER SCIENCE PUBLISHING COMPANY, INC.
52 Vanderbilt Avenue
New York, N.Y. 10017
U.S.A.

Library of Congress Cataloging in Publication Data

Main entry under title:

Large-scale energy projects.

   (Studies in regional science and urban economics ;
v. 12)
   Includes index.
   1. Energy industries--Social aspects--Case studies.
2. Energy industries--Environmental aspects--Case
studies. I. Lakshmanan, T. R., 1932-
II. Johansson, B. (Börje) III. Series.
HD9502.A2L373 1985   338.4'7621042   85-1607
ISBN 0-444-87724-X

PRINTED IN THE NETHERLANDS

INTRODUCTION TO THE SERIES

Regional Science and Urban Economics are two interrelated fields of research that have developed very rapidly in the last three decades. The main theoretical foundation of these fields comes from economics but in recent years the interdisciplinary character has become more pronounced. The editors desire to have the interdisciplinary character of regional sciences as well as the development of spatial aspects of theoretical economics fully reflected in this book series. Material presented in this book series will fall in three different groups:

- interdisciplinary textbooks at the advanced level,
- monographs reflecting theoretical or applied work in spatial analysis,
- proceedings reflecting advancement of the frontiers of regional science and urban economics.

In order to ensure homogeneity in this interdisciplinary field, books published in this series will:

- be theoretically oriented, i.e. analyse problems with a large degree of generality,
- employ formal methods from mathematics, econometrics, operations research and related fields, and
- focus on immediate or potential uses for regional and urban forecasting, planning and policy.

Åke E. Andersson
Walter Isard
Peter Nijkamp

THE INTERNATIONAL INSTITUTE FOR APPLIED SYSTEMS ANALYSIS

is a nongovernmental research institution, bringing together scientists from around the world to work on problems of common concern. Situated in Laxenburg, Austria, IIASA was founded in October 1972 by the academies of science and equivalent organizations of twelve countries. Its founders gave IIASA a unique position outside national, disciplinary, and institutional boundaries so that it might take the broadest possible view in pursuing its objectives:

To promote international cooperation in solving problems arising from social, economic, technological, and environmental change

To create a network of institutions in the national member organization countries and elsewhere for joint scientific research

To develop and formalize systems analysis and the sciences contributing to it, and promote the use of analytical techniques needed to evaluate and address complex problems

To inform policy advisors and decision makers about the potential application of the Institute's work to such problems

The Institute now has national member organizations in the following countries:

Austria
The Austrian Academy of Sciences

Bulgaria
The National Committee for Applied Systems Analysis and Management

Canada
The Canadian Committee for IIASA

Czechoslovakia
The Committee for IIASA of the Czechoslovak Socialist Republic

Finland
The Finnish Committee for IIASA

France
The French Association for the Development of Systems Analysis

German Democratic Republic
The Academy of Sciences of the German Democratic Republic

Federal Republic of Germany
Association for the Advancement of IIASA

Hungary
The Hungarian Committee for Applied Systems Analysis

Italy
The National Research Council

Japan
The Japan Committee for IIASA

Netherlands
The Foundation IIASA–Netherlands

Poland
The Polish Academy of Sciences

Sweden
The Swedish Council for Planning and Coordination of Research

Union of Soviet Socialist Republics
The Academy of Sciences of the Union of Soviet Socialist Republics

United States of America
The American Academy of Arts and Sciences

PREFACE

This book is the outcome of a collaborative research project between the International Institute for Applied Systems Analysis (IIASA), Laxenburg, Austria, and the Center for Energy and Environmental Studies, Boston University, Boston, USA. The rationale for the research derives from the need to learn, in industrialized countries, to manage the transition from the pre-1973 world of cheap and abundant oil supplies toward newer flexible energy systems that are better adapted to the likely future economic and energy structures. In the last decade, energy exporters have attempted to expand their capacities for production and export, while energy-importing countries have tried to combine energy conservation and energy supply augmentation strategies. Such large-scale adjustments in energy systems have pervasive effects on the economy, environment, and the social and institutional fabric. Consequently, the ability to implement such changes and attain energy security depends upon the capacity to manage their consequences to be consistent with other socially valued objectives (e.g., price stability, full employment, environmental quality). The project represents an effort to survey the various models and methods used for assessing the consequences of large-scale energy projects and understand, in a comparative framework, the various approaches to manage those consequences in the different decision frameworks and institutional settings of four countries. The results of the project embodied in this book could serve as a reference guide to policy analysts and decision makers concerned with *ex ante* assessments of large-scale energy initiatives.

The project has its origin in a suggestion of the late Boris Issaev, Leader of the Regional Development Group at IIASA, and benefited from his advice and encouragement. The scope of the project was elaborated in discussions with Folke Snickars of Umeå University, Sweden, and the project advisory group comprising Peter Nijkamp, Norman Glickman, Lars Lundquist, and Leen Hordijk. Drawing freely on these discussions, we prepared, jointly with Sam Ratick of Boston University, the project definition paper.

A major component of this study is a review of models and inference structures used in analysis of energy project impacts (economic, institutional, and environmental) − the supporting databases, and the uses of such information in pertinent policy analysis. In this effort, our study emphasized the regional dimension of impact analysis. Second, in order to capture the rich and complex pattern of energy initiatives, their multidimensional impacts, and methods of assessment of such impacts, five case studies of large-scale energy projects in four countries were commissioned. Large-scale adjustments in energy supply and demand, and in economic and environmental systems are inherently surrounded by technological and political uncertainties. Further, these countries — Canada, the USA, Sweden, and the USSR — vary considerably in the objective conditions of energy supply and demand, in their policy formulation and decision frameworks, and in their policy implementation settings. The case studies were consequently intended to elucidate, in these diverse decision-making and implementation contexts, the antecedents and development of the energy investments: how energy crises were perceived; how they were transformed into public policy issues by the various national and regional interest groups; how the scope of energy impact assessment studies was defined; what methods and databases were used in impact analysis; and how these technical study results interfaced with policy-making groups or influenced the energy investment outcomes. The overall study attempted to integrate these two prongs of analysis — the comparative study of impact assessment models and management methods and the rich, complex delineation of energy development case studies — into a broad understanding of the process of policy formulation and decision making on large energy initiatives.

In this task of integration, the study reached beyond the case studies into the broader experience of IIASA and Boston University, in the analysis of interactions between the economy, energy, and the environment on the one hand, and in the understanding of the relationships between scientific analysis and policy formation and decision making in different societies on the other. Further, we sought to bring together individuals trained in different disciplines and operating in a variety of institutional roles in an IIASA workshop with a specially designed format. For each case study, two discussants were selected that were from a different institutional context from that of the case study author. During the workshop, the discussants reviewed the case studies, often providing fresh perspectives to the case study authors and other workshop participants.

The book attempts to capture the salient features of the process of assessment and decision making on large-scale energy initiatives, from initial specifications of the energy problem, through impact assessments, to the final stage of using such studies in policy decisions. Part I of the book presents the case studies of assessment studies and planning efforts in the four countries. The major response of the USSR and Canada to the 1973 energy discontinuity was to increase energy production and exports. The USSR case study focuses on the plan to alleviate a variety of constraints on the production and export of natural gas from a resource frontier to energy-consuming regions in the USSR and Western Europe. The Canadian case study presents the system of monitoring the environmental impacts of tar sands exploitation. The US and Swedish case studies reflect the more complex strategies of energy conservation combined with energy supply augumentation in resource frontier regions as well as in major consumption centers accompanied by major fuel switching.

Part II provides an overview of various models and inference structures used in the assessment of consequences of energy developments from four perspectives. Chapter 6 surveys the variety of national and regional economic models, identifying both the trend in the design of linked models that provide assessments of various economic dimensions of energy project impacts and the various policy issues that have eluded attention in these models. Chapter 7 presents the various policy issues and models developed to assess the effects of boom towns — dynamic developments of the settlements associated with energy resource frontiers such as Colorado, Alberta, western Siberia, Scotland, Norway, etc. Chapter 8 provides a comparative review of the institutional and legal frameworks for assessing the environmental impacts of energy projects in the four countries, and of the variety of models used. Chapter 9 provides an overview of information systems needed to support the assessment of regional impacts of energy projects.

Part III focuses on the decision frameworks and institutional settings in which energy issues are defined, analyzed, and projects are decided upon. The decision and institutional framework in each country reflects the political structure, the constellation of interest groups, and the ground rules for their interaction and conflict management. In the case of energy, when there are sharp changes in the objective conditions of energy supply and demand and where the need for closely coordinated decisions between energy and economic growth, environment, and income distribution exists, decision structures become very complex. Part III delineates the morphology of these decision structures, and the "stylized" links between scientific impact assessment and policy decisions — how the scientific scope of the assessment study is defined and the results used in decision making — in the USSR, the USA, and Sweden. Finally, Chapter 11 provides a retrospective view of the project. It opens with a broad overview of the process of energy decision making and implementation in a comparative framework, to provide a backdrop for identifying the full agenda for impact assessment studies and the effective interface with decision making and implementation. This permits us to highlight the mutual learning from comparative studies and the nature of the tasks to be addressed in future studies of this type.

As in any project of this type, the participants have come away with many subtle unanticipated intellectual dividends. We trust that this book conveys the excitement of this rich intellectual harvest and provides some signposts for policy analysts and decision makers not only in the energy field, but more generally in many fields where large-scale projects are initiated.

A variety of individuals, not all named here, contributed in many valuable ways to the project. We would be remiss if we do not acknowledge in particular the help of Lillian Funk of Boston, Elfriede Herbst, Jean Bolton, Olivia Carydias, and Judy Pakes at IIASA for their efficient, organizational and secretarial assistance — cheerfully delivered in contexts charitably described as hectic. Robert Duis and Val Jones helped in editing the text and coordinating the production of the book. To all of these individuals, we acknowledge our deep debt.

T.R. Lakshmanan
Börje Johansson

LIST OF CONTRIBUTORS

Anderson, W.P., Boston University, Boston, MA, USA
Bolton, R., Williams College, Williamstown, MA, USA
Chalmers, J.A., Mountain West Research, Southwest, Inc., Denver, CO, USA
Chang-i Hua, Boston University, Boston, MA, USA
Creed, S., Boston University, Boston, MA, USA
Hordijk, L. International Institute for Applied Systems Analysis, Laxenburg, Austria
Johansson, B., International Institute for Applied Systems Analysis, Laxenburg, Austria
Lakshmanan, T.R., Boston University, Boston, MA, USA
Lee, R., Oak Ridge National Laboratory, Oak Ridge, TN, USA
Lonergan, S.C., McMaster University, Ontario, Canada
Lundqvist, L., Royal Institute of Technology, Stockholm, Sweden
Nijkamp, P., The Free University, Amsterdam, The Netherlands
Ratick, S.J., Boston University, Boston, MA, USA
Rylander, G., Boston University, Boston, MA, USA
Snickars, F., Umeå University, Umeå, Sweden
Takayama, T., The University of Western Australia, WA, Australia
Watson, W.D., US Geological Survey, Reston, VA, USA
Wilbanks, T.J., Oak Ridge National Laboratory, Oak Ridge, TN, USA
Williams, T., US Department of Energy, Washington, DC, USA

CONTENTS

Large-Scale Energy Projects: Assessment of Regional Consequences
T.R. Lakshmanan and B. Johansson (Editors)
Elsevier Science Publishers B.V. (North-Holland)
© IIASA, 1985

1

CHAPTER 1

Consequences of Energy Developments: An Approach to Assessment and Management

T.R. Lakshmanan and B. Johansson

Introduction

The sharp increases in the price of energy in the 1970s, and rising demand, imposed a serious strain on both the energy supply systems and the economies of many nations. A major mechanism for coping with this situation has been a twofold strategy of promoting conservation policies and increasing the supplies of domestic resources to ensure energy security.

As a consequence of these measures a number of large-scale energy projects have been initiated in several countries. These include projects to extract and convert primary energy in resource frontiers (Canada and the US); the development of large-scale primary and secondary energy supply systems (USSR); and integrated projects combining conservation and conversion of primary energy, distribution of secondary energy, and transmission of final energy (Sweden). While these projects may be localized spatially, their consequences are incident on various activities at many spatial levels (local, regional, national, and international), and have diverse environmental, economic, social, and institutional effects that may persist over long periods of time. In this chapter we outline the characteristics of such large-scale energy developments and their impact pathways, and identify the complex multidimensional and pervasive nature of their impacts.

Such wide-ranging consequences may threaten other social goals (e.g., price stability, full employment, environmental quality) in affluent societies where there is a high demand for amenities. The successful implementation of such large-scale projects to ensure energy security depends upon society's capacity to manage their consequences to be consistent with other valued social objectives. A crucial prerequisite for such management is the compilation of information tracing the chains of interactions from energy projects through economic, social, and environmental pathways to welfare outcomes at the national, regional, and local levels. However, the traditional approach to this analytical problem has generally failed to take into account policy-making structures. Since there is considerable division of responsibility for the control of the determinants of welfare, the role of institutions and their actions affect the processes by which ultimate impacts are incident on society.

In this chapter we explore relevant ideas of organizational and political analysis so as to outline the context of decision making on energy issues. We also examine how institutions cope with uncertainty and how this affects their structure and decision-making information requirements. We proceed to provide a comparative perspective on decision systems in four countries characterized by various degrees of political pluralism.

Out of this broad, integrative discussion of energy decision systems, we adopt a two-pronged approach. The first aspect comprises case studies of four countries, which provide a detailed look at the development of energy projects and the methods and data used in impact analysis, against the background of the diverse technological and institutional settings. The second aspect, consisting of comparative studies, focuses on the models, supporting data systems, and the uses of information in policy analysis that are needed to manage the impacts of energy developments. This book brings together the two strands of analysis in order to develop a broad understanding of the energy impact process.

Energy Developments and Impact Pathways

Prior to the increases in crude oil prices in 1973, national/regional energy planning had to a large extent the character of exercises with aggregate trends. The increases caused shifts in the world economy as regards international income flows and the distribution of purchasing power. Although these shifts were viewed at the time as a major discontinuity, history may judge them to have been very modest. But their effects on the world economy have been far from modest.

For a variety of nations and international organizations, the oil price increases galvanized a wide spectrum of inquiries into energy systems in order to investigate and evaluate possible transitions from current supply systems towards ones that are more resilient and better adapted to the changing perceptions of possible energy futures and corresponding new economic structures. Such perspectives imply that nationwide systems analysis should be brought into the main focus. This also means that long-term changes in energy supply systems should be analyzed as part of structural change in the economy as a whole, including changes in the spatial patterns of activities and settlements. Moreover, this approach cannot avoid taking into account energy developments on a global scale.

Integrated systems analysis of this kind, however, still has a long way to go before it reaches maturity. Attempts to follow a systemwide, comprehensive approach have hampered analyses of regional aspects of changes in energy supply systems and the associated grids, despite the fact that many important effects of the new development are felt at the regional level. Also, the problems of combining and balancing complementary supply systems have to be resolved at the regional level, in a multiregional context. Finally, investments in new supply systems are spatially localized, even though their impacts are spread over space and time. This study focuses on the methods used to assess local large-scale energy developments, as well as the institutional arrangements with which their associated consequences are managed, and attempts to analyze the ways in which development plans are formulated in local, regional, and multiregional contexts.

Energy conversion chains

From a global point of view, the connection between energy supply systems and the spatial distribution of energy demand can be seen as a network of "energy conversion chains", as shown in Figure 1.1 (Häfele 1981). The first stage in such a chain relates to the recovery of primary energy from natural sources: flowing water, wind, natural gas, uranium, oil, coal, peat, and wood materials, etc. Generally, these resources have to be converted to secondary energy (e.g., electricity, gasoline, and gas) and final energy before useful energy is obtained. Secondary energy is thus in a form suitable for transportation and distribution to its end-use locations, but the transformation inevitably results in conversion losses, and its distribution to consumers involves transmission losses. Energy in a boiler exemplifies final energy, while the associated useful energy is hot water for cleaning and for heating.

Schematically, one may identify the sites for primary energy recovery as sparsely populated resource frontier areas, and the end-use locations as urban agglomerations with high levels of energy consumption. This general characterization of energy systems applies on the international, national, and regional levels.

As indicated in Figure 1.1, it is possible to economize at different stages of the energy conversion process, and attempts to increase the efficiency of these processes generally involve technological improvements. However, when such large-scale investments are directed towards a specific point in the energy chain, this is not only a technical issue, and clusters of such projects will have global income distribution effects. The reason for this is evident: not only are primary energy resources and reserves unevenly spatially distributed (both within and between

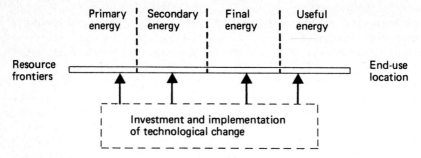

Figure 1.1. Energy conversion chain.

countries), but the various conversion systems along the energy chain are also unevenly distributed. Investments in new processes to reduce end-use energy consumption will thus reduce the demand for all the preceding forms of energy back along the chain. A similar effect also occurs with the introduction of new conversion and transmission systems.

One should also note that increases in the prices of existing primary resources have two effects: (i) it becomes more profitable to invest in more costly processes for extracting primary resources; and (ii) at the same time, these higher prices provide incentives to invest in more costly conversion and transmission systems, including end-use technologies. Of course, the timing of such investments is indeed a decision problem with a game-like structure in which the players are both governments and multinational corporations. Many of these decisions involve "irreversibilities", since once an energy supply system has been installed, the investment costs are really sunk costs.

Development of Energy Supply Systems

From the energy conversion chain in Figure 1.1 it is possible to distinguish several types of large-scale energy developments relating to such processes as:

- extraction of primary energy resources and their conversion to secondary energy for transportation to locations where transformation to more refined forms is possible;
- conversion and distribution of secondary energy to different locations; and
- transmission of final energy to convey useful energy to consumers.

The case studies in this book provide examples of different parts of the conversion chain. There are two examples of large-scale projects for extracting and converting primary energy: the Athabasca tar sands project in Canada, and the synfuels development program in the US. The

network for distributing natural gas from Siberia to markets in Western
Europe is given as an example of a large-scale supply system for primary
and secondary energy. Finally, the integrated process for the conversion
of primary energy, the distribution of secondary, and transmission of
final energy in Sweden is described.

The analysis and assessment of the consequences of a large-scale
energy project may be divided into two aspects. One concentrates on
direct factors such as investment costs, rate of return on investments,
the uncertainty of costs and income flows, etc. The background necessary for assessing such factors requires an analysis of the demand for the
type of energy considered, competition from other energy sources, and
market conditions in general, extending from the local to the international level.

The second aspect of large-scale energy project assessment involves
indirect consequences, such as impacts on the local economy (e.g.,
demand for labor, and the capital required for housing, transportation,
infrastructure, and public services). Other effects include changes in the
pattern of local public expenditures, tax rates, local and national changes
in patterns of energy demand and supply, environmental effects such as
air and water pollution, solid wastes, etc., and the long-term effects on
ecological systems. At the local level all of these impacts affect the distribution of costs and benefits between individuals and groups in society.
Some of these consequences, however, may in turn be related to an
uneven distribution of investment costs, public programs, etc., between
municipalities and jurisdictions.

The assessment of all these impacts requires a complex evaluation
and decision-making structure, as is demonstrated in the Canadian and
US case studies. The degree of complexity is increased in the case of the
design of a new energy supply system, such as the introduction of a district heating system in the Stockholm region. In such cases, the analysis
has to take into account severe synergistic effects; i.e., features of the
system may change drastically when particular parts of it are altered.
Also, the nature of the problem requires a simultaneous analysis of
changes in the supply system and urban structure with corresponding
changes in the spatial distribution of energy demand.

The need for an integrated systems analysis is even greater when
transitions to new combinations of energy supplies for an entire country
are deliberated. The moratorium on nuclear power in Sweden illustrates
such a case; another is the plan to construct a natural gas pipeline from
Siberia to Western Europe.

Scale of Developments and Scale of Impacts

The exploitation of new fossil fuel resources in response to increasing energy demand (apart from some important exceptions) has followed
the Ricardian law: the most productive resources are exploited first, and
as they are gradually exhausted, less productive and thus more expensive

resources have to be utilized. To compensate for this, resource recovery methods have increased in scale, and the search for new resources has extended into less developed and less accessible areas. In such cases, large-scale projects have given rise to the phenomenon of the "boom town".

The rising demand for energy, despite its higher cost, has imposed serious strains on energy supply systems, as well as severe tensions in many national economies. One class of strategies for coping with this new situation has been to promote energy conservation policies, to exploit domestic resources, and to combine various systems into effective grids. The individual programs associated with such strategies are usually small in scale, but together they result in complex system changes and thus can cause large-scale impacts. Such simultaneous processes of reshaping energy supply networks in densely populated areas may not create boom town problems, but more large-scale coordination problems may occur within decision units.

Local Energy Projects as Parts of System-Wide Changes

Large-scale energy projects generate consequences that usually spread over time from the local/regional to the national level. When several such projects are clustered in time, the consequences become even more obvious. To investigate the acceptability of such projects, one may either contemplate impacts of the development on the national economy, or construct economic scenarios to determine the frames within which that development must fit. A more comprehensive approach is to combine these two alternatives, as illustrated in Figure 1.2. Clusters of energy projects will generally have systemwide, lasting economic, societal, and environmental impacts. Given their size, indivisibility, durability, and uncertain pay-back profiles, decisions on such investments must be based on long-term forecasts/scenarios of economic and structural development. These must in turn be founded on energy supply—demand forecasts in which future markets are integrated with international political strategies. Overall assessments such as those illustrated in Figure 1.2 should also be checked for multiregional feasibility; i.e., interregional economy—environment interactions, siting and spatial connections of grids, and associated interregional cooperation/conflict problems.

One has to consider the impacts on several spatial scales: local, regional, national, and international. At the local level the project may create new settlements or boom towns, depending on the nature and the location of the activity. Other consequences may emerge as the need to invest in support services and infrastructure increases, such as distribution networks and transportation systems, housing, schools, etc., as well as public capital and public and private services.

The secondary effects of large-scale projects include both investment efforts and problems of social organization. For the municipalities

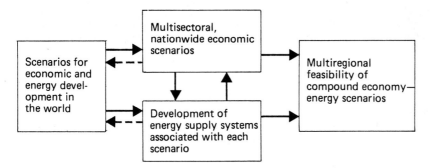

Figure 1.2. Analyzing long-range overall compatability between economic structure and composition of energy supply systems.

that have to provide the necessary capital, this may create severe budgetary problems, since expenditure is required before income from property taxation and external financial support can be raised. Moreover, costs and benefits may be irregularly distributed among the municipalities affected by a project. The distribution of environmental consequences is also complex, since these may be felt in distant areas, e.g., in other states, provinces, or countries.

A model of an impact universe

Causality and Interdependences over Time

In general, impact analysis presupposes the existence of a causal model. Schematically, impact analysis may be based on the following assumptions:

- It is possible to identify and specify the magnitude of an impact generator, $g(t)$, which (possibly in the form of a vector) takes on values for different points in time within a time interval $(0, T)$, so that $g(t)$ is defined for $t \in (0, T)$.[1]
- It is possible to observe or specify a vector of consequences, $c(t)$, $t \in (0, T)$.[1]
- A forecasting model may be represented by a consequence mapping F_t for each time t. If we measure the generated disturbances and consequences in discrete time, this then yields $F_t: [g(0), \ldots, g(t)] \to c(t)$ or, in compressed form, $F_t: \bar{g}(t) \to c(t)$, where $\bar{g}(t) = [g(0), \ldots, g(t)]$.

---

[1] This specification includes the case in which $g(t)$ and $c(t)$ contain 0–1 variables indicating the existence or nonexistence of a phenomenon.

In this procedure there could be a reference trajectory $g*(t)$ and an associated trajectory of outcomes or consequences, $c*(t)$, of the process. In this setting $\bar{g}(t)$ indicates deviations from $g*(t)$, and $c(t)$ signifies deviations from $c*(t)$. With marginal disturbances the analysis is illustrated in Figure 1.3; a partial analysis is sufficient, and the analyst will usually have reliable information on F_t, which relates the time sequence of consequences with the impact-generating process. The less marginal the disturbances are to the system, the greater is the likelihood of structural change. In relation to Figure 1.3 this implies that the structure of the impact mapping F_t becomes more complex. Also, in this case, information on F_t will generally not be available without special research efforts.

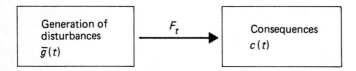

Figure 1.3. The case of standard impact analysis with reliable information on F_t.

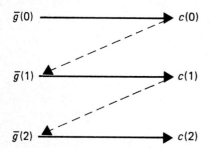

Figure 1.4. Time dependence between system disturbances and consequences.

With non-marginal disturbances the socioeconomic and environmental impacts will be spread over a larger area, so that a partial analysis is no longer sufficient. A wider spectrum of interdependences thus has to be considered, often involving nonlinear repercussions, etc. Moreover, the uncertainties about system responses over time will increase. One way of compensating for this is to increase assessment efforts by utilizing more elaborate forms of systems analysis that can incorporate structural changes and responses from the policy-making process. However, this requires a closer connection between the process of assessment and policy analysis on the one hand, and the actual planning and decison-making process on the other.

Another reaction to situations in which information on F_t is slight may be to concentrate efforts on effective monitoring of impacts and to design adaptive strategies for the decision system. Figure 1.4 illustrates one way of depicting repercussions when the impacts are non-marginal. Over time causes and effects may strongly interact in a dynamic process. Primary effects may become secondary causes at a later stage, leading to unexpected and/or uncontrollable trajectories.

Dimensions of an Impact Space

A fundamental requirement of impact analysis is the specification of an impact space. Which consequences should be derived and specified, and which should not? The way in which this problem is resolved, as indicated in the case studies, naturally reflects the institutional context, since the basic reason for tracing and specifying consequences is to create decision support information.

The consequences that are studied in any particular case may be organized into several broad categories, as indicated in Figure 1.5, where energy project impacts are related to different systems. The classification in Figure 1.5 gives only a rough description of the possible impact dimensions. Large-scale projects generally have multidimensional as well as multilevel and temporal impacts; those associated with different geographical areas and regional levels will have to be dealt with by a hierarchy of decision-making bodies. When all these factors are taken into account, we then obtain an impact universe, as shown in Figure 1.6.

Consequence Dimensions

The four impact categories or areas specified in Figure 1.6 may be subdivided into smaller substantive categories. An outline of such a structure is given in Table 1.1, which illustrates the organization of impact variables into categories.

The different types of impacts evolve along distinct trajectories and extend with time over specific geographical areas. With regard to the spatial dimension one may distinguish between "study area" and "spatial linkages". The study area may be local, regional (subnational), national, or international in scale, and various parts of the study may focus on different spatial areas. For example, a study of resource extraction may analyze consequences at the local level for the assessment of available resources, at the regional level for air quality impacts, and at the local, regional, and national levels simultaneously for some economic effects. To some extent, these examples also demonstrate various types of spatial linkages, as illustrated in Figure 1.7. The spatial category defines the degree to which the analysis incorporates interactions within and between different spatial scales.

The temporal dimension can be represented by two categories: "projection horizon" and "time dependence". The projection horizon denotes the time scales used within the assessment. Distinct types of impacts may require different horizons within one study. If these consequences are interdependent and interact over time, it is essential to capture the

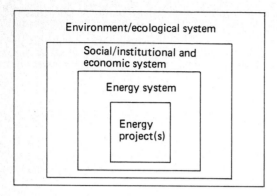

Figure 1.5. Consequences relating to different system categories.

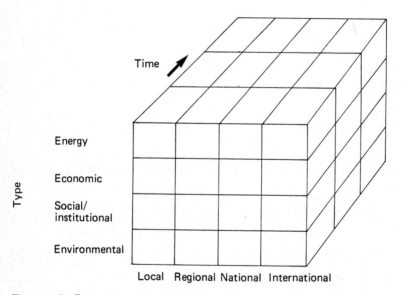

Figure 1.6. Categories of impacts.

time dependences. This cannot be done using a static approach with one single-period analysis or with a non-temporally related multiperiod model.

Managing the Consequences of Energy Projects

The impacts of large-scale energy projects are incident on the national and regional economy, on the energy system, on social and institutional structures, and on the environment in complex and pervasive

Table 1.1. Types of consequences.

ENERGY

- *Demand:* Level and composition; shifts between types (forms of energy and between local/regional and external supply sources; changes in energy-use technologies.
- *Supply of primary energy:* Identification and utilization of resources and reserves.
- *Supply technologies:* Composition of the system of energy conversion chains. Technical change.
- *Other systemic effects:* Complementarity and substitution between components of the supply system.

ECONOMY

- *Production/supply and demand:* Development of sectors such as industry, transportation and communication, residential, services.
- *Capital formation:* Construction and installation of fixed capital; financing investments.
- *Employment:* Supply and demand for labor; employment and participation rates.
- *"Market" effects:* Prices, wages, shortages, queues, etc.; export/import balances; fiscal effects.
- *Household/welfare:* Income and wealth, employment opportunities; distribution between individuals and socioeconomic groups.

SOCIAL SYTEM/INSTITUTIONS

- *Migration and population change:* Number and categories of migrating households; turnover rate for categories of households, etc.
- *Community growth:* New settlements, new infrastructure, and public capital.
- *Social tensions:* Household stability, criminal activity, etc.
- *Tensions in the public sector:* Public sector budgeting, financing investments in schools, health care, etc.
- *Institutional spatial conflicts:* Distribution of costs and benefits between municipalities; interregional, interstate and intercountry impacts like acid rain, etc.
- *Land-use patterns*
- *Induced governmental decisions*

ENVIRONMENT

- *Atmosphere:* Air quality: pollutants, visibility, etc.
- *Water system:* Water quality: pollutants, temperature, etc.
- *Land-use patterns:* Changing areas for production, recreation, wildlife, etc.
- *Ecological systems*
- *Solid and hazardous wastes*
- *Climatic changes*

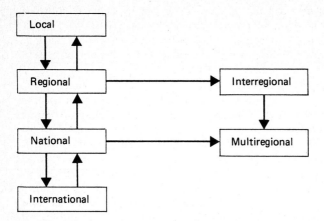

Figure 1.7. Illustration of various categories of spatial linkages.

ways. Prudent policy development and management of an energy supply program must therefore ensure that such projects do not pose serious adverse consequences or threaten other valued social objectives, such as economic growth, full employment, price stability, environmental quality, etc.

A crucial prerequisite to such management is the compilation of information tracing chains of impacts of energy projects through economic, social, and environmental pathways to welfare outcomes at the national, regional, and local levels. Analytically, this is a problem of isolating relationships between the activities of institutions that produce the incremental energy services or those that make decisions affecting energy production and the quality of life. This can be formulated as a problem of developing relationships between energy inputs, policies, and programs, and the resulting social outcomes. Framed in this manner, it is soon evident that the identification of such variables and their relationships is not only crucial to energy policy research, but also to broader problems of evaluation research and policy analysis.

Researchers from a variety of disciplines have attempted to identify and develop these relationships. The current economic paradigm, with its emphasis on the analysis of choice under conditions of scarcity, is a familiar starting point for such analysis. A major drawback of the basic economic model[2] in addressing complex energy impacts, however, is its incompleteness and crucial neglect of the major determinants of welfare outcomes. Individuals or groups rarely control the full chain of events

[2] The basic economic model identifies four sources of variability in welfare outcomes: (*a*) price structure for goods and services; (*b*) production activities and resource use; (*c*) consumer control over and preferences for goods and services; and (*d*) consumer technology used to process resources or goods and services into welfare outcomes.

that link energy investments to ultimate welfare outcomes. In industrialized societies there is considerable division of responsibility — among
groups, private and public institutions, and political bodies — for the generation of social welfare, so that a variety of private, public, and semi-
public institutions affect various aspects of the linkages between energy
developments and final social outcomes.

Consequently, in order to obtain a more complete representation of
the energy impact process, the traditional economic framework of impact
analysis must be broadened to include the roles of institutional structures and networks in this process. One way to accomplish this is to synthesize to some degree two important traditions in decision analysis
(Garn *et al.* 1976): economics (the analysis of choice under conditions of
scarcity) and political and management sciences (the analysis of choice
under conditions of uncertainty). In this section we outline some
relevant ideas of organizational and political analysis. Specifically, we
sketch out the process by which institutions cope with uncertainty and
how this affects their information requirements with regard to energy
decision making. We then provide a comparative perspective on decision
systems in countries with different degrees of political pluralism.

The context of energy decision making

Coping with Uncertainty

Theorists in management and political sciences view organizational
decision making as an effort to cope with uncertainty while making pur-
posive choices (see, for example, Simon 1957, Cyert and March 1963, Dahl
and Lindblom 1953, Thompson 1967). In this view, actors in private or
public institutions attempt to relate goals to available means in a purpo-
sive manner, while making decisions in which they face a wide variety of
uncertainties. Three broad types of uncertainty can be distinguished
(Thompson 1967):

(1) The *internal structure* of the institution: what are the characteris-
     tics of its elements, and how homogeneous are they? Is the struc-
     ture stable or unstable? How routine are the functions of each
     element?
(2) The *external environment* of the institution: how complex is it?
     How stable is the environment in which institutional goals have to be
     validated and from which resources are obtained? How amenable is
     the environment to manipulation by institutional actors?
(3) The level of knowledge about *causal relationships* between institu-
     tional goals and the means available to achieve them at any point in
     time. Examples of such causal knowledge available to decision mak-
     ers include such items as accepted notions of how to manage full
     employment, or how emissions from power stations lead to acid rain.

Decision makers in these institutions collect and use information to help them reduce these types of uncertainties. Such information concerns events or activities and decision-making rules that can order the data in terms of crucial goals/means relationships. This information is then in two forms: (*a*) specific data providing descriptive detail, and (*b*) different kinds of models or inference structures implicit in the behavior governing these data.

While there is general agreement about the need for both types of information, there is considerable dispute among decision theorists about the decision frameworks in which such information is eventually used. Some argue that institutional behavior should be directed by formal rules that ensure either maximum efficiency from a given level of resource inputs, or maximum effectiveness at a given resource level (Hitch and McKean 1965, Quade 1965). Others stress the multiple uncertainties surrounding decision making and postulate an arena of "bounded rationality" in which decision makers search, learn, and work towards solutions in a semistructured context (Simon 1960).[3]

It should be noted that each of these frameworks may be appropriate in different decision arenas. The institution selects a behavior pattern that is relevant in relation to the requirements of its internal structure and external environment. For example, the corporation that is unsuccessful in its efforts to coordinate various subelements will suffer in the market place. Similarly, public bodies or political actors who fail to respond to well articulated values will experience unpleasant feedbacks, so that functional decision-making behavior is learned over time.

In any large organization such as a corporation, government agency, or regional planning agency, the levels and types of uncertainty dictate, in the interests of effective decision making, some division of responsibility in terms of coping with uncertainty. Actors at different levels specialize in particular classes of uncertainty. From this perspective, one can identify decision-making arenas concerned with three levels of authority and control (Anthony 1965):

- *operational*, concerned with the performance of relatively routine tasks;
- *managerial*, dealing with the coordination of linkages between subunits of the institution and the agencies using its outputs; and
- *strategic*, dealing with the relationship between the institution and its environment.

At each of these levels, the functions performed, the primary sources of uncertainty, and the appropriate models and performance standards vary considerably (Table 1.2).

---

[3] Some of this discussion in the field of political science is related to the debate between goal-oriented decision processes and incremental processes. We review this later.

Table 1.2. Structural characteristics and appropriate model structures at different decision-making levels. Adapted from Anthony (1965) and Garn *et al.* (1976).

Level	Functions performed	Major sources of uncertainty	Appropriate model structures and performance criteria
Operational	Operate and control routine tasks	Available causal knowledge on production and consumption processes	Well defined causal models (e.g., from economics, operations research, etc.); universal criteria related to efficiency and effectiveness
Managerial	Manage interdependences between operational level units and the outside world, which supplies inputs and receives outputs	Nature of interdependences within the organization and between the organization and its environment	A "bounded rationality" involving learning—solving sequences. Organization specific tests of effectiveness
Strategic	Mediate between the organization and the environment	Broader environment, particularly in relation to the organization's sector	Loose unstructured procedures for surveillance and focus on major opportunities and challenges

Largely buffered from external influences, actors at the operational level face relatively stable, homogeneous, and responsive environments. They carry out relatively standardized tasks under sets of objectives defined by higher-level actors. In such activities as manufacturing, transportation, construction, energy production and distribution, decision makers must address choices with rigorous, closed-system inference structures or models that indicate choice on the basis of specific efficiency or effectiveness criteria. The rich lode of positivist and normative models in social sciences and systems analysis come into play here.

Functional modes of choice at the managerial level, where there is greater organizational diversity and complexity, and ambiguity and openness with reference to the external environment, are closer to the paradigm of "bounded rationality" with its "satisficing" procedures. These decision procedures involve continuous monitoring of organizational tasks and direct relationships with the environment in order to work out satisfactory solutions to the problems of interrelationships and coordination.

At the strategic level, where institutional resources are mobilized and the overall performance of the institution is accounted for, the

Table 1.3. Major attributes of alternative models of political decision arenas. Adapted from Wilson (1980).

Model / Attribute	Rational	Incremental	Mixed scanning	General systems	Learning–adaptive
1. Key concepts	Structured rationality; scientific empiricism; efficiency, optimization	Disjointed incrementalism; muddling through; process rationality	Self-guiding society; active social self; societal knowledge	Holistic, interdependent, purposive open systems; system design; redesign	New humanism; flexible, adaptive, societal–learning
2. Locus of power	Policy scientists; political leaders	Fragmented among different political leaders and interest groups	Balanced between active public groups and high-level guidance units	System-wide but vertically centered and integrative	Communal and participative; loose networks of small groups
3. Planning and decision process	Problem and goal definition; identify options, evaluate, and choose best; make plan	Fragmented, adaptive; small changes, reactive and remedial; no grand questions	Mixed scanning, long-range scanning and goal setting with short-term probing	Systemic, participatory value search; change processes creative and integrative	Self-organizing learning system, participating and adaptive
4. Role of planners	Professional scientific analysts	Mediators, active participants	Active, integrative mediators among societal knowledge decision-making and consensus-building units	Interactive change agents; dynamic system designers/managers	Stimulator and process designers
5. Political implications	Elitist	Pluralist/ elitist	Combination of communal and high-level elites	Multilevel communal but hierarchically coordinated	Communal, participatory in loose networks

	Positivism	Positivism	Critical of positivism but ambiguous	Systems	Phenomenology
6. Epistemology	Positivism	Positivism	Critical of positivism but ambiguous	Systems	Phenomenology
7. Disciplinary origin	Economics, public administration, management science	Political science, economics	Sociology, political science	Mathematics, physical sciences, management sciences	Social psychology, behavioral sciences
8. Major advocates	Dror, Lasswell, Tinbergen	Lindblom, Wildavsky	Etzioni	Ackoff, Bertalanffy, Gross	Michael Schorr
9. Treatment of values	Initially value-free but values now assessed as factors in analysis	Values emerge as output of process	Efforts to set and realize societal values	Continuous exploration of shared evolutionary values	Both individual and societal values key
10. Major methods	Cost–benefit analysis, decision theory, model building, information technology, systems analysis	Advocate analysis in a competitive bargaining process	Consensus building; new information and feedback	Holistic model building; cybernetic technology	Widespread social learning; innovation and adaptation
11. Major criticisms	Unattainable ideal crippling. Cognitive and data demands social engineering. Reductionistic. Too much focus on technique and methods	Pro status quo, too atomistic, no shared values, can't handle rapid social change	Synthesizing and therefore too compromising	Underdeveloped techniques; mechanistic	Nonrigorous, weakly developed theory; naive, utopian

decision procedures are loose and comprise unstructured surveillance of the environment so as to identify and work on opportunities and challenges.

Many formal organizations approximate the broad outlines of this threefold division of decision arenas. In addition, decision makers in these organizations pursue their goals by not only acting within the constraints set by the given institutional framework, but also by attempting to modify these constraints in their favor. Thus, each institution attempts to influence the authority of the state and to define its own interests in a way that helps the institution. This activity takes place in the political arena, which is mediated by the informal processes of political interaction.

The primary functions of the political arena are to reduce conflicts between social groups and institutions (which constantly attempt to maintain or improve their relative positions), and to make decisions that will influence social outcomes. The level of uncertainty confronting decision makers in the political arena is often higher than that facing them in any other, because of the large array of heterogeneous participants involved. We proceed now to a brief characterization of these political arenas through the use of alternative models of political decision making.

Alternative Approaches to Political Decision Making

Decision theorists suggest that actors in the political arena, surrounded by uncertainty, ambiguity, and conflict, adopt a variety of alternative approaches to decision making. These reflect the varying structures of political arenas as perceived by actors. Five such approaches, as distinguished in the abstract analyses of decision theorists and planners, offer reasonably representative "world views" of actual political behavior. These approaches are (Table 1.3): the rational or goal-oriented approach, incrementalism, mixed scanning, general systems, and the learning–adaptive approach.

The *rational* or *goal-oriented approach* is the dominant view, and has grown out of economic, urban, and defense planning traditions. This approach works in the context of consensual collective demands of citizens willing to accept goals as achieved through instrumental policies and actions. Performance is judged by the ability of decision makers to achieve desired results, such as combating unemployment, ensuring adequate energy supplies, and providing desired levels of environmental quality. Such outcomes are pursued from a positivist perspective, rather than undisciplined speculation. Although there are several factors of positivism, they all influence the logical structure of scientific theory and promote the use of mathematics in the form of decision models from social sciences, management, public administration, etc. This approach is the fundamental paradigm for multilevel decision making in planned economies such as that of the USSR. Although popular for some time, the attachment to one notion of an efficient standard of the public interest has been problematic. There are often wide disparities between the planner's view of rationality and the outcome of political processes in societies where institutions with conflicting interests compete in the decision arena. Thus, the positivist orientation of this rational model has posed serious problems for planners in dealing with the values and goals of individuals and institutions.

The *incrementalist approach*, first advanced by Lindblom (1965), represents a recognition of the uncertainty, ambiguity, and conflict in the political context. Political leaders, faced with disparate demands, try to compromise, bargain and "muddle through". Grand questions and broad goals are avoided, and conflicts are managed without threatening established interests in the form of short-term, incremental adjustments. Small changes — reactive and remedial — emerge from advocate analysis in a competitive bargaining process between interest groups. Such disjointed incrementalism may fit situations of incremental changes in social systems, rather than large-scale or pervasive change. The latter type of change is typified by the implementation of a large-scale energy project, in which excessive fragmentation in constructive policy making, as in incrementalism, can be dangerous.

Given that most political arenas exhibit both universalistic (rational) and particularistic (incremental) attributes, many decision makers employ a combination of goal-oriented and incremental modes of choice. This combination is termed the *mixed scanning approach* (Etzioni 1968), and requires two sets of mechanisms: a high-order, fundamental policy-making process to set basic directions; and an incremental process that prepares for new fundamental decisions and then revises them after they have been reached. When rapid changes occur in the environment or society, with prolonged mismanagement leading to increasing difficulties, the higher-order fundamental review process becomes operative. In democratic societies the mixed scanning model tends more towards incrementalism (because of its need to build consensus), whereas less democratic societies are more able to implement long-term plans. The decision-making behavior of many parliaments, the US Congress, or large government departments exemplify this pattern.

The *general systems approach* views the political arena as open, pluralistic, and integrative. Political processes are viewed as multilevel, communal, and hierarchically coordinated (see Table 1.3). In its ambitious analytical versions, the range of holistic model building, system simulation, and cybernetic technology is brought into play.

The newest, and also the most amorphous, approach is the *learning—adaptive approach*, which has emerged from the humanistic counterculture view of the world. The essence of this phenomenological approach is its view of decision making as social learning. The view here is that society and its institutions are in a continual process of transformation and must learn to guide and manage those transformations. The approach is to invent and develop institutions that are learning systems. Such an approach is relevant to certain multilevel decision contexts where all levels are involved in the participatory decision processes, such as in "boom town" developments.

The above discussion of the attributes of decision arenas suggests that the many institutions involved in decisions on large-scale energy developments — energy companies, production and construction enterprises, national, state or provincial governments, regional planning agencies, and boom town communities — display some mix of the attributes of these five models. The data requirements and model structures for decision making in such contexts will depend upon whether rational or incremental or learning–adaptive modes predominate in the institution. When efficiency or effectiveness criteria predominate (e.g., energy systems choice, etc.), the data and model structures focus on the determination of various impacts on society of different state actions and policies that promote certain energy systems. A variety of positivist models that describe the relationships between public actors and policies and social conditions (with the specification of sectoral influence) will then be brought into play.

While the decision systems in the case study countries share to some degree many of the attributes sketched above, the remaining differences warrant a brief comparative perspective, to which we turn next.

Comparative perspectives on decision systems

Governments are sufficiently similar that institutional decision-making contexts exhibit broad areas of shared attributes. One such attribute is *pluralism*, which describes the interplay of multiple influences in the determination of public policy (Levine 1980). In pluralistic environments, many interests and viewpoints influence public policy through many channels and in many forms. Beyond this, however, the similarities between the USA, Canada, Sweden, and the USSR are limited. The US is more pluralistic than most other Western democracies, reflecting partly its size, its ethnic heterogeneity, and its federal political system. The constitutional structure of the US, with its division of power, magnifies and institutionalizes pluralism. Policy-making power is divided among the executive and legislative branches, and the ability to influence this power resides among various broader institutions and different public and private interest groups. An analogous condition (though characterized by less pluralism) prevails in Canada, with its large size, geographic distinction between energy production and consumption areas, and its federal structure. This high degree of pluralism has important implications in the way energy policy decisions are made, where the complex and multidimensional impacts of energy projects have widespread income distribution and regional effects, thereby increasing the play of pluralism.

In Sweden, in spite of its demographic homogeneity, small size, and its tradition of a social contract, pluralism is evident in the expression of multiple viewpoints (e.g., on the nuclear power issue, on new energy technologies) through many channels. In the USSR pluralism is manifest in the incorporation in the decision process of different perspectives of central planning agencies, ministries, regional groups such as territorial production complexes (TPCs), state governments and the various sectors.

A common feature of all the case study countries is the basic tension in the determination of public policy between the interpretation of public or common interests and the efforts of various partial (or special) interests to improve their positions and to bargain over the distribution of social outcomes (Levine 1980). The distinction between public and special interests lies in the different ways they influence events. The public interests do this through arguments, by suggesting that a recommended policy is preferable for the majority, whereas partial or special interests focus on their own interests and use their political power, collective bargaining, or other forms of power to increase their share of resources (Flathman 1966).

In pluralistic politics, events are influenced in both directions, and the reality of policy analysis (as distinct from the theory of policy analysis) is determined by how both these modes — public or partial interests — mix. Public interest rationality is clearly a strand in which public decision making and well conceived policy analysis (with its battery of arguments) can increase its role. But narrower interests also play roles that vary according to circumstances (Sundqvist 1968).

For instance, US national energy policy in the late 1970s was formulated as a public interest case to reduce demand for scarce imported liquid fuels, and involved a variety of sophisticated market devices to promote conservation and greater use of indigenous resources such as coal and solar power. However, a variety of special interests — some domestic producers (in the south and west), allied with some regional energy-importing interests (in the northeast) whose profits would be adversely affected — reacted against this. What finally emerged was some common interest considerations allied with many partial interest viewpoints. As Levine (1980) points out, even this case, where the role of public interests in the final policy outcome was weak, argues for a greater role for policy analysis in the future. What is needed, however, is a new kind of public policy analysis that focuses on the concept of rational achievement of the common interest but which still incorporates into its concept of rationality the idea that perspectives of partial interests are relevant to the final legislative outcomes.

Such policy analysis will clearly vary from country to country. For instance, in Sweden, with its financially and politically independent municipalities, and its dependence on energy imports, public interest arguments predominate in policy determination. What is common to all countries, however, is the notion that these political institutions and their effects must form a key part of energy policy analysis.

Towards a more comprehensive analysis of energy impacts

The major thrust of the above discussion has been the idea that significant roles are played by a wide variety of institutions and networks in the process by which energy decisions operate through the energy system, and economic, social, and environmental pathways to welfare outcomes at all spatial levels. Unfortunately, studies of the impacts of energy projects (or other public actions) often fail to take account of the institutional structures through which such activities occur and which are highly relevant to both the level and nature of social outcomes. Similarly, approaches developed for policy analysis from disciplines such as political science leave out other important perspectives such as the effects on the distribution of resources or levels of welfare.

If we are to move towards a more complete analysis of energy programs and policies, we should develop bridging paradigms that can be learned and utilized by representatives of various disciplines. These paradigms should identify important relationships between the major conceptual and methodological concerns of partial research traditions used in decision analysis. They should permit both the effective integration of analyses carried out within narrower disciplinary bounds, and should also promote research based on models that combine the analytical power of the component disciplines.

It has been suggested that such a framework may emerge from bridging two important traditions in policy research — the analysis of choice under conditions of scarcity and the analysis of choice under conditions of uncertainty (Garn *et al.* 1976). Such a synthesis would permit both the objectives and processes of choice to be taken into account simultaneously. Such an interactive approach is needed not only from an aesthetic viewpoint of intellectual completeness, but also to help in the avoidance of critical failures in many areas of policy analysis.

What currently exists in the form of such synthetic frameworks are, however, little more than broad range of conceptual sketches that need quite a bit of refinement of their frameworks and demonstration of usefulness in a variety of policy studies. Although we have no such integrative model to follow, we now use the implications of the above discussion as a guide with which to structure our study of large-scale energy projects.

The Study Strategy

The objective of this book is to provide an international comparative analysis of the experiences with models and methods of assessing the regional impacts of large-scale energy projects. To this end, we adopt a two-pronged approach, involving case studies and comparisons of assessment methodologies, that is broadly consistent with the characteristics of the energy impact process detailed above.

The analysis of energy impact processes is a field of research that lends itself particularly well to the case study approach, since we can classify the specific decision context, analyze the sequence of policy decisions, and the strategy choices that are made over time. Such an approach also has the advantage that features unique to one case study can be taken into account, as well as those that are generic. These qualities account for the widespread use of case study material.[4]

It is useful to draw attention to three broad categories of generalization that can be drawn from the case study findings (Adelman *et al.* 1977). The first involves generalizations from particular case features to a multiplicity of classes by reference to formal theories in experimental research. This is perhaps the most poorly developed of the three categories, and least expected in our study. The strength of the case study method lies essentially in the other two categories of generalization: (*a*) generalizations from the case being studied to other cases assumed to be in the same class, and (*b*) generalizations about the case itself that follow from a detailed investigation.

Such "between-case" generalizations may suggest limited comparisons, whereas "within-case" generalizations add detail in terms of project history and development, the policy issues posed, analytical methods and data systems, and the reality of policy analysis. With reference to the latter, as each case study clarifies the institutional decision context, we learn about the interactions between analysts and policy makers, the role of policy analysis in decision making, and the interplay between policy analysis and other inputs to decision processes, such as precedent, partial interests, etc.

The comparative review studies, on the other hand, represent a series of cross-cutting analyses of specific elements of impact analysis. Such studies focus on (i) models and methods for assessing economic, environmental, and local/regional impacts of energy investments; (ii) the nature of information systems for impact assessment; and (iii) role of policy analysis in theory and in practice.

Methodologically, we are attempting to bring together people from several disciplines — economics, geography, operations research, urban planning, management science, policy analysis, and environmental systems — to focus on the problem and see if they can *talk to and listen to* one another. We have asked some of these specialists to play amateur historians while they prepared and commented on the case studies. When an author of a comparative study listens to an amateur history of a

---

[4] The pioneer development of the case study method by the Harvard Business School to train management students was to alert students to the range of possibilities and uncertainties surrounding management decisions (Dewing 1954). Another example is the preparation of case studies by the OECD documenting development control processes that facilitate greatly the international transfer of the urban management experience (Masser 1982).

case study, he acquires a large body of facts and descriptions — with some explanation as to why things happened the way they did — somewhat buried in the folds of the narrative. When amateur historians listen to a comparative study of models and decision systems they will find tightly developed arguments based on carefully defined terms and relations, but not open to the rich and complex detail of the case study experience. It is our hope that this book brings together these two prongs of analysis, to combine the fertility and the sensitive regard for individual experience of one with the formal rigor of the other, and thus develop a broad under-standing of the energy impact process.

References

Adelman, C., Jenkins, D., and Kemmis, S. (1977) Rethinking case study: Notes from the 2nd Cambridge Conference. *Cambridge Journal of Education* 6:139–50.

Anthony, R.N. (1965) *Planning and Control Systems: Framework for Analysis* (Cambridge, MA: Harvard University Press).

Cyert, R.M. and March, J.G. (1963) *A Behavioral Theory of the Firm* (Englewood Cliffs, NJ: Prentice-Hall).

Dahl, R. and Lindblom, C.E. (1953) *Politics, Economics and Welfare* (New York: Harper and Row).

Dewing, A.S. (1954) An introduction to the use of cases, in P. McNair (Ed) *The Case Method at the Harvard Business School* (Cambridge, MA: Harvard University Press).

Etzioni, A. (1968) *The Active Society* (New York: Free Press).

Flathman, R.E. (1966) *The Public Interest* (New York: Wiley).

Garn, H.A., Flex, M.A., Springer, M., and Taylor, J.B. (1976) *Models of Indicator Development*. Urban Institute Working Paper 1206-17 (Washington, DC) April.

Häfele, W. (1981) *Energy in a Finite World: A Global Systems Analysis* (Cambridge, MA: Ballinger).

Hitch, C.J. and McKean, R.N. (1965) *Economics of Defense in a Nuclear Age* (Boston, MA: Atheneum).

Levine, R.A. (1980) Analyzing United States policy making, in C.R. Foster (Ed) *Comparative Public Policy and Citizen Participation* (New York: Pergamon) pp 3–26.

Lindblom, C.E. (1965) *The Intelligence of Democracy* (New York: Macmillan).

Masser, I. (1982) The analysis of planning processes: Some methodological considerations. *Environment and Planning* B9:5–14.

Quade, S. (1965) *Systems Analysis*. Rand Analysis Memorandum, Santa Monica, California.

Simon, H.A. (1957) *Administrative Behavior* (New York: Macmillan).

Simon, H.A. (1960) *The New Science of Management* (New York: Harper and Row).

Sundqvist, L.J. (1968) *Politics and Policy* (Washington, DC: The Brookings Institution).

Thompson, J.D. (1967) *Organization in Action* (New York: McGraw-Hill).

Wilson, D.E. (1980) *The National Planning Idea in US Public Policy: Alternative Approaches* (Boulder, CO: Westview Press).

PART I

Regional Consequences of Energy Projects in Four Countries

This book attempts to capture important aspects of the regional consequences of the siting of large-scale energy projects and assessments of their effects in four countries. It considers the entire assessment process from the stage of problem identification and formulation to the final stage of transforming the results of an assessment to the policy conclusions.

Part I describes case studies in four countries. It provides information about how various methods have been used in practice and gives insights into how institutional frameworks and decision contexts influence the design of assessments and the selection of methods and approaches.

Chapter 2 reports on assessments and planning efforts related to natural gas development in Western Siberia. Chapter 3 examines studies of tar sands developments in Alberta, Canada. Chapter 4 contains two reports: one investigates environmental feasibility studies initiated to support decisions relating to President Carter's Synfuels Acceleration Program, and the second describes an impact information system in Colorado, which was designed to bring about a better coordination between investment plans of industry and associated decisions made by state authorities and local governments. Chapter 5 reports on one nationwide and one regional study in Sweden. The aim of the first study was to support a referendum on the abolition of nuclear power, and the second was initiated to evaluate alternative ways of redesigning the energy supply system of the Stockholm region.

In Chapters 3–5 the case study reports are followed by one or two review sections that evaluate the reports from a broader, international perspective. The reviews comprise critical evaluations of the methods applied, gaps in the analyses, and the policy relevance of the studies. They also compare the studies with other, similar assessments performed in the same, as well as other countries, so that the generic aspects of each case are identified. Moreover, the reviews shed light on the possibilities of transferring experiences of one case to other institutional and decision contexts.

For each assessment study the corresponding review investigates its objectives and the associated policy issues. It describes the category of clients, sponsors, and interest groups that formed the decision context and policy importance of each study. The assessment results are presented, and the interface between analysts, study results, and the policy-making process is examined.

Each assessment project is also characterized in terms of impact dimensions, types of methods utilized, time scales of the consequences traced, and the spatial scales covered by the analysis.

Large-Scale Energy Projects: Assessment of Regional Consequences
T.R. Lakshmanan and B. Johansson (Editors)
Elsevier Science Publishers B.V. (North-Holland)
© IIASA, 1985

CHAPTER 2

The Development of Natural Gas Deposits in Western Siberia[1]

F. Snickars and B. Johansson

The West Siberian Plain: National and International Perspectives

Size and location of the gas resource

In recent years industrialized countries have revealed a growing interest in natural gas as an energy source. There are two obvious reasons for this change in attitude. First, in the 1970s the world gradually became aware of the imminent exhaustion of oil resources, which would be accompanied by increasing scarcity prices of oil products. Second, processes using gas cause less environmental damage than those based on oil, coal, and similar fossil fuels. This has caused the USSR to view Europe as an important and growing market for its gas exports. The USSR's internal demand for oil products has been satisfied by domestic resources in the past, but recent demand and supply projections imply that this situation may become gradually more difficult to maintain. An obvious way to continue the established state of self-sufficiency is to utilize the country's vast gas resources and to substitute gas for oil. Hence the Soviet plans to develop the Siberian natural gas deposits at an accelerated rate stem from a combination of international and domestic conditions.

It is indeed relevant to consider the West Siberian gas fields in a global perspective, since the resource potential is also significant in a world market context. East of the Urals, the West Siberian basin occupies an

---

[1] This chapter is based on a paper by Yurij Maximov, which was delivered to the workshop at IIASA in February 1983: an equally important source is Kotchetkov (1984). Additional information comes from earlier work done at IIASA.

area of over 2 million km^2. The northern part contains the world's largest concentration of oil and gas reserves: about 18 billion barrels of oil
and 545 trillion cubic feet (Tcf) of gas. The resource potential has been
estimated to include an additional 54 billion barrels of oil and at least 948
Tcf of gas (Meyerhoff 1980, 1982).

As shown in Figure 2.1, the basin is bounded on the west by the
Urals, on the east by the Siberian platform, and in the south by the Kaza-
khstan fold belt. One of the fields in the basin, Urengoy, is the world's
largest, and contains more proved gas than is left in the entire United
States (Meyerhoff 1982). This field may soon supply much of the nation's
gas, as well as a sizeable amount of the gas consumed in Europe.

Figure 2.1. The West Siberian plain.

The role of West Siberian development in the national economy

The USSR is a petroleum-oriented country; only 30% of its energy
needs are supplied by coal, and more than 60% by oil. In 1980, about 60%
of the oil and more than 30% of the gas came from Western Siberia (Meyerhoff 1982, Maximov 1983). A major part of future expansion in energy
consumption is also expected to be covered by increased supplies from
this region, which implies that an increasing share of the demand growth
west of the Urals will be met by supply from regions east of the Urals.

Table 2.1 describes the composition of various energy sources in the
Soviet energy supply system. The table also shows that in the period

Table 2.1. Energy sources in the Soviet energy system: composition and change (from Maximov 1983).

	Production level 1980	Annual growth 1965–80 (%)
Gas ($10^9 m^3$)	435	8.2
Electric power (10^9 kWh)	1295	6.3
Oil (10^6 tons)	603	6.1
Coal (10^6 tons)	716	1.4
Total energy (million tons coal equivalent: 10^6 tce)	1970	4.7

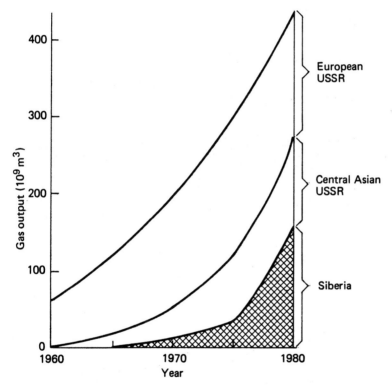

Figure 2.2. Geographical composition of Soviet gas output, 1960–80 (Maximov 1983).

1965–80 the fastest growing source was natural gas, while the supply of coal stagnated. Projections for 1980–90 indicate that energy production in the USSR will increase by 35–45%, and that the share of gas in the energy balance will grow significantly (Maximov 1983). An expanding proportion of the gas output is expected to come from Western Siberia, following the trend developed during 1965–80 (see Figure 2.2).

The West Siberian gas development project will play an important role in the plans for the entire Soviet economy; in particular, it will contribute significantly to the future national energy balance. Potentially it will also generate substantial export sales, and the project has been designed in such a way that it will promote further industrial development east of the Urals.

The West Siberian gas project is a gigantic territorial production complex (TPC), and this stresses its national importance. TPCs are the instruments through which long-term goal-oriented programs in the USSR are implemented; they constitute a form for designing such elements in the spatial organization of production which aim to achieve goals of overall national importance (Issaev 1982). They can also be considered as fundamental methods of inducing and stimulating structural change in the economy.

National and international gas demand

According to Maximov (1983) the West Siberian TPC has been developed to fulfill the following objectives:

- to compensate for the depletion of high-grade energy resources in the Urals region and the regions west of the Urals;
- to stimulate the location in Siberia of energy-intensive enterprises and chemical industries that will use gas as an input;
- to accelerate the installation of gas services in the region; and
- to enlarge the basis for exports of natural gas and derived products such as synfuels.

The focus on the possibility of exporting gas to Europe seems to be a natural reaction to the development of international energy markets in the 1970s. However, as already pointed out, the internal problem of matching consumption and production of energy is regarded as the main driving force behind the intensified investments in the resource frontiers east of the Urals. From this perspective, the plans for the gas network to Western Europe have been motivated by reasons of economics of scale.

As indicated in Figure 2.1, the distances between the extraction and consumption centers are enormous. Maximov (1983) reports that between 1960 and 1970 the length of gas pipelines increased more than threefold; between 1970 and 1980 the length was more than doubled, and reached an average of 135000 km in 1981. This corresponds to huge infrastructural investments that require a high capacity utilization in order to be economically feasible. Thus, an extended export market with long-term contracts can help to ensure such economic utilization. It should be emphasized that the gas pipelines and associated facilities comprise only a part of the infrastructural investments. The whole West Siberian region has no more than 9 million inhabitants, and the future exploitation of the gas fields will require large investments in road networks and settlements.

With this background, project planning has involved careful delibera-
tion of the export potential and projections of price patterns of energy
products. As an illustration of the understanding in the USSR about the
future energy situation in Western Europe, Maximov (1983) has presented
the projections shown in Table 2.2. The construction of pipeline networks
in Western Europe has also been used as an indicator of the potential
market for gas deliveries. At the same time, estimates of price changes
of oil and coal products have also been essential in the evaluation of the
competitiveness of Soviet gas exports. As regards the West Siberian gas,
transportation accounts for 70% or more of the total supply costs.

Table 2.2. Energy consumption structure in Western
Europe (%). From Maximov (1983); see also OECD
(1980).

	1974	1985	1990	1995
Oil	58.7	48.2	48.3	49.8
Coal	21.2	21.9	20.4	19.0
Gas	11.7	14.2	13.9	13.5
Nuclear	1.7	7.3	8.8	10.1
Other	6.7	8.4	8.6	7.6

Characterization of the Gas Development Project

National and international assessment dimensions

The West Siberian TPC (WS-TPC) constitutes an investment project of
a size that goes far beyond the size of others considered in this book.
Moreover, the project aims at integrated regional development, so that
assessment and evaluation have to be truly multidimensional and
comprehensive.

As in all other TPC projects the top-down perspective dominates the
evaluation. However, as described below, multiregional consistency is a
fundamental constraint, so that bottom-up exercises must also be
included in the assessment process. At the national level the evaluation
must comprise (i) the allocation of capital to natural resource areas; (ii)
institutional development in the regions considered; and (iii) standards of
living in the regions (i.e., the aspect of equalization between regions; see
Aganbegyan 1982). This includes assessment of intersectoral compatibil-
ity over time, feasibility of interregional transportation, and national and
multiregional aspects of labor force allocation.

The size of the project is also such that it will have significant
impacts on the gas market in Europe, and on the international energy
market in general. The time span considered in the national assessment
is indicated by Maximov (1983). Two sequential phases are considered:

1966–85 and 1985–2005, although some parts of the national and international analyses extend to the year 2020.

Regional assessment dimensions

Chapter 1 specified four assessment and design categories: (i) the energy system, (ii) the economy, (iii) the social system, and (iv) the environment. With regard to WS-TPC these dimensions can be organized as follows:

*   *Energy system.* Resource assessment; assessment and design of extraction technology; assessment and design of distribution systems.
*   *Economic system.* National linkages in TPC design; assessment and design of the integrated TPC production system and its operational organization; implementation analysis of investments in plants, transportation and distribution systems, and settlement systems; regional development outside the TPC organization.
*   *Environment and social systems.* Assessment of boom town phenomena; analysis of social problems specific to Arctic regions; ecosystem analysis.

Available information indicates that the assessment of West Siberian energy resources has only gone through an initial phase. Oil exploitation activities in the area started as early as 1912, with more serious exploration only after 1948; intensive geophysical surveys were carried out only after 1953. Of particular interest is the question of whether the area contains oil below the gas condensate at the lowest examined levels. According to Meyerhoff (1982) drilling has not been sufficiently deep to determine whether the gas condensate in the northern part of the plain is just above the oil window or not. He believes that the oil window may not yet have been reached. Also, large areas of potential gas resources are as yet unexplored. Maximov (1983) includes unconventional sources such as crystalline hydrates as other potential resources in the region. New extraction technologies to be used in 1985–2005 and thereafter are mentioned by Maximov (1983) as ongoing assessment problems. He also discusses the distribution of liquefied gas as a future option to be examined, with the distribution of chilled gas as the short-term solution.

The WS-TPC is one of the country's largest national programs so that both national and international aspects are covered in national long-term planning. However, the regional organization of the TPC is also assessed and designed at the national level, as described below. The focus of economic analyses has changed, concentrating on oil and gas extraction in 1966–85 and power plant construction in 1985–2005. Plans for the latter period also include the creation of integrated complexes for the petrochemical, chemical, and power industries.

Climatic conditions in the area continue to be fundamental factors in the assessment of economic, social, settlement, and environmental aspects of the WS-TPC. Most of the basin is low and flat; the spring thaw begins in the south and causes flooding early in the year. This flooding converts the entire region north of the Middle Ob River into a quagmire in which field operations become extremely difficult and expensive, so that construction activities can only take place in winter. Maximov (1983) characterizes the region as comprising taiga, tundra, lakes, swamps, numerous rivers and tributaries, permafrost, and sharp temperature and weather contrasts.

All these features require careful planning of the construction of pipeline networks and compressor stations, interfield roads, storage and transshipment terminals, as well as settlements such as centers for interregional systems, local centers of production, industrial centers, and temporary and permanent industrial villages.

The ecosystem in the northern part of the region is very sensitive to disturbances. For inhabitants in the area, biological clocks easily fail to synchronize with the length of days in mid-winter and mid-summer, leading to a high frequency of the so-called "Rusca reaction" (the Finnish name for "autumn depression") that starts at the onset of winter and which may cause psychotic states (Rey 1982).

The TPC Concept and the Planning Process

Overview of the planning process

In overall economic planning in the USSR, regional and multi-regional aspects are extremely important: regional plans are not just regional breakdowns of national plans — the latter also have to satisfy multiregional consistency. Naturally, this is complicated by the structural changes introduced in the form of TPCs.

It is important to observe that in the USSR planning includes all activities to ensure the fulfillment of plan targets (Issaev 1982) so that, to a certain degree, the plan *is* the economic system. Theoretically, the planning system is the form in which the socioeconomic system functions. Figure 2.3 gives a simplified schematic picture of the basic elements in the planning system, and shows how TPC elements cut through all levels of the system.

Special resource-oriented assessment and planning (such as TPCs) include large-scale projects such as oil and gas extraction in Western Siberia, the construction of large hydropower plants, railway network developments in Eastern Siberia, and brown coal extraction. As a project is gradually completed and its operation stabilizes, then the TPC planning is phased out and is replaced by less centralized regional planning (Issaev 1982).

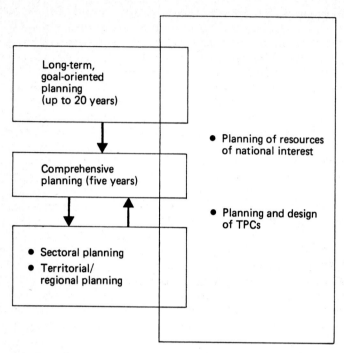

Figure 2.3. Schematic representation of the Soviet planning system, and its integration with TPC design.

TPC design activity represents development planning, and has three main objectives: (i) to determine the principal directions of national plans and resource allocation for specific areas and projects; (ii) to promote intraregional cooperation and to assign labor to areas of intense economic development; and (iii) to formulate regional policies that utilize labor-saving technologies and encourage technologies suitable for the climatic conditions in Siberia (Aganbegyan 1982).

In parallel with normal planning activities, resource development in Siberia has also been analyzed in qualitative, overall assessment studies (Granberg 1982). In order to ensure multiregional feasibility and consistency between national and regional levels (see Figure 2.3), coordination planning and assessment of multiregional feasibility is carried out (Baranov and Matlin 1982). The assessment and planning of projects at detailed regional levels also makes use of implementation-oriented design analysis (Alekseyev 1982).

Multiregional assessment of West Siberian development

The importance of multiregional analysis in national economic planning in the USSR is in particular due to extremely diverse socioeconomic
and resource conditions in the different regions and the immense distances between regional centers. Background studies, with special reference to the West Siberian development, have been carried out with the
help of interregional input–output optimization models such as SIREN-
OPT or IIOM (Granberg 1982a,b). In such models a Chenery–Moses
approach is applied to capture interregional couplings. Granberg
discusses two aspects of exercises conducted with SIREN-OPT: (i) centralized preplanning at the national economic level, and (ii) coordination of
regional designs.

A basic SIREN-OPT model includes regional balances of sector outputs, transportation, labor resources, and regional and national investments. The main endogenous variables are regional production, consumption, and interregional deliveries. The primary use of the model is to find
the optimal national consumption, given prespecified lower consumption
levels in the different regions, so that Pareto-optimal solutions are generated. By varying the regional constraints one can obtain assessments
of alternative priorities in multiregional policies in the form of trade-off
information. Such analyses have been used for two time periods, 1966–75
and 1976–90. With regard to the first period the model results indicated
that development rates for Siberia would exceed those for the Soviet
economy as a whole, and that priority should be given to the development
of mining in Siberia. This finding was based on dual prices of production
capacities that were used to identify bottlenecks in production.

Special assessment analyses of Siberian development have been carried out, which confirmed that relocation of labor to this region would
increase national consumption levels. The same conclusion was also
drawn from analyses of increasing the investment proportions allocated
to Siberia. Recommendations and conclusions of this type are likely to
have contributed to preplanning considerations, although the type of
modeling represented by SIREN-OPT is not included in the final Gosplan[2]
development analyses and plan formulation processes.

TPC planning: Assessment and design

For each TPC, demographic factors, service systems, and the natural
environment are analyzed simultaneously to produce the targets and
objectives defined at the national level. Not all aspects of TPC planning
are analyzed with formal models. According to Aganbegyan (1982), the
long-term optimization models of production and spatial patterns are the

---

[2] Gosplan, the Soviet state planning agency.

most advanced components.. Medium-term simulation models are also used.

The WS-TPC comprises a system of facilities that adheres to inter-related national economic sectors. These are organized in accordance with a specially devised plan that considers labor and natural resources. The plan ensures that resources are utilized efficiently according to national criteria, that environmental restrictions are not violated, and that ecosystems (renewable resources) remain in balance. The plan also contains designs for the infrastructure associated with TPC production systems (Bandman 1982).

Within a TPC development priority is given to those resources that can be efficiently utilized with respect to the national economy, and from this one obtains a specification of the tasks of the TPC. This criterion also determines the degree to which a resource should be used, and to which it should be processed and refined within the TPC. TPC components are not evaluated individually, but as interrelated parts of the TPC as a whole. Hence, TPC design aims at system optimization (Bandman 1982). The structure of the WS-TPC up to 1985 is described in Table 2.3, which shows that the share of gas in total output has been increasing steadily, while the planned expansion of power, chemical, and petrochemical output has had to be realized at later stages of development.

Table 2.3. Industrial structure of the WS-TPC (%). From Maximov (1983).

Industries	1960	1970	1975	1980	1985
Oil	—	19.4	38.8	46.0	34.8
Gas	—	3.4	5.3	14.3	22.2
Power generation	1.2	1.8	3.0	3.5	4.5
Machinery and metal products	14.7	17.3	13.8	11.5	12.4
Chemical and petrochemical	2.3	2.1	0.8	0.5	4.3
Building materials	2.5	3.7	3.3	2.8	3.3
Food	41.9	22.6	14.7	7.2	6.4
Pulp and paper	24.6	18.2	10.3	5.5	4.8
Light industry	12.8	11.5	10.0	8.7	7.3
Total	100.0	100.0	100.0	100.0	100.0

Assessment of multiregional feasibility: Coordination analyses

In the 1970s the model SMOPP was used for coherent optimization of sectoral and regional planning with special attention to transportation of certain important products, and with specific constraints on labor allocation and the use of natural resources (cf. Issaev 1982). In 1980 a more refined approach was developed under the name SMOTR. This model is used to simulate and evaluate alternative policies, and operates with a three-level system of models (Baranov and Matlin 1982):

(1) National level. Production patterns for 18 aggregate industries are determined in accordance with goals for national socioeconomic development.
(2) National level, but production is disaggregated into 260 different products. Sectoral and regional indicators are checked against corresponding national aspects of the plan.
(3) Regional/local level, which is assigned to detailed calculations with regard to industrial complexes and for entire regions.

In various modules the system covers such aspects as population and labor resources, income and consumption, service supply, financial balances, foreign trade, natural resources, and the environment. On the first level an interactive dialogue technique is used to obtain consistency, while the second level applies an iterative aggregation procedure to make the 260-product pattern compatible with the 18-sector pattern. At the same time, regional indicator consistency is checked.

Implementation-oriented design analysis

The TPC analysis is broken down not only to intraregional interactions but also to the design of the interactions between specific operational systems. At the regional level network models are used to assess and design transport accessibility linkages, resource delivery linkages, technological constraints for construction, operational distribution linkages, and interactions between interrelated plants.

Alekseyev (1982) describes the structure of those network models which adhere to the tradition of the program evaluation review technique (PERT) and the critical path method (CPM), both of which are established operations research tools for large coordination problems in which time schedules are important. Combinations of simulation and programming approaches have also been used. Network models are included in detailed TPC planning. Also, when the formal framework is less sophisticated than that described by Alekseyev (1982), the models reflect that basic approach to TPC planning.

Overview and Conclusions

Development consequences in Western Siberia

The gas and fuel TPC projects in Western Siberia will have strong and lasting consequences for the future development of the region. Granberg (1982a) has outlined certain overall expected consequences as follows:

- The problem of labor supply in Siberia is likely to be aggravated because of a sharp fall in the birth rate and an increase in migration from the region.
- Demand for investments will continue to grow due to capital-intensive industries and the necessary infrastructural developments.
- It has been estimated that Siberia's share of the national output will increase by around 2% per annum in the 1980s. At the same time, the region's share of total national investments may grow by more than 15% per annum.
- There will be a rapid increase in the number of settlements in the region, and large-scale labor force relocations will be necessary.

National and international consequences

Gas deliveries to population centers to the west of the Urals will compensate for the projected future depletion of energy supplies in these areas. Maximov also mentions that there will be a cost effect. In the European USSR the cost of using West Siberian gas will be around 60% of that of using coal from the Moscow basin. At the same time, there will be a continuing strong competition between the two sides of the Urals as regards the allocation of investment funds.

The increased gas supply from Siberia will have strong effects on West European markets. First, there will be an impact on the development of prices of various energy carriers in those markets. Second, if the West European countries respond in the 1980s to the potential change in supply by extending their gas pipeline network systems, this will cause permanent structural change in European energy markets. Maximov (1983) presents assessments of the project "Gas Pipes", which is described as a set of agreements between the USSR and a number of West European countries on deliveries of Soviet gas. According to initial plans deliveries will continue over a 25-year period starting in 1984. A full-scale implementation of this project may lead to a situation at the end of the century in which Soviet gas deliveries will account for about 30% of the West European gas market. Currently, the main importers are expected to be the FRG, France, Italy, and Belgium, while competitors in the same export market would be North Africa, Norway, and Denmark, given that the other gas-producing countries in Europe are regarded as domestically oriented suppliers.

Within this long-term perspective, the USSR may also enter the market for liquefied gas expected by the end of the century, by which time this market in Western Europe may have reached 30 billion m^3 (Maximov 1983).

Reflections on the assessment methodology

The assessment approach and planning system outlined above is extremely schematic; the planning procedures involve much more than just model exercises. Of particular importance are the negotiations between planning bodies for the various sectors and organizations responsible for national and regional aspects of the plan documents. From this point of view one could perhaps describe the planning system as being composed of interactions between assessment analysis, negotiation, and final plan determination. It is also important to observe that to a large extent, plan formulations emerge from routine procedures in which the existing socioeconomic system and other forms of inertia play a stabilizing role. In this sytem TPC design procedures represent an offensive component that is able to bring about structural change in the system as a whole.

As a complement to evaluations of the official planning system Maximov (1983) has suggested a focused study of the WS-TPC through the following steps:

- projections of expected changes in Soviet energy demand patterns;
- analyses of possible changes in world prices of fossil fuel input materials and in products that utilize such inputs;
- analyses of structural changes in the composition of Soviet energy supplies;
- assessments of possible changes in West Siberia's share of the total national gas output;
- analyses of the impact of technological innovations on the WS-TPC development.

Such an approach could add to the understanding of uncertainties and the sensitivity of existing plans to possible disturbances. This type of information should be valid with regard to the formation of strategies for including adaptability in longer-term plans.

Maximov (1983) also indicates that the flexibility and reliability of the plans for Western Siberia for 1975–80 were greater than those for 1971–75. For this latter period measures of plan reliability (degree of plan fulfillment) are reported to have been far from completely successful: 90% for gas output, 94.5% for gas pipeline development, and 81% as regards investment in gas production. The improvement between the two periods is said to have been achieved by making the regional information in the plans more specific. As a result, equipment and technologies have been adapted to suit climatic conditions and the characteristics of distribution and supply systems in various parts of the region.

References

Aganbegyan, A.G. (1982) Regional economic modeling in the USSR, in Albegov *et al.* (1982).

Albegov, M., Andersson, Å.E., and Snickars, F. (Eds) (1982) *Regional Development Modeling: Theory and Practice* (Amsterdam: North-Holland).

Alekseyev, A.M. (1982) Modeling regional development projects, in Albegov *et al.* (1982).

Bandman, M.K. (1982) Territorial production complexes: The spatial organization of production, in Albegov *et al.* (1982).

Baranov, E.F. and Matlin, I.S. (1982) A system of models for coordinating sectoral and regional development plans, in Issaev *et al.* (1982).

Granberg, A.G. (1982a) Regional economic interactions in the USSR, in Albegov *et al.* (1982).

Granberg, A.G. (1982b) Experience in the use of multiregional economic models in the Soviet Union, in Issaev *et al.* (1982).

Issaev, B., Nijkamp, P., Rietveld, P., and Snickars, F. (Eds) (1982) *Multiregional Economic Modeling: Practice and Prospect* (Amsterdam: North-Holland).

Issaev, B. (1982) Multiregional economic models in different planning and management systems, in Issaev *et al.* (1982).

Kotchetkov, A. (1984) *Institutional Framework for Regional Development in the USSR*. Working Paper WP-84-24 (Laxenburg, Austria: International Institute for Applied Systems Analysis).

Maximov, Yu.I. (1983) *Regional, National and International Implications of the Developments of Natural Gas Deposits in the North of the West Siberian Plain*. Paper delivered to the IIASA Workshop on Regional Consequences of Large-Scale Energy Projects, February 1983. International Institute for Applied Systems Analysis, Laxenburg, Austria.

Meyerhoff, A.A. (1980) Petroleum basins of the Soviet Arctic. *Geol. Mag.* 17(2):101–86.

Meyerhoff, A.A. (1982) *Energy Resources of Soviet Arctic and Subarctic Regions*. Paper presented at the Conference on Arctic Energy Resources, September 22–24, 1982. Det Norske Veritas, Høyvik, Norway.

OECD (1980) *Energy Policies and Programs of the IEA Countries* (Paris: OECD).

Rey, L. (1982) *The Arctic Regions in the Light of Industrial Development: Basic Facts and Environmental Issues*. Paper presented at the Conference on Arctic Energy Resources, September 22–24, 1982. Det Norske Veritas, Høyvik, Norway.

Large-Scale Energy Projects: Assessment of Regional Consequences
T.R. Lakshmanan and B. Johansson (Editors)
Elsevier Science Publishers B.V. (North-Holland)
© IIASA, 1985

CHAPTER 3

Tar Sands Development in Canada: A Case Study of Environmental Monitoring

3.1. Resource Extraction in Canada: Modeling the Regional Impacts

S.C. Lonergan

Introduction and Historical Background

Canada's energy situation must be an enigma to those unfamiliar with the spatial distribution of energy supply and demand and the development of the country's vast resources. Since the discovery of conventional oil at Leduc, southwest of Edmonton, Alberta, in the late 1940s, Canada has become a net energy exporter (one of only four developed countries in the world), yet until quite recently more than 30% of the country's crude oil supply was imported (this percentage declined rapidly in 1981—82 due to the world recession). Per capita energy consumption and consumption per dollar of output (GDP) are the highest of any developed nation, yet the clamor for energy self-reliance in the 1970s[1] was made in the context of regulated prices to final demand. Ontario, Quebec, and the eastern provinces produce little more than 15% of the total energy consumed, while Alberta's supply of liquid hydrocarbon reserves and resources is greater than that of the entire Middle East.[2] In

---

[1] *Energy Futures for Canadians* (1978). Although the concept of self-sufficiency had been espoused prior to 1978, the LEAP report explicitly presented self-reliance as the primary energy objective for Canada over the next 20 years. Decreased dependence on imported oil was the main concern.

[2] *Energy Alternatives* (1981).

addition, large natural gas reserves are located in Alberta; British Columbia has substantial coal deposits; Ontario and Quebec are spawning large hydroelectric projects; and potential oil reserves exist in offshore areas, particularly in the Arctic and off the coast of the Maritime Provinces (see Figure 3.1). The magnitude of these reserves and resources and the high levels of energy consumption indicative of industrialized nations have resulted in an emphasis, at both federal and provincial levels, on large-scale energy projects (in terms of dollars invested, extent of impacts, and energy produced). These range from the Baie James hydroelectric project, sponsored by Quebec Hydro, with a potential power production of 12 GW (Bourassa 1973), to the construction of artificial islands in the Beaufort Sea for offshore oil drilling, to the further mining of the tar sands in Alberta, at the present capital cost per plant of $11 billion.

The concern with energy development has been explicitly manifested in federal policies; a strong reliance on non-renewable energy resources to meet forecasted demand in the near future has aroused interest in frontier resource development. There has, however, been a relative lack of information on the social, environmental, and regional economic consequences of such development. Research on regional impacts has been "after-the-fact", rather than part of any formal decision involving resource development. The only institutional requirement is the submission of an environmental statement with a development proposal (see Chapter 4). Such submissions often lack detailed information, but these concerns are usually overshadowed by the priority given to energy development. Note the following statement made by Alberta's Environment Minister on tar sands development: "We know that major information gaps exist in respect to baseline environmental data in the entire area. Nevertheless, in light of Canada's critical energy balance, it did not and does not appear prudent to delay oil sands development until all needed information is available" (Pratt 1976).

The pervasive preference for energy "megaproject" development in the absence of information on the consequences has largely been due to the acceptance of demand forecasts and, in turn, to the unqualified belief that domestic supplies must be stimulated to meet this demand as soon as possible.

This paper reflects the degree to which social, environmental, and economic impacts have been addressed in the assessment of the consequences of resource extraction projects in Canada, concentrating specifically on tar sands operations, and the types of modeling frameworks that are presently being used for policy determination.

The Syncrude project and its historical context

The development of the Athabasca tar sands has been a focus of federal and provincial energy planners since the decision by the government of Alberta to place the operation in the hands of private firms in

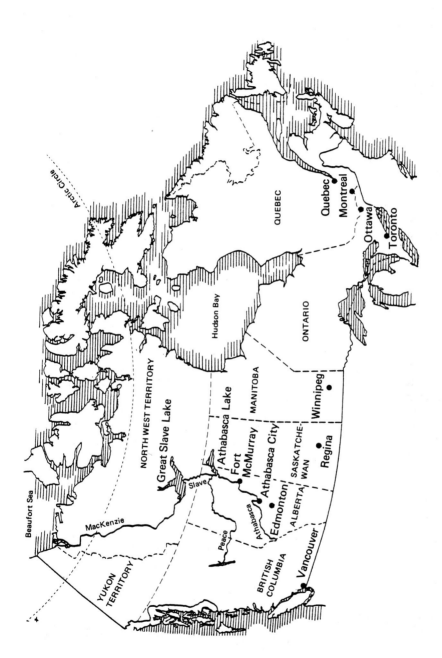

Figure 3.1. Canada.

1951. The size of the resource (estimated at over 900 billion barrels[3]), the present capital costs of an extraction plant ($11 billion), and the question of federal/provincial shares combined to elevate tar sands projects to a key position in Canada's quest for energy self-sufficiency. Additionally, the establishment of the Alberta Oil Sands Environmental Research Program (AOSERP) in 1975 as a joint federal/provincial environmental research project on the tar sands reflects the contemporary emphasis on the methodology of large-scale energy project impact assessment. AOSERP can be viewed as Canada's initial excursion into acknowledging and attempting to assess the regional impacts of such projects. The formal assessment procedure mentioned above was not yet in place, and the joint program appeared as much politically motivated, to allow for the concerns of environmentalist groups, as designed to provide the standard for regional impact assessment in Canada. The evolution of the program seems to bear this out: a number of reorientations in the project, drying up of federal funds, changes in program administration, and disparities between objectives and research led to an ineffectual program. Although AOSERP must be evaluated in light of budget cuts and administrative chaos, it remains a useful example of the methodological approach to regional impact assessment that is indicative of present Canadian policy. The remainder of this section will deal specifically with the Syncrude project, the second tar sands operation (begun in 1979), and the associated study of the regional consequences of that specific plant, as undertaken primarily through AOSERP.

Syncrude was initially a consortium of four oil companies. Leases and permits in the tar sands area had been purchased by these firms in the 1950s, but not until 1971 did the consortium receive approval for a 125 000 barrels per day (bpd) complex. Restrictive government policies in the 1960s required potential developers to secure export markets beyond the reach of the conventional oil industry, a restriction that became severely limiting for tar sands development (it appeared) with the discovery of oil on Alaska's North Slope in 1968.

Negotiations on the Syncrude project between the four oil companies and Alberta developed in late 1972, and were completed in 1975 in an atmosphere of concern over energy prices and the dependence on foreign oil. The Canadian political environment in the early 1970s was (and is) extremely important in resource extraction decisions and was instrumental in shaping not only the elements of the Syncrude project, but also the extent to which comprehensive impact assessment studies were undertaken prior to project completion (1979). Specific concessions granted to the consortium by the Alberta government included:

---

[3] *Oilweek*, 22 March 1982.

(1) royalty agreements, including a guaranteed annual rate of return on investments;

(2) infrastructure support, including a highway between Edmonton and Fort McMurray;

(3) environmental concessions, including Syncrude involvement in Clean Air and Clean Water Act policy changes and five-year operating leases to reduce uncertainties regarding alterations in environmental regulations;

(4) a government guarantee of no-strike conditions during construction.

The potential impacts, both social and environmental, of the Syncrude project were largely unknown and, for the most part, of little concern to decision makers. The only survey of the possible ecological impacts, in 1973, concluded that "the environmental effects of eventual multi-plant operations over the extent of the Athabasca tar sands could be enormous" (Pratt 1976).

Tar sands are a mixture of crude bitumen, water, and sand. The crude bitumen is a viscous, tar-like substance that must be either mined and subsequently combined with hot water and steam, or recovered by *in situ* techniques such as steam injection or fire flooding. The bitumen is then processed to remove contaminants such as nitrogen and sulfur, and the resulting product is a high-quality synthetic crude. The two tar sands plants presently in operation, Suncor and Syncrude, both use massive open-pit mining operations to extract the tar sand (at the ratio of approximately 2 tonnes of sand/barrel of crude), and, accordingly, cause ecological disruption typical of any strip mining operation. In addition, liquid waste disposal and the nature of the tailings ponds may have significant environmental effects. The concern for the potential consequences of tar sands development, while not having a significant impact on the development decision *per se*, was taken into consideration by the federal and provincial governments in designing a joint research venture to provide a framework within which these questions could be addressed, as well as to provide inputs to future tar sands project decisions.

The Alberta Oil Sands Environmental Research Program (AOSERP)[4]

The Canada–Alberta agreement on AOSERP was signed in 1975 and developed as a joint research effort based on the need for extensive, long-term efforts to assess the possible effects of Athabasca tar sands development. The agreement was restricted to investigations of the

---

[4] The material presented in this section was taken from reports published by the program and, to a greater extent, from the AOSERP 1975–80 Research Summary Report.

environmental aspects of renewable resources, and was not intended as a study of extraction technologies. The initial agreement called for a ten-year effort at a cost of not more than $4 million annually, with each party contributing not more than $2 million per year. The specific objectives of AOSERP, as set out in 1975 and amended in 1977,[5] were:

(1) To identify the baseline states, processes, and absorption capacity of the environment that may be affected by tar sands development.

(2) To identify the nature of interactions between the various environmental components and the various components of proposed development activities.

(3) To predict, in part from information obtained by meeting objectives (1) and (2), the individual and cumulative effects of anticipated developments on the environment.

(4) To develop methods necessary to protect the environment, and finally to return the biotic environment to a productive state.

(5) To advise regulatory and management agencies and industry of new scientific and technological information pertinent to their jurisdictions to minimize adverse and maximize beneficial environmental effects.

(6) To use existing agencies within the administration of the parties involved wherever possible, and to use other sources when necessary. Taking inventories was not considered as part of the objectives under this program, except where necessary.

(7) To establish research priorities, and to assign these priorities in the light of an Alberta development strategy.

(8) To coordinate projects within the program so as to provide an inter-disciplinary study of environmental problems.

(9) To promote an environmental research program to ensure cooperation between provincial and federal governments, industry, universities, and other institutions.

(10) To compile, assess, and disseminate research reports resulting from the program.

It is worth noting that the societal effects of tar sands development was not an explicit objective until the 1977 amendments were made. At its conception, AOSERP was divided into eight autonomous technical research committees (aquatic fauna, hydrogeology, hydrology, human environment, land use, meteorology, terrestrial fauna, and vegetation), each with research links to a federal and a provincial department. The first two years entailed extensive data collection activities, mapping, and planning future directions, in order to provide reliable scientific information; any impact evaluation work was given low priority.

---

[5] Canada–Alberta Agreement on AOSERP, 1977.

The program was, at least superficially, redirected in 1977 to consolidate existing technical research committees, and to adopt a systems approach in all further research. The program was restructured to include four systems under which all research activities were undertaken. These systems (comprising air, land, water, and human) were designed to receive direction from a single source and, accordingly, to be more responsive to government policy and to identify independently future research needs and deficiencies. The structure of AOSERP is outlined in Figure 3.2.

Two years after the program was redirected to a general systems orientation, the federal government decided to relinquish its funding obligation as of 1980. Provincial funding was maintained at the rate set prior to 1979, but the reduced level of total funding necessitated additional reorganization, and in 1980 the program was subsumed under the Research Management Division of Alberta's Department of Environment. The general systems structure has been maintained superficially, but the $2 million in annual provincial funds is now channeled into one of the department's 11 existing programs. Funding will be terminated in 1985, as the interest in tar sands extraction and its associated regional impacts has waned considerably since the demise of the Alsands project (which was to be the third, and largest, plant), due to the failure of the consortium and provincial and federal governments to reach agreement on revenues.

Nevertheless, AOSERP provides an interesting perspective on the pervasive governmental ideology on regional impact assessment in Canada and offers an interesting contrast to the analytical models discussed elsewhere in this volume. Each of the systems or research sections that comprise AOSERP has a number of specific objectives, but all can be subsumed under the general categories data acquisition, description of regional characteristics, and modeling the system under consideration. Most of the following discussion will be on modeling and predictive elements (see AOSERP *Research Summary Report*, 1975–80).

Air Systems

The primary analytical focus of the air systems section has been air quality modeling efforts, including the adaptation of related models to the Athabasca region and the development of a working air quality model that reflects airshed management requirements and use needs. An initial focus, once the air quality data acquisition network and meteorological data acquisition program were in place, involved the use of available data to test the applicability of atmospheric and air quality management models in the region. Models tested included the US Environmental Protection Agency's CRSTER model (Padro and Bagg 1980), and the Lawrence Livermore Laboratory's LIRAQ and ADPIC systems (Reid *et al*. 1974). Gaussian frequency distribution models were used primarily to predict SO_2 dispersion. Criticisms of these models (as well as other, less detailed

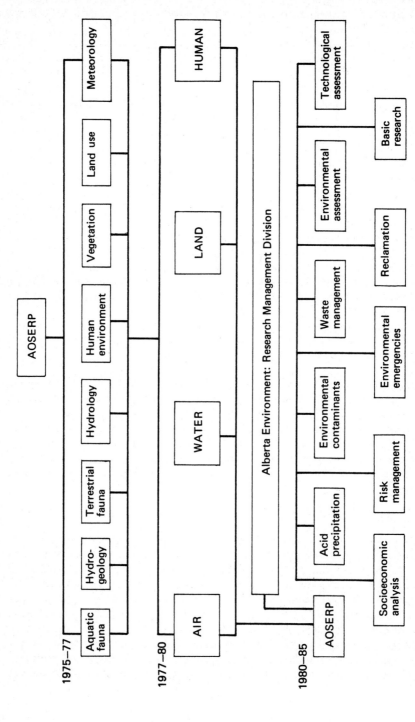

Figure 3.2. The structure of the Alberta Oil Sands Environmental Research Program (AOSERP) since its inception in 1975.

studies) ranged from their inapplicability to the area, to the need for more data and an expanded monitoring effort before the model results could be accepted.

One of the objectives of AOSERP was to supply advice and scientific information on meteorology and air quality to regulatory agencies and industry to aid in environmental management decisions. The perceived inadequacy of existing modeling efforts as applied to the Athabasca region necessitated the development of a specific air quality management model of the area. The basic model developed by Davison and Leahy (1980) is a Gaussian frequency distribution model that provides output on the ground-level concentration of a given pollutant over time. The simple framework (similar to the CRSTER model mentioned above) was modified to include three other characteristics:

(i)   The sensitivity of a particular receptor can be included. The model enabled any ground-level concentrations to be weighted according to any meteorological parameter. The sensitivity of plant or animal species at certain time, for example, can thus be accounted for.

(ii) Pollutant concentrations are generated in time series at any location. Estimates of time periods between peak concentrations can be made relative to air quality regulations and recovery times for certain species.

(iii) Flexibility is allowed in source specification. Ground-level concentrations can be assessed using a single source or group of sources, and marginal contributions can be calculated.

Although the development of a Gaussian frequency distribution model has been the most sophisticated AOSERP modeling effort, the lack of data on near-ground air movements and on interregional pollutant transfers has foreclosed its application to estimate the impact of emissions from proposed plants. The impact of acid precipitation outside the immediate tar sands region has not been assessed. Within the region, it was assumed that lakes are not sensitive to acid precipitation because they are well buffered.

Land Systems

The majority of the work on the land system by AOSERP involved baseline data accumulation, soil mapping, and animal and vegetation surveys. Preliminary studies, primarily literature reviews, were conducted in an attempt to link pollutant output (mainly SO_2) to ecological damage. All experimental work was species- and pollutant-specific and intended as "useful input to more comprehensive studies" (AOSERP *Research Summary Report* 1975–80). Although the development of a conceptual or analytical model with which to estimate the ecosystem effects of tar sands plants and to identify outputs that act as limiting elements in ecosystems development are two explicit objectives, no such work has yet been undertaken. The sensitivity of numerous plant species to SO_2 has been estimated, but no significant effects of emissions from Syncrude (or Suncor, operating since 1967) have been detected. All of the studies to date have been concerned with baseline measurements, so that a discussion of spatial and temporal dimensions is, accordingly, not applicable.

Water System

The Athabasca tar sands region contains two major river systems, the Clearwater and the Athabasca, at the confluence of which stands Fort McMurray. The systems are used for transportation, recreation, domestic water supply and sewage dilution, and industrial water supply. Again, baseline data acquisition was the focus in the initial three years of study, followed by a forecast of total water demand up to 2010 and estimates of the toxic effects of tar sands plant effluents.

Total water use over the next 30 years was estimated with a simple simulation model, the results of which suggest that water supply may be a serious problem as early as the year 2000 (Staley *et al.* 1983). With this exception, no aquatic system modeling has been undertaken, although much of the necessary background studies have been completed. The susceptibility of lakes in the region to acidification is low, since all are well buffered (Hesslein 1979). Significant concentrations of heavy metals were noted in certain stream segments, but no evidence of a connection with industrial operations was revealed (Korchiniski 1978). Primary productivity in the water bodies up and downstream of the oil sands plants was not significantly different (Hickman *et al.* 1979). Tar sands development may, however, have substantial impact on fish populations, by degrading the quality of spawning grounds and altering the water quality along major fish migration routes (Seberak and Walder 1980). Recent work has centered on establishing an aquatic biomonitoring network in the region (McCart and Mayhood 1980).

Increased heavy metal loadings and organics resulting from tar sands operations have not significantly affected microbial populations or other aquatic life in the Athabasca River, but smaller tributary systems and lakes have not been studied. The spatial dimension has been entirely limited to the major river; no interregional transfer of pollutants or short- versus long-term effects have been studied.

Human System

The direction of research in the human system paralleled the other three systems: baseline data acquistion, with some interest in social impact assessment. One of the requirements of the human system research after its inception in 1977 (two years after the other projects had begun) was the development of a conceptual framework within which to identify information needs and to propose avenues for further investigation. Four basic approaches were utilized:

(a) *Historical studies.* The gathering of oral histories and the history of socioeconomic development (Parker and Tingley 1980), focusing on the integration of local people into the labor force, and their employment patterns (Deines *et al.* 1980).

(b) *Inventories.* Recreation, culture, and leisure activities were inventoried for 1972, 1976, and 1979 in an attempt to link sociocultural variables to tar sands developments, as well as changes in housing stock, demographic composition, and infrastructure (MTB 1980).

(c) *Surveys.* A survey of the adult population was conducted to assess the impacts of tar sands development on Fort McMurray society. Selected social indicators were used to facilitate data analysis: demographic composition, perceived quality of housing and services, labor force activity, incomes and standards of living, social participation, and subjective responses on lifestyles (Cartrell *et al.* 1980).

(d) *Estimates.* Using different scenarios for future tar sands developments, basic population forecasts were generated, in five-year increments, and service and infrastructure demands estimated as simple linear functions of population size.

These four approaches describe the present extent of research on the human system. The only modeling efforts have focused on population forecasts and the associated demand for goods and services. Research on the human system has concentrated on changes that have occurred, and are likely to occur, in the social and demographic character of the region. The population has increased tenfold since 1960, and the mean age has fallen significantly. The impact on local residents, in terms of employment, has been negligible; their integration into the workforce is little different from the rest of Canada and the Fort McMurray area prior to tar sands development.

Socioeconomic Analysis Associated with AOSERP

Boom town models of Fort McMurray

The Alberta Department of Municipal Affairs, although not directly associated with AOSERP, has been involved in one aspect of the human system: simulation modeling of the housing market in Fort McMurray. The "BOOM-H" model is an application of systems dynamics (Forrester 1971a,b) to a region experiencing rapid resource development, and was built at Los Alamos Scientific Laboratory (Ford 1976). BOOM-H attempts to estimate the impact of exogenous changes on the municipal system by recognizing a series of feedback loops that control temporal behavior (Power *et al.* 1980, 1982). Figure 3.3 illustrates the five model sectors and one of several feedback loops that, in this case, results in a lower quality of life (measured by facilities per capita). The primary objective of the

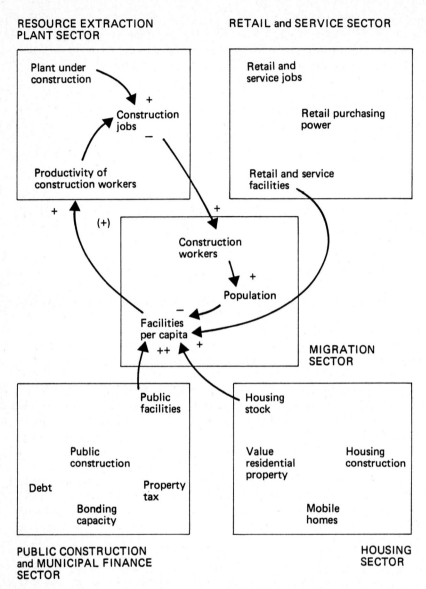

Figure 3.3. Sectoral composition of the BOOM-H model (from Power *et al.* 1982).

model was to test the sensitivity of the variables to public policies aimed at minimizing the "shocks" to the boom town system.

BOOM-1 was developed to simulate the social and economic effects of large-scale energy projects on small communities (this includes a "boom" period during project construction and a corresponding "bust" following

facility completion). The model has five sectors (Ford 1976): power plant
(the project for which BOOM-1 was initially developed); housing; public
construction and municipal financing; retailing and services; and migration. The relationships within and between sectors are then depicted in
detail diagrammatically (see Figure 3.3) and mathematically, and the
simulation is run under different sets of assumptions. A typical model
output to a project simulating a boom town response (described as "business as usual") might be as follows:

- rapid growth in construction jobs, population, and temporary housing stock;
- reduction in public services per capita and increases in local property tax rates;
- a modest increase in permanent housing and no change in retail and
  service capital.

Subsequent to project construction, the boom may yield to a "bust"
phase, and the model would generate the following response:

- a rapid decline in construction jobs, population, and temporary
  housing;
- an increase in public services per capita (often to levels greater than
  pre-boom conditions), and a reduction of property tax rates; and
- little change in permanent housing or retail and service capital.

Using the basic generic framework of BOOM-1, BOOM-H was developed
for Fort McMurray in anticipation of future tar sands development (Power
et al. 1980). BOOM-H differs from BOOM-1 only in the housing sector,
which is treated in more detail to facilitate an understanding of the vola-
tility of housing supply, demand, and prices resulting from boom town
phenomena, and to gauge the impact of predevelopment policies on the
housing sector. The sector comprises three aspects: permanent housing
− supply and demand; temporary housing − supply and demand; and land
uses and land values. A causal loop diagram of the permanent housing
aspect is illustrated in Figure 3.4. The model has been tested against the
construction boom that occurred in Fort McMurray during Syncrude project development and was found to be reasonably successful. It has
proved useful in forecasting trends in housing rents and supplies relative
to boom town growth and in determining the effects of potential impact-
mitigating policies (Power *et al.* 1980). It is interesting to note, however,
that the development and application of this model ws instigated
privately rather than from a government policy initiative. A more complete discussion of boom town models can be found in Chapter 7.

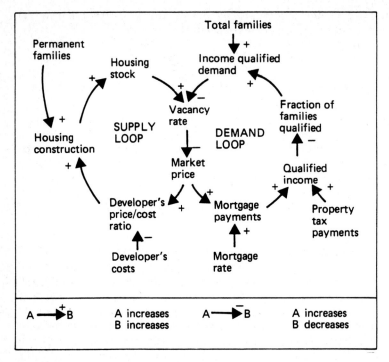

Figure 3.4. Causal loop diagram of the permanent housing sector in the BOOM-H model (from Power *et al.* 1980).

Interregional input—output modeling

The Canadian Energy Research Institution, a cooperative organization partially sponsored by the Alberta Department of Energy and Natural Resources, has provided an additional technique to those developed within AOSERP: an input—output analysis to estimate the interregional economic impacts of the proposed Alsands project over a 30-year period (Douglas and MacMillan 1982). The analysis used the federal government's 1974 interprovincial input—output model of the structure of the Canadian economy. Economic impacts were decomposed, by province, into direct, indirect, and induced, given assumptions on plant construction and operating expenditures, employment, and urban and residential development expenditures.

The estimation of economic impacts within an input—output framework provides one measure of the benefits and distributional consequences of project development. It is particularly significant when weighing the funding of AOSERP (initially $40 million spread over 10 years) relative to the gross benefit of a single tar sands plant ($54 billion).

Nevertheless, it provides only a single model, and is unable to address broader questions of social and environmental impacts.

Alternatives to AOSERP

AOSERP provides an interesting perspective on methodological approaches to regional impact assessment at the provincial/federal level. Although few other comprehensive efforts to assess the impacts of large-scale energy projects in Canada exist, two particular models are worthy of note and provide distinctive alternatives to AOSERP: the Alberta energy resources allocation model (AERAM), and the Helliwell natural gas pipeline model.

The Alberta energy resources allocation model (AERAM)

The extensive hydrocarbon resource base of Alberta has raised much concern over how best to manage it, in light of future needs and present policies. One of the more sophisticated analytical efforts to address this concern was the Alberta Research Council's development of a dynamic linear programming (LP) model to suggest the optimal allocation of the province's resources to satisfy national and regional demands (McConaghy and Quon 1977, 1980). AERAM is a regional extension of the Brookhaven energy system optimization model (BESOM) that provides a comprehensive energy framework within which technical, environmental, economic and policy constraints are expressed. Supply side models typically incorporate a minimum supply cost objective, subject to supply and demand conditions and other constraints. In BESOM, an LP framework is used to determine the optimal allocation of resources subject to such constraints, one set of which is environmental conditions. These are simple linear multipliers on resource supply (e.g., kg SO_2/MW electricity produced from coal) and any impacts (e.g., on lakes or humans), must be estimated externally to the model. As a result, environmental and social impacts can only be viewed as costs that result in suboptimal allocations rather than in any dynamic sense.

The structures of BESOM and AERAM are identical, with the exception of context, and the latter includes fewer variables. Basic inputs to AERAM include:

(1) *Alberta energy resources:* coal, crude oil and natural gas, oil sands, renewables, nuclear.
(2) *Demand categories:* national (oil and gas), provincial, export markets.

(3) *Competing energy sources:* imported crude oil, frontier gas and oil.
(4) *Non-energy inputs to energy projects:* land, water, labor, infrastruc-
     ture, capital.

AERAM does generate some information that is useful for estimating the
direct impacts of resource allocation. The cost of land acquisition relative to the opportunity cost of using the land for agriculture or forestry is
incorporated into the model, as is the direct water consumption associated with each energy supply system. Pollution emissions are not
included, however, so that very little environmental impact information
is generated. Social considerations are also absent and must be considered externally to the model output.

The Helliwell model

     AERAM is indicative of a very small set of Canadian interregional or
national models relating to energy distribution and demand. Only one
extensive analytical effort has been developed in the Canadian context to
evaluate the costs and benefits of a large-scale energy project: a group at
the University of British Columbia, under the guidance of John Helliwell,
developed a dynamic simulation model of proposed Alaskan natural gas
pipeline projects (Helliwell *et al.*, 1980a,b).
     Similar to most decisions on energy project development, the pipe-
line proposal was not based on an extensive study of the consequences of
pipeline construction, but on the concern for providing the US and
Canada with a link to natural gas reserves in the Mackenzie delta in
extreme northwest Canada. In an attempt to provide a quantitative
framework within which to assess project impacts, the major components
of the Helliwell model were an engineering cost-minimizing model to
determine capital costs, operating costs, and the quantity of gas used in
transmission, given throughput, pipeline diameter, and pressure. The
engineering portion was initially linked to a quarterly macroeconomic
model of the Canadian economy to estimate the effects of pipeline construction on certain national economic indicators; income, employment,
prices, interest rates, international trade and capital flows, and foreign
exchange rates (Helliwell *et al.* 1980b). The approach was strictly
macroeconomic in nature and did not explicitly include any environmental or social variables, but it has been the only attempt to model the
consequences of an energy project in Canada to date.
     A second phase of the model was developed to account for the overall
benefits and costs of long-term Arctic development projects and
integrated the demand for and supplies from the primary energy sectors
in Canada (Helliwell *et al.* 1980a). The dynamic model is run over a
period of 50 years and is divided into five major regions. Energy prices
for each region are calculated, treating the world oil price as exogenous,
and the total primary energy demand by region is calculated

econometrically as a function of prices and GNP. The resultant demands are then distributed by a translog share model to the respective energy sectors. The structural components of the model are:

(1) Domestic energy prices are set exogenously to the model.
(2) Given the above prices, total energy demands are estimated as a function of GNP, and supplies allocated between electricity, coal, natural gas, and oil.
(3) Nonfrontier oil production varies endogenously to meet demand; once present reserves are exhausted, supply deficiencies are met by offshore oil and imports.
(4) Four tar sands projects are treated as domestic supply (as mentioned previously, only two plants are now in operation).
(5) The nonfrontier natural gas sector is treated in the same way as the nonfrontier oil sector, except that supply deficiencies are not met by imports, but stimulate Arctic gas development.
(6) Taxes, subsidies, and levies are given detailed treatment in the allocation model to facilitate estimating efficiency and distributional impacts.

The model-based research on natural gas pipelines by the Helliwell group concluded that Arctic gas is unlikely to be needed in Canada before the mid-1990s. This conflicted with government predictions, and it was suggested that the National Energy Board (NEB) had overestimated future demand and underestimated nonfrontier natural gas supplies (McRae 1978). The model results were, accordingly, useful in forcing the NEB to reconsider their interest in the immediate development of an Arctic gas pipeline.

Appropriate Methodological Frameworks for Impact Assessment

The methodological approach to regional impact assessment by Canadian federal and provincial governments, as characterized by AOSERP, must be viewed in light of the funding and administrative turmoil surrounding the program since its inception. The (initially) joint effort explicitly recognized the types of consequences that do occur, and through a combination of descriptive studies and baseline data acquisition sought to improve the identification of the nature of the consequences.

The disinterest in interregional work was, to a large extent, due to AOSERP's mandate: concern was for the Athabasca region only, and little mention was made of other spatial dimensions. Dynamic considerations were also lacking; only the simple extrapolations conducted by the human system research dealt with future impacts of development. These

models were primarily population forecast simulations and demand projections for services and infrastructure based on these estimates. Time
horizons were guided by federal energy planning: ten tar sands plants
were expected to be in operation in the region by the year 2000.

The AOSERP approach to impact assessment is in marked contrast
with other Canadian models mentioned in this paper. Table 3.1 presents
a comparison of the attributes of these models with respect to dimen-
sionality, types of impacts, and policy implications. The Helliwell model
is, at first glance, the most distinct from the reductionist approach
developed within AOSERP, yet it is unclear whether the policy implications of either are at all significant. Canadian energy models, whether
privately or publicly developed, tend to fit into very traditional analytical
frameworks (input–output, LP), and are directed toward economic
impacts or objectives. AOSERP, on the other hand, sought to address the
environmental and social issues involved in energy projects, yet did not
develop a consistent framework that could cover the scale necessary in a
study of this type. The failure of AOSERP to consider interregional issues
and long-term dynamics, however, reflects both the fundamental problems evident in such models and the government's interest in energy
supply. Given the size of the resource and the desire for energy self-
sufficiency, a major effort took place to exploit the energy value of the tar
sands. Although tar sands development was a singular component of the
national program to increase supplies through megaproject development,
it was, initially, a major one. The projects were designed to supplement
energy exports in markets not served by traditional oil supplies, but the
increasing dependence on foreign oil necessitated the consideration of
synthetic crude from the tar sands for domestic use. The incentives
(financial and otherwise) granted to the consortia involved in tar sands
development were substantial, which is quite understandable in light of
the income benefits attributable to a single plant ($54 billion). Neverthe-
less, it is apparent that both dynamic and interregional considerations
should — and could — have been addressed by AOSERP without altering
their basic methodological approach.

AOSERP and National Energy Policy

The evolution of Canadian energy policy has been guided by the fundamental belief that tapping the country's vast resources will solve the
problems of increasing energy demand and self-sufficiency. Implicit in
this position is an acceptance of the benefits of megaproject development
over the costs or consequences. The fact that there is a dearth of
research on the social and environmental consequences of energy projects in Canada must be attributable to that position. At its inception
AOSERP was the first major federal/provincial effort aimed at assessing
the possible impacts of large-scale energy projects. The objectives of the

Table 3.1. Dimensions of impact assessment methodologies.

Modeling framework description	Dimension				Types of impacts	Policy impacts (level)
	Temporal		Spatial			
	Horizon	Dependence	Area	Linkages		
1. AOSERP Resource extraction orientation, systems approach, baseline data acquisition, descriptive, reductionist.	Near, short term	Static	Local	–	Environmental, social	0 (at present)
(*a*) *BOOM-H.* Project development impacts by economic sector, systems dynamics, simulation	Medium term	Dynamic	Local	(Has been adapted to three regions)	Economic, infrastructure	+ (provincial)
(*b*) *Input–output.* Impacts on economic sectors, linear model of the economy	Medium term	Static	Regional (provincial)	Inter-regional	Economic	++ (national)
2. AERAM Energy supply orientation, dynamic LP model, aggregate, regional decision making	Short, medium term	Dynamic	Regional, national, international		Energy, economic (minimum environmental)	++ (provincial)
3. Helliwell Transportation of energy orientation, integrated model, dynamic simulation, minimum cost, aggregate	Long term	Dynamic	Regional, national		Economic	+ (national)

program were appealing, ranging from information assessment to conceptual and operational modeling of the systems involved. The project budget, additionally, was quite substantial; $4 million per year for ten years. What has AOSERP accomplished?

The research contracted by the program focused primarily on baseline data acquisition and information review; only a few of the almost 200 reports published attempt to estimate the impacts of tar sands projects or forecast consequences that might be expected from further development. The modeling goals that were explicit in the objectives in each section were not addressed, nor, it appears, will be addressed in the remaining two years of the program.

The interaction between systems, such as the impact of rapid population growth on water supply and quality, is of particular interest in areas experiencing development pressure. The systems identified by AOSERP as research sections were autonomous in control and little effort, as measured by the outcomes, was made to integrate the information obtained by research on one system with another. Again, this was in large part a result of the focus of the program.

Explicit in the statement of objectives was the foreclosure of "inventory taking" as part of the program; this point seems to have been neglected in the consideration of baseline states. With the exception of baseline state identification, none of the substantive objectives in the federal/provincial agreement on AOSERP was met. The techniques used were confined to those necessary for reductionist research rather than for comprehensive or integrated perspectives. The only analytical techniques of note were simple air dispersion models and the extrapolations of the human system group. Other techniques included monitoring biophysical processes, survey techniques, and basic inventory taking.

The information gained by AOSERP was extremely important in defining the existing state of the region from a variety of perspectives, but its usefulness for public policy purposes and for estimating the consequences of further development of the Athabasca tar sands was minimal. The capability for innovative or comprehensive approaches to assess the consequences of tar sands development was set within the bounds of the federal/provincial pact on AOSERP; the development of alternative methodologies or an exploration of possible approaches available to address impact assessment, however, has been conspicuously lacking from the entire research effort.

The deficiencies in the existing AOSERP research are not likely to be rectified in the remaining two years of the program. The third proposed tar sands project, Alsands (a consortium of private concerns plus Petro-Canada, the national oil company) was set aside in the spring of 1982, due to a perceived inadequate rate of return for private companies. Other potential tar sands projects have also become low priority in terms of energy project investments. The funding for AOSERP, accordingly, has been dramatically reduced, as has the potential for future comprehensive modeling efforts undertaken by AOSERP.

The impact of AOSERP on policy, either at the federal or the provincial level has been minimal. The Syncrude consortium specified in its operating agreement with the respective governmental concerns that they would have a major input into revisions of water and air quality regulations, ensuring a strong lobbying effort on the part of the energy extraction sector. Little of the information obtained is of use for the purposes of public policy, although it is not clear that major modeling efforts would have any more of an effect (e.g., the Helliwell model was not allowed as evidence in the Berger Inquiry on natural gas pipeline proposals because it addressed national issues that were not within the commission's mandate). Given that the impact of tar sands development has only been addressed by the human system group, and in a cursory manner, the research is of little use in assessing the regional consequences of future tar sands projects. Canada is firmly committed to megaproject development; such development has occurred in the absence of any substantive input as to environmental or social impacts. AOSERP, a major program designed to estimate the consequences of energy projects, has done little to rectify this problem.

Large-Scale Energy Projects: Assessment of Regional Consequences
T.R. Lakshmanan and B. Johansson (Editors)
Elsevier Science Publishers B.V. (North-Holland)
© IIASA, 1985

CHAPTER 3

Tar Sands Development in Canada:
A Case Study of Environmental Monitoring

3.2. On Canadian Energy Impact Assessments

Lars Lundqvist

Introduction

In this paper I review the Canadian case study and evaluate the Canadian achievements in the light of European (particularly Swedish) experiences. I will discuss the Canadian case study from the perspective of regional systems analysis, focusing on a scheme of regional, national, and global aspects of socioeconomic developments and energy supply systems. Based on this approach, I evaluate the characteristics of Canadian energy studies (including some not mentioned by Lonergan).

The Canadian energy policy context

Canada is extremely rich in terms of energy resources, is a net exporter of energy, and has the highest per capita energy consumption and aggregate energy intensity of the developed nations. In spite of her net energy exports, however, Canada imported as much as 30% of the crude oil consumed during the 1970s. This dependence on foreign oil and growing energy demand (at regulated prices) have raised great interest in large-scale resource development projects, including hydropower, natural gas, tar sands, and offshore oil.

The abundance of energy resources has obviously influenced Canadian energy policy in a supply-oriented way. The case study mentions no

social cost—benefit analysis of this supply expansion strategy as compared with other energy policy options. Resource development projects
are spatially distributed in very different ways: while huge liquid hydrocarbon and natural gas resources are located in Alberta, coal deposits are
situated in British Columbia, hydropower projects have been launched in
Ontario and Quebec, and offshore oil reserves exist in the Arctic and off
the east coast. From a regional policy point of view, various energy supply strategies seem to have quite different development potentials.

A short review

The AOSERP Research Program

The initial approach of AOSERP (1975) was restricted to environmental impacts but, after a redirection in 1977 a "systems approach" was
adopted, as illustrated in Figure 3.5. Although predictions of the impacts
of tar sands developments and the modeling of each system were high-
priority goals in the program (both before and after the 1977 amendments), most of the work has been devoted to data acquisition and
descriptions of regional characteristics in the base year. The modeling
efforts were confined to a Gaussian frequency distribution model of air
pollution dispersion (air system), water demand simulations (water system), and population growth projections with associated forecasts of
infrastructure demands (human system). In Lonergan's words: "The
modeling goals that were explicit in the statement of objectives ... were
not addressed, nor, it appears, will be addressed in the remaining two
years of the program."... "The techniques used were confined to those
necessary for reductionist research rather than those needed for
comprehensive or integrated perspectives."

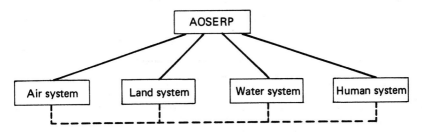

Figure 3.5. The systems approach adopted by AOSERP after 1977.

These criticisms of AOSERP are seemingly justified. Apart from the
lack of genuine modeling as a basis for impact assessment, the following
shortcomings of the program can be pinpointed:

- The lack of studies of interactions between subsystems.
- The focus on baseline system status and measurement of impacts that have already occurred emphasize the short-term character of mainstream research.
- The project addressed only local impacts and is thus only a partial impact study from a regional point of view.
- Very little is said about the treatment of uncertainties. Various scenarios have been specified for population growth and related infrastructure demands, but no comprehensive strategy for treating the total set of uncertainties stemming from different subsystems seems to have been developed.
- Distributional impacts and conflicts of interest are not mentioned. Even though the initial focus of the study was on environmental impacts, the intertemporal and spatial impact profiles should be of interest from a distributional point of view.

In a regional systems analytic perspective, this characterization is depressing indeed. The points raised are normally considered crucial in any application of systems analysis to impact assessment. The main conclusion on impacts from two plants currently in operation is that the direct effects of air pollution and water-borne pollutants seem to have been small.

Boom Town Models

The case study touches upon systems dynamics modeling of the transient local impacts of large-scale construction work. Here model relationships play a fundamental role and the analysis is explicitly dynamic. The modeling work has been initiated to aid the development of housing and migration policies in order to minimize the "shocks" of the boom and bust phases of tar sands plant construction. Systems dynamics is an attractive simulation framework capable of dealing with some of the characteristic features of boom town phenomena (disequilibrium, dynamic feedback effects, etc.), although often in an *ad hoc* manner. The test against the historic development of Fort McMurray was considered reasonably successful and positive policy impacts are reported in the summary table (Table 3.1).

It is interesting to observe that the BOOM-H model for Fort McMurray has some properties that were not addressed by AOSERP. It represents modeling as a base for impact assessment, traces the dynamic impacts over an extended construction period, and treats explicitly interactions between subsystems of the boom town. The Fort McMurray study was initiated independently from AOSERP, even though it would have been natural to utilize BOOM-H in the analysis of the human system.

Interregional Input—Output Model

An interregional input—output model of the Canadian economy (INTERREG) has been used to study income and employment effects of a proposed tar sands project over a 30-year period. Clearly, the method focuses on the interregional distribution of impacts from large-scale energy projects. The results show that a considerable proportion (30—40%) of income and employment effects will materialize outside the tar sands province itself.

The Alberta Energy Resources Allocation Model (AERAM)

AERAM is a regional version of BESOM developed for comprehensive analyses of energy systems, which optimizes resource extraction, energy conversion, and energy utilization subject to technology and policy constraints. Various choices of objectives and constraints are possible, making the model a flexible tool for energy policy. AERAM focuses on the energy supply system with various exogenous energy demand categories. It is dynamic in the sense that it includes intertemporal linkages between four time periods 1977—95. It incorporates non-energy resource requirements in terms of land, water, manpower, capital, and infrastructure costs. Even though AERAM concentrates on the costs incurred by these non-energy resources by using simple relationships, it would be possible to use these constraints in other ways:

- to enforce strict resource limits in non-monetary terms;
- to add complexity to the calculation of resource requirements; and
- to use the model as a consistent device for simulation of total non-monetary impacts on the environment, land, water, and infrastructure systems.

Given the simplicity of AOSERP models in these resource areas, AERAM has the potential of acting as an attractive integrating tool linking impacts on the four basic AOSERP systems to the total development of energy resources in Alberta.

The Helliwell Models

Under the guidance of John Helliwell of the University of British Columbia, a number of models have been developed to assess the costs and benefits of pipelines connecting gas reserves in Alaska and the Mackenzie River delta with US and Canadian markets. The later work of the Helliwell group included the development of an integrated model of primary energy demand and supply in Canada, as illustrated in Figure 3.6.

The pipeline model determines capital and operating costs and the quantity of gas used in transmission as a function of throughput and design parameters. Thus the whole model can be seen as a linkage of an engineering submodel with an integrated model of supply and demand. This way of linking a detailed, project-specific model with a wider energy system model is of great interest in impact studies. The policy impact of Helliwell's cost—benefit studies has been mainly indirect; the results pointed out inconsistencies in official arguments and forced parties to

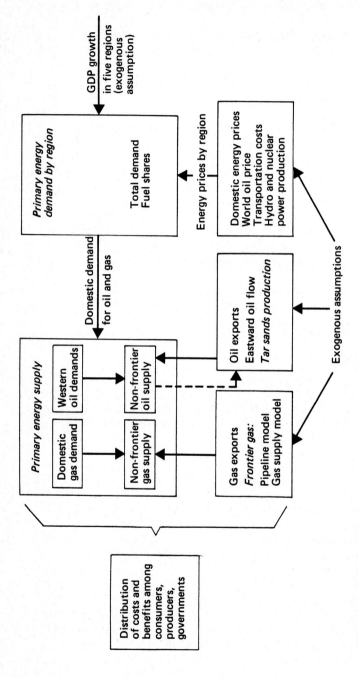

Figure 3.6. The Helliwell model of primary energy supply and demand.

integrate their views, to be more explicit about their procedures, and to raise the standard of research underlying the arguments in hearings and inquiries.

The achievements of the Helliwell group can be summarized as follows:

* an interesting linking of an engineering model of energy project design with an integrated model of energy demand and supply;
* only economic consequences within the energy system are studied;
* the approach is basically long-term oriented;
* there is no linking between the energy system and the (regional) economic system;
* the model has been used to shed light on uncertainties in energy supply and demand conditions;
* the model has been used to study distributional consequences of pipeline and tar sands projects;
* institutional and policy-relevant control variables are built into the model framework (pricing rules, revenue-sharing systems, etc.);
* the treatment of the energy system is far from complete in a 50-year perspective.

Discussion and Critical Evaluation

A scheme for energy impact analysis

The Canadian impact assessment studies provide a fairly rich family of analyses in terms of scope and characteristics (see Table 3.1). As a basis for discussion and critical evaluation of studies with different properties, we sketch a multilevel picture of society in which we can distinguish between socioeconomic (demand) and energy system (supply) components (see Figure 3.7). Assessments of the effects of large-scale energy projects will naturally start from investments in the energy system of a single region. Various impact studies differ in terms of their treatment of spatial (and temporal) linkages, as well as their modeling of supply–demand relationships.

A very rough classification of the five studies covered by the Canadian case study is presented in Figure 3.8, together with eight additional tools that could be used in energy impact studies (Ziemba and Schwarz 1980). The scheme shows that the studies discussed by Lonergan constitute a representative sample of Canadian energy impact assessment methods, although with a certain bias towards the supply side. Energy demand is only modeled in the Helliwell studies, and the only example of interactions between the energy system and the interregional socioeconomic system is the INTERREG model. This is somewhat surprising since both regional energy demand modules and national

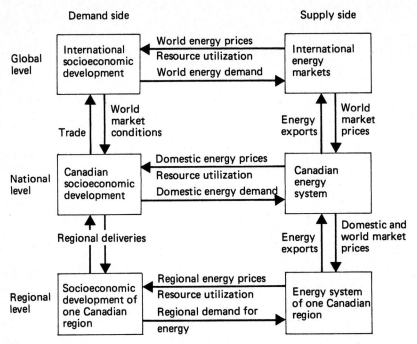

Figure 3.7. Socioeconomic (demand) and energy system (supply) components of society.

macroeconomic models with a certain level of detail on energy sectors are available.

Critical evaluation

The supply-oriented nature of the Canadian energy policy context has been reflected to some extent in the studies reviewed by Lonergan. Of the five studies, three are purely local or regional (AOSERP, BOOM-H, AERAM); one covers the national oil and gas market with regional demand estimations (Helliwell); and one depicts the interregional economic system (INTERREG).

The Alberta energy planning model (AEPM) is similar to AERAM, but comprises the national energy system with a detailed treatment of Alberta energy technologies. The model also includes price-sensitive demand mechanisms. The network model of Debanné is a multiregional counterpart of AEPM, while the Fuller–Ziemba model is a two-region extension of the ETA–MACRO model framework for energy technology assessments in the US.

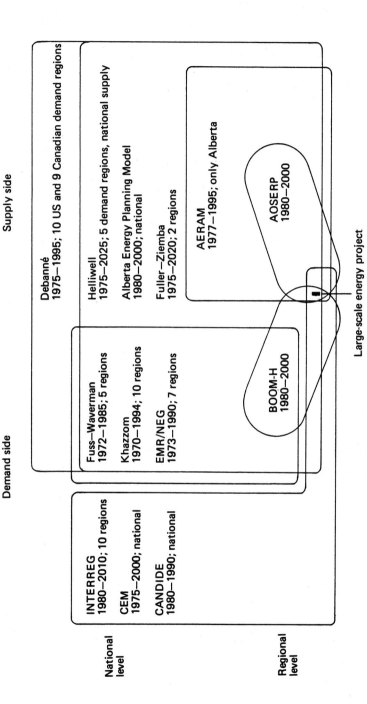

Figure 3.8. Classification of the analyses used in Canadian energy impact studies.

The Fuss–Waverman, Khazzom, and EMR/NEB (Energy, Mines and Resources/National Energy Board) studies are all purely oriented towards regional energy demand. They estimate the demand for various kinds of energy in different sectors econometrically. The Khazzom model focuses on lagged responses to price changes due to durable capital stocks. These demand modules normally need information from macroeconomic models as inputs. Similar demand modules have been linked to supply systems in the Helliwell, AEPM, and Fuller–Ziemba models.

The CEM and CANDIDE macroeconomic models have enough detail on the energy sector to be interesting options for energy–economy studies. The Helliwell group has carried out studies linking engineering pipeline models to national macroeconomic models. The INTERREG results illustrate the potential of multiregional extensions.

The Canadian set of tools for energy impact assessments provides a wide variety of models covering both regional and national aspects of energy supply and demand. Lonergan has shown that this potential has only partially been used, however, and that the influence of impact assessments on actual policy decisions has been small. The AOSERP research overemphasized data acquisition and short-term monitoring at the expense of analysis and prediction models. The academic nature of the Helliwell studies, the questioning of the "official truth" and, in part, the integrated national perspective, were all factors that worked against their acceptance. However, the Helliwell group argues that the long-term teaching function may have important effects on the future decision-making climate.

In my view, the Canadian energy policy context is a very interesting arena for multiregional assessments of changes in the energy system. The large and regionally heterogeneous base of energy resources, the close links with the US energy–economy system, the availability of both non-frontier and frontier energy resources, the high energy intensity in domestic uses, the implications of Canadian geography for energy transportation and transmission are all factors that favor integrated and systematic investigations concerning the interrelationships between the energy system and multiregional development patterns.

There are several ways of integrating the effects of large-scale energy projects from energy and/or socioeconomic systems points of view:

- national or multiregional energy system studies;
- national or multiregional socioeconomic studies;
- regional integration of energy system and socioeconomic studies; and
- national or multiregional integration of energy system and socioeconomic studies.

Conclusions

In the Canadian context many factors would tend to favor integrated socioeconomic energy frameworks for impact assessment:

- the growth rate of energy demand is controversial;
- the profitability of frontier resource use is uncertain, at least in the short term;
- "megaprojects" consume large investment resources; and
- regional imbalances are extensive and may be considerably affected by energy developments.

In order to assess energy projects comprehensively, both national and regional (or multiregional) perspectives are generally needed. My experiences from the Swedish context tell me that impact analyses starting from the national level need regional considerations in order to be policy-relevant, and vice versa. The regional, multiregional, and national assessment methods briefly touched upon in this paper constitute a good starting point for integrated regional/national energy impact assessments in Canada. Although previous attempts in this direction have not met immediate acceptance, continuing efforts may eventually indicate whether or not the current supply-oriented energy policies are supported by efficiency and/or distributional arguments.

Large-Scale Energy Projects: Assessment of Regional Consequences
T.R. Lakshmanan and B. Johansson (Editors)
Elsevier Science Publishers B.V. (North-Holland)
© IIASA, 1985

72

CHAPTER 3

Tar Sands Development in Canada:
A Case Study of Environmental Monitoring

3.3. Technical Review of the Canadian Case Study

William D. Watson

A study with the title "Regional Consequences of Large-Scale Energy Development"[1] connotes many different dimensions. First, there are the effects on the regional economy and environment, which become visible with time. To these we must add what I term informational and adaptive consequences. *Informational consequences* refer to the general ability of scientists and systems analysts to identify future states of nature with enough precision that forecasts of expected trade-offs can be judged to be either significantly similar or significantly different under alternative development patterns. *Adaptive consequences* refer to the general ability of institutions such as the market place and the political system to filter information and broker preferences so that outcomes or consequences are pushed in the direction of minimizing losses in welfare.

In my opinion, the focus of the problems addressed in this book is on informational and adaptive consequences, and our main concerns center on two questions:

(1) whether or not we are really smart enough to garner sufficient data and do adequate modeling so that forecasts are sufficiently precise in the sense I have described; and

---

[1] This was the title of the workshop preceding the finalization of the contributions to the book.

(2)   whether or not the ability to make sufficiently precise forecasts extending more than a few years matters. Another way of stating this second question is to ask whether or not the incremental coping mechanisms of the market place and the political system are sufficiently vigorous to ensure no-regret outcomes?

These two questions are not independent of each other. The market and political systems need information and forecasts; still, there is an important distinction. If costs and benefits are internalized, markets and political systems could continuously replan and, if appropriate, redirect development toward no-regret outcomes. There can be built-in incentives to be flexible and adaptive. The degree of flexibility — for example, redundant measures to protect the environment — would probably be related to the amount and the precision of information on environmental consequences. Just as importantly, internalization in markets and political systems can provide incentives leading to efficient provision of scientific information and analyses. Thus "having a stake" can provide dual pay-offs to an energy development project both in the form of redirection and in the form of data/forecasting efforts.

The contrast of this benign situation with policy or project planning conducted when a large part of costs and benefits are not internalized, is striking. In this case, objectives are narrow, the approach is fragmented and piecemeal, information gathering and analysis is focused on narrow objectives, and flexibility or the ability to undertake corrective actions can be severely constrained.

Nonetheless, an important choice facing society is the degree of internalization. If internalization is confined to narrow financial interests, as it usually is in most market transactions, then costs and benefits, adaptation, planning, and information generation will be prescribed accordingly. Widening the sphere of internalization can lead to increased adaptability and attempts at more comprehensive balancing of costs and benefits, but may not necessarily result in an improved outcome. There is a temptation to assume that just because markets are failing that non-market intervention in the form of attempts at enhanced internalization is justified. But this is not so; market failure can be followed by non-market failures of an even more damaging nature.

An ideal decision criterion, under the extreme assumption of certain (but scarce) information about the future, is that society should choose that degree of internalization, accompanying level of information generation, and project scale and location for which net present worth is maximized. Relaxation of the perfect information assumption requires modification to a criterion of maximizing expected net present worth if risk neutrality holds. A strong case can be made that the cumulative or stock effects from the build-up of environmental pollutants could result in irreversible effects. In these cases it may be desirable to reduce project benefit streams below their risk-neutral values because the possibility for irreversibility can reduce the options available to society.

In the final analysis, the treatment of uncertainty, risk, and information generation in project analysis and decision making will involve some measure of judgment. An issue that ought to concern the builders of analytical models to treat these difficulties, should be the identification of the attributes and expected outcomes for alternative degrees of internalization in project planning and development.

With regard to studies of regional consequences, three implications can be drawn from the foregoing discussion:

(1) Projects dominated by uncertainty (i.e., those for which alternative configurations generate equally likely net benefits) provide an opportunity for "learning-by-doing". Project design should integrate information acquisition and project flexibility. However, if unknown external effects are judged to be large and irreversible, then learning-by-doing should proceed with extreme caution.

(2) An efficient method for integrating information acquisition and project flexibility is to internalize costs through market and political system incentives. Examples of market incentives include environmental clean-up bonds paid by developers that are forfeited if environmental limits are exceeded and negotiable effluent charges based upon a review of the latest industry and government data on environmental impacts. Internalization by the political process could involve joint infrastructure planning by communities and developers, including revenues for financing additions to infrastructure.

(3) A situation of all-eggs-in-one-basket should be avoided. A variety of internalizing situations ranging from conventional internalizations that focus on immediate financial interests to more comprehensive designs should be allowed and investigated.

These three principles can be applied to the study of the regional consequences of Alberta tar sands developments. At a very general level, the Canadian approach would appear to be to generate information and to assess regional consequences under the narrow constraints of private financial returns, as tempered by national energy policy. Not surprisingly, information generation has taken the form of baseline studies and monitoring studies.

Lonergan's description of the Canadian experience indicates that the agencies concerned may not have been particularly deliberate in their planning efforts. AOSERP is one of the first Canadian efforts to assess possible impacts of large-scale energy projects. I would speculate that the Canadian scientific community made a convincing argument that assessment and especially forecasting could not be conducted until baseline data were gathered and until forecasting models, like the air dispersion models, were validated. In my judgment, validated models and a broad, well defined database are essential for defensible impact analyses. Also, it would appear that the Canadian planning agencies made the judgment, perhaps implicitly, that there was little likelihood that large, adverse, or cumulative irreversible environmental effects would result from tar sands development. Thus came the emphasis in AOSERP on baseline data and environmental monitoring programs. I would characterize all of the elements of the Canadian approach as learning-by-doing.

My assessment of what AOSERP has accomplished differs in emphasis from the answer provided by Lonergan. If AOSERP and any follow-on planning efforts are regarded as an experiment in learning-by-doing, then I think it is too early to evaluate and grade AOSERP. The baseline data are being gathered and the monitoring programs are being put in place. To date, judging from Lonergan's description, it would appear that no impacts have been detected that had not been anticipated to some degree. Perhaps some new set of environmental impacts will be detected and project development plans revised accordingly. If it is later judged that these impacts could have been detected only through a learning-by-doing approach and that any necessary adjustments are low cost, then I would conclude that the Canadian planning exercise for Alberta tar sands development merits high marks.

Finally, I applaud the Canadian effort to gather comprehensive baseline data and validate models. Canada's southern neighbor, the US, should take note. In some instances, US national and regional planning agencies have proceeded to make extensive superficial and artificial forecasts of environmental and economic impacts. The ability of the Canadian agencies to refrain from such practices is refreshing.

References

AOSERP *Research Summary Report* 1975–80, AOSERP Report 118 (Edmonton: Alberta Environment).

Bourassa, J. (1973) *James Bay* (Montreal: Harvest House).

Cartrell, J.W., Krahn, H., and Sunahera, F.D. (1980) *A Study of Human Adjustment in Fort McMurray*, AOSERP Report 112.

Davison, D.S. and Leahy, D. (1980) *Development of an Airshed Management Model*. INTERA Environmental Consultants Ltd, AOSERP Project AS 5.0.

Deines, A., Littlejohn, C., and Hunt, T. (1980) *Native Employment Patterns in Alberta's Athabasca Oil Sands Region*, AOSERP Report 103.

Douglas, G. and MacMillan, J. (1982) *Interregional Economic Impacts of the Alberta Sands Project*, Canadian Research Institute Report No. 82-2 (Calgary).

Energy Alternatives (1981) (Ottawa: Supply and Services Canada).

Energy Futures for Canadians (1978) Long-Term Assessment Program (LEAP) (Ottawa: Energy Mines and Resources Canada).

Ford, A. (1976) *User's Guide to the BOOM 1 Model*, LA-6396-MS (Los Alamos, NM: Los Alamos Scientific Laboratory).

Forrester, J.F. (1971a) *Principles of Systems* (Cambridge, MA: Wright-Allen).

Forrester, J.F. (1971b) *Urban Dynamics* (Cambridge, MA: Wright-Allen).

Helliwell, J.F., Kendricks, K., and Williams, D.B.C. (1980a) Canadian perspectives on the Alaska Highway pipeline: Modeling the alternatives, in W.T. Ziemba and S.L. Schwartz (Eds) *Integrative Energy Models*, vol. II (Boston, MA: Martinus Nijhoff).

Helliwell, J.F., *et al.* (1980b) An integrated simulation approach to the analysis of Canadian energy policies, in P.N. Nemetz (Ed) *Energy Policy, The Global Challenge* (New York: Elsevier) pp. 283–94.

Hesslein, R.A. (1979) *Lake Acidification Potential in the AOSERP Study Area*, AOSERP Report 71.

Hickman, M., Charlton, S.E.D., and Jenkerson, C.G. (1979) *Interim Report on a Comparative Study of Benthological Primary Productivity in the AOSERP Study Area*, AOSERP Report 75.

Korchiniski, M.K. (1978) *Interaction of Humic Substances with Metallic Elements*. Fisheries and Environment Canada (unpublished report).

McCart, P.J. and Mayhood, D.W. (1980) *A Review of Aquatic Biomonitoring with Particular Reference to its Possible Use in the AOSERP Study Area*, AOSERP Project AS 3.5.

McConaghy, D.J. and Quon, D. (1977) *AERAM: Alberta Energy Resources Allocation Model* (Edmonton: Alberta Research Council).

McConaghy, D.J. and Quon, D. (1980) The Alberta energy resources allocation model, in W.T. Ziemba and S.L. Schwartz (Eds) *Integrative Energy Policy Models*, vol. II (Boston, MA: Martinus Nijhoff).

McRae, R.N. (1978) A quantitative analysis of primary energy demand in Canada. Paper presented at the *IASTED Symposium on Simulation Modeling and Decisions in Energy Systems*, Montreal.

MTB (1980) *Analysis of the Leisure Delivery System, 1972–1979, with Projections for Future Servicing Requirements*, AOSERP Report 103 (MTB Consultants).

Padro, J. and Bagg, D. (1980) *Applications of the CRSTER Model to the Oil Sands Region.* Prepared for AOSERP by Environment Canada, Atmospheric Environment Service.

Parker, J.M. and Tingley, K.W. (1980) *History of the Athabasca Oil Sands Region, 1880 to 1960*, AOSERP Report 80.

Power, G., Gillespie, W., Wittkowski, D., and Rink, R. (1980) Computer modeling of boom town housing: The Fort McMurray study. *Canadian Journal of Regional Science* 3(1):29–48.

Power, G., Cadden, P.G., and Rushdy, S. (1982) *The Choice of Housing Policies for New Resource Towns: An Application of the BOOM H Simulation Model.* Presented at the 6th Annual Meeting, Canadian Regional Science Association, June 1982.

Pratt, L. (1976) *The Tar Sands* (Edmonton: Hunting).

Reid, J.D., *et al.* (1974) *An Assessment of the Models LIRAQ and ADPIC for Application to the Alberta Sands Area*, AOSERP Report 66.

Seberak, A.D. and Walder, G.L. (1980) *Aquatic Biophysical Inventory of Major Tributaries in the AOSERP Study Area*, AOSERP Report 114.

Staley, M., Everitt, R.R., Jones, M., Sonntag, N.C., and Birdsall, D.A. (1983) *Simulation Modelling of the Environmental Effects of Athabasca Oil Sands Development*, AOSERP Report 132.

Ziemba, W.T. and Schwartz, S.L. (Eds) (1980) Energy policy modeling: United States and Canadian experience, in *Integrative Energy Policy Models*, vol. II (Boston, MA: Martinus Nijhoff).

Large-Scale Energy Projects: Assessment of Regional Consequences
T.R. Lakshmanan and B. Johansson (Editors)
Elsevier Science Publishers B.V. (North-Holland)
© IIASA, 1985

CHAPTER 4

Synfuels Development in the USA: Case Studies of National Environmental Feasibility and Local Socioeconomic Impacts

4.1. The US Synfuels Acceleration Program: An Environmental and Regional Impact Analysis

Ted Williams

Introduction

This paper describes an assessment of the regional, environmental, resource, and socioeconomic impacts of a US national policy to accelerate the exploitation of synthetic fuels — liquids and gas from coal and gas shale. The policy was first proposed by President Carter in July 1979, at which time phase I of this regional assessment was completed to support the assertion that it would be feasible to develop an industry that could produce over 1 million barrels of crude oil equivalent per day (b.p.d.) without severe environmental consequences. The policy was implemented about a year later by the US Congress in the form of the Energy Security Act (1980), about six months after the final draft of the more complete assessment described here was made available for public review. The Act called for the setting up of the US Synthetic Fuels Corporation (SFC) with funds of up to $88 billion for the rapid commercialization of synfuels technology. The SFC continues, but has not accelerated synfuels development at levels anticipated by the Carter Administration. This is because of a number of factors, including slow economic growth, inflation, and high interest rates in the early 1980s, and the present low cost of naturally light crude oil. However, for a variety of reasons, it appears that both the policy and the supporting assessments have facilitated synfuels development in the US.

The assessment prepared by the Department of Energy (DOE 1979b) centered on a regional analysis of environmental impacts on an unprecedented scale; it covered all relevant environmental topic areas, and was done for all major US coal and shale resource areas. The study's findings — that there would be minimal and manageable impacts — acted as a benchmark for the assessment of environmental feasibility. Previously, finance and environmental regulations had been considered the two main inhibitors to synfuels commercialization; afterwards, environmental factors continued to be major constraints, but they were generally believed to be manageable.

The History of US Synfuels Policies

Just as synfuels applications are not new in the US but go back well over a century, assessments of the environmental impacts of large synfuels facilities did not begin with the DOE study. In 1976 a major assessment of potential environmental impacts was carried out by the Energy Research and Development Administration (ERDA 1976) to implement a portion of the set of initiatives proposed by "Project Independence", a crash study of energy supply alternatives by the Federal Energy Office after the oil crises of 1973–74 (FEO 1974).

The ERDA results were similar to those of several previous partial environmental studies on synfuels, stating that a great number of uncertainties existed because the technology was innovative and the projected size of any single facility was itself sufficient to suggest large impacts even if the proposed technologies had pollutant streams similar to those of existing industries. Further, the synfuels-process pollutants and wastes appeared to require controls that, at that time, had not been proven. A classic problem noted was that of the huge volumes of waste from shale retorts; equally vexing was the lack of information on the incidence and magnitude of new toxics and carcinogens in both products and wastes.

The Administration proposed in 1976 that Congress authorize the Energy Independence Authority (EIA), even though the projected environmental problems had been noted in the ERDA study. The EIA would be a temporary, quasi-public corporation that would provide up to $100 billion to private investors through loans, guarantees, product purchases, and ohter incentives. The aim of the EIA was to produce 2.5 million b.p.d. of synfuels by 1985. But Congress did not authorize the EIA proposal; in fact, it never came to a general debate, primarily because of the concerns over potential environmental impacts and existing energy supply patterns.

Even though the establishment of the DOE in 1977 had pointed to the national commitment to continue a policy of becoming "energy independent" by the 1990s, synfuels was only a minor energy supply proposal in terms of anticipated relative supply levels needed to meet mid-term commitments. As late as spring 1979 the projected level of synfuels development in the Second National Energy Plan (DOE 1979a) was only 1–2 million b.p.d. for the year 2000 — far less than the 1985 EIA goal proposed in 1976. The main reason for this low emphasis on synfuels was the fear of potentially catastrophic environmental damage, and that a lengthy period of environmental R&D based on demonstration plants would be necessary before any general commercialization could take place (DOE 1979c).

The spring and summer of 1979 brought another world oil crisis, and several proposals were considered by the Carter Administration to foster domestic fuel development, particularly synfuels. This was a major turnabout in the perception of the utility and safety of synfuels facilities after the defeat of the EIA proposal in 1976.

The Carter synfuels acceleration program, announced in July 1979, was similar to that of the Ford Administration for the EIA. Yet the new proposal received much more favorable consideration in Congress and within one year the Synthetic Fuels Corporation (SFC) was authorized. The SFC program expected to achieve a similar production level of 1.5 million b.p.d. (in 12 rather than 10 years), but a major change was in the findings of the regional environmental assessment that accompanied the Carter proposal (DOE 1979b): these were optimistic that the potential impacts of synfuels were manageable.

The scope of the 1979 assessment, plus the generally more positive (and detailed) regional findings, had a major impact on the acceptance of the SFC by Congess. Certainly the memory of the most recent oil crisis was fresh, R&D had progressed since 1976, and process economics appeared to have improved, but also the new environmental assessment appeared to verify that facility permits were more likely to be granted, pollutants would be known and manageable, and planning could minimize expected regional growing pains. The early congressional debates raised many questions as to the potential impacts, but the availability of detailed assessment results and the continued substantiation of results by follow-on studies shortly turned the impacts discussion to one of management — with the acceptance that all of the problems would be manageable.

Table 4.1 provides a chronology of the major actions that led to the enactment of the SFC legislation by Congress (column 2) and the primary activities connected with the preparation of the environmental analyses (DOE 1980) reported in this paper (column 3).

Many parties are involved in national policy actions. After extensive debate in Congress draft legislation is returned to the President for rejection or acceptance. But even after the SFC was accepted, other private elements had to respond to the initiative since the SFC was set up to

Table 4.1. Major events in the Synfuels Acceleration Program, May 1979 to August 1980.

	General legislative actions	Supporting environmental analysis actions
May 1979	Synfuels accelera-tion proposal (DOE)	Environmental appendix assigned to DOE (phase I report).
May–June 1979	Interagency analysis for president's review	Initial phase I draft provided for presidential review.
July 1979	Presidential pro-posal for legislation sent to US Congress and announced to public	Phase I report made available to Congress, public, for com-ment. Amplifying phase II report planning begun. Initial state questions asked.
August–November 1979	General public discussions	Report publicized in press. Phase II contractor reports begun; special reports for CO_2 and acid rain prepared.
September–November 1979	Congressional committee hearings on SFC	General environmental hear-ings held in September; special hearings on water held in November.
January 1980		Draft phase II report distributed to state agencies, Congress, interest groups, public.
February 1980	Congressional com-mittee legislation finalized	150 comments received, DOE peer review completed.
June 1980	Final congressional votes on SFC	Final phase II environmental report printed.
30 June 1980	President signs SFC into law	
July–August 1980	Special US congres-sional committee hearings on oil shale implementation	Special long-term (year 2000) analyses presented at hearings in Colorado.

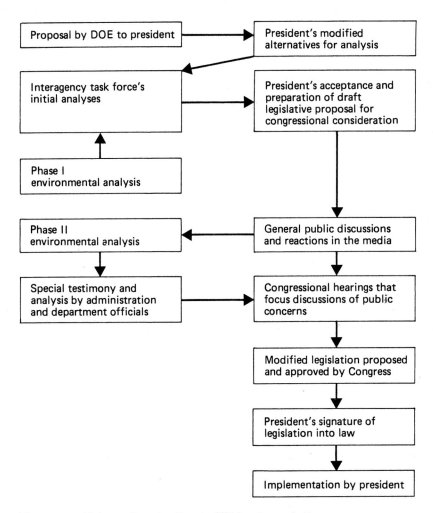

Figure 4.1. Major actions leading to SFC implementation.

accelerate anticipated private developments (see Figure 4.1). Much of this process involves discussion and refinement of policy concepts, but in order for these to be effective, a series of supporting analyses are needed. The DOE regional environmental analysis was one of several specialized reports compiled by the Administration.

In the year following the formation of the SFC, a vigorous project stimulation program was carried out by the DOE, but with the change of administrations in 1981 the activities of the SFC were slowed down. Several private initiatives appear likely to maintain the synfuels (especially oil shale) development momentum, although the present world economic situation has caused these to be slowed down or halted. The SFC continues to make proposals to stimulate development; for example, a plan to support six shale, peat, and coal conversion facilities costing up to $15 billion was put forward in April 1983.

To complete this historical background, it is appropriate to cite similar assessments and related analyses that have been prepared since the publication of the final DOE report in June 1980, including those of the Environmental Protection Agency and the Office of Technology Assessment. Under the sponsorship of the DOE an industry advisory group (the National Petroleum Council) and a national environmentalist group (the National Wildlife Federation) each updated the DOE assessment with their own reports (NPC 1981, Masselli and Dean 1981). Certainly the tones of these follow-on reports differ, but their factual findings are quite similar and are consistent with the DOE results.

After two years of intensive study by other groups, the DOE findings – that the environmental impacts would not be as severe as predicted in mid-1979 – have been confirmed time and again. This suggests that as synfuels initiatives are again advanced, the earlier perceived potential constraint of environmental impacts is no longer a major impediment, but rather a manageable constraint.

Phase I of the DOE Synfuels Assessment

In May 1979, during the second major oil crisis, the primary proposal by the DOE to President Carter was to reduce oil imports over the "mid-term period – 1985–2000" by developing synfuels technologies using domestic coal and oil shale. A crash development–stimulation program was proposed with alternative national goals for 1990 of 1, 2, or 5 million b.p.d. Because of concerns about technological feasibility and environmental impacts, however, these goals were rapidly scaled back to 0.5, 1, or 2 million b.p.d., and an interagency task force was set up to carry out a set of more detailed impact assessments, headed by the DOE Office of the Environment. The DOE assessment was also reviewed by the EPA and the staff of the Council for Environmental Quality (CEQ).

Phase I assessment methods

Because of the short time available in which to conduct the assessment (eventually lengthened to one month), the DOE used simple, existing tools and dealt only with a review of the adequacy of major resource areas to deal with environmental impacts. Since there was no way to estimate development schedules for proposed facilities, even though it was recognized that past studies had not been accepted because they lacked regional-level impact analyses, the report was designed as follows (see Figure 4.2):

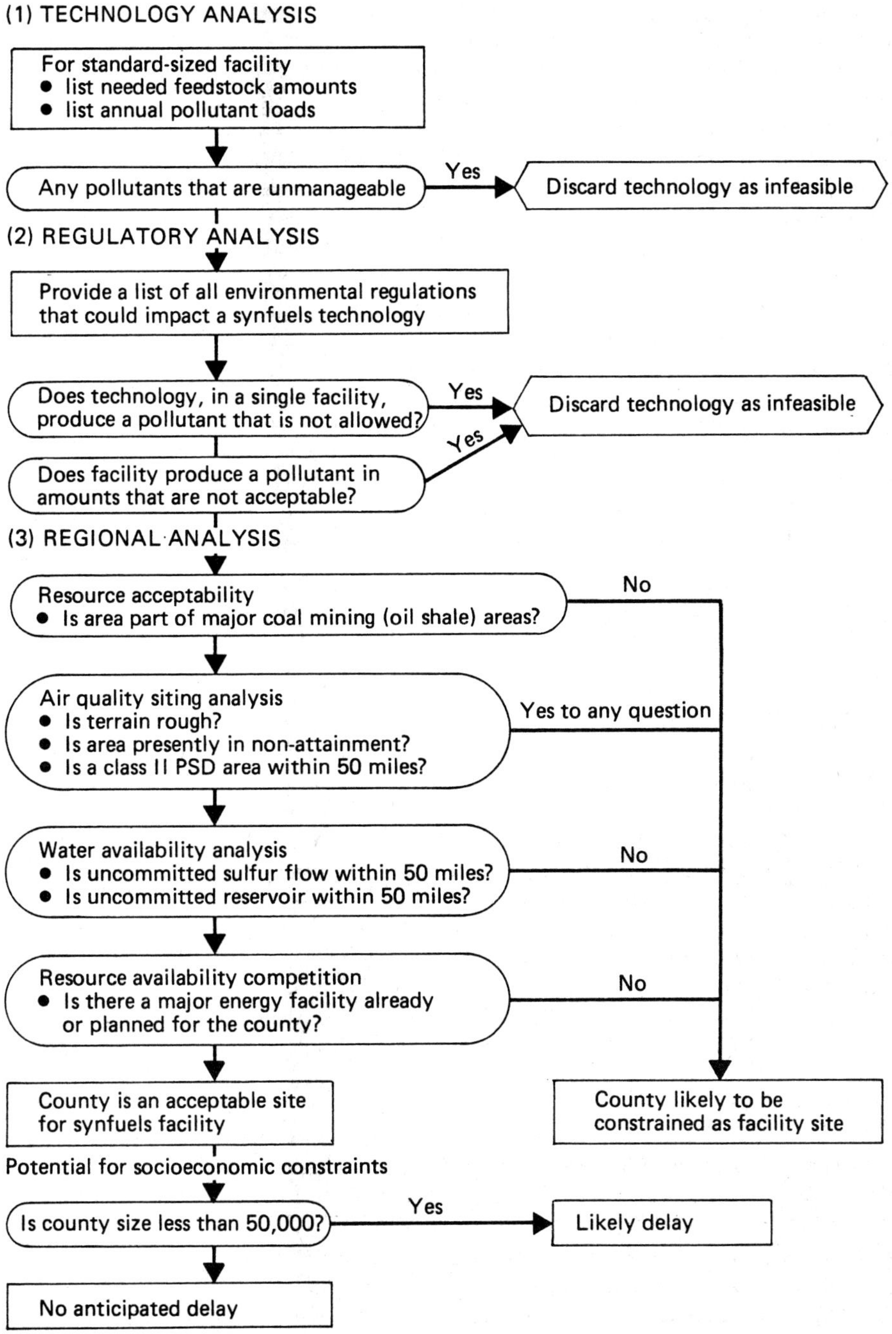

(1) TECHNOLOGY ANALYSIS

For standard-sized facility
- list needed feedstock amounts
- list annual pollutant loads

Any pollutants that are unmanageable — Yes → Discard technology as infeasible

(2) REGULATORY ANALYSIS

Provide a list of all environmental regulations that could impact a synfuels technology

Does technology, in a single facility, produce a pollutant that is not allowed? — Yes → Discard technology as infeasible

Does facility produce a pollutant in amounts that are not acceptable? — Yes →

(3) REGIONAL ANALYSIS

Resource acceptability
- Is area part of major coal mining (oil shale) areas? — No →

Air quality siting analysis
- Is terrain rough?
- Is area presently in non-attainment?
- Is a class II PSD area within 50 miles? — Yes to any question →

Water availability analysis
- Is uncommitted sulfur flow within 50 miles?
- Is uncommitted reservoir within 50 miles? — No →

Resource availability competition
- Is there a major energy facility already or planned for the county? — No →

County is an acceptable site for synfuels facility

County likely to be constrained as facility site

Potential for socioeconomic constraints

Is county size less than 50,000? — Yes → Likely delay

No anticipated delay

Figure 4.2. Phase I assessment methods.

(1) Existing and probable federal environmental regulations, standards, and permitting procedures were analyzed to determine the major constraints. Five areas of potential regulations were suggested that, in their most severe forms, could prevent the use of some specific synfuels technologies.

(2) For each available technology and typical facility size, a quantitative analysis of major pollutant emissions and resource requirements was done. From this the principal environmental constraints for each technology, and the necessary information with which to assess the magnitude of potential constraints at each site were identified.

(3) A generalized regional analysis dealt with some crucial factors not considered in (2) – at how many sites could the needed resource and environmental conditions be met, and could several facilities be located at one site? This was done on a county level for the four major coal resource areas and for the western oil shale areas (see Figure 4.4). Apart from the availability of energy feedstocks, the major factors considered were air quality, water availability, environmental demands of other nearby energy facilities, and socioeconomic constraints. It appeared that some counties could meet the siting requirements; and the national aggregate number of counties was larger than the expected number of facilities at the anticipated development level. However, because the most favorable areas were the western resource areas, secondary socioeconomic and ecological impacts could cause construction delays.

(4) A permitting constraints analysis was done as part of the environmental impact assessment. In the past, permitting slowdowns and uncertainties have delayed or halted development of several large new energy facilities. While the analysis proposed some procedural improvements, it showed no general pattern that this viewpoint has been generally true.

Phase I assessment results

The results of phase I (DOE 1979b) provided positive support for the national proposal to stimulate synfuels development. The general finding was:

> Assuming application of the most effective environmental control technologies and practices, deployment of synthetic liquids facilities on an accelerated schedule to 1990 appears feasible in terms of current environmental constraints. A set of first-generation technologies (surface oil shale retorting, indirect liquefaction, and biomass conversion) at the low (500 000 barrels per day (b.p.d.)) and medium (1 000 000 b.p.d) levels of production have sufficient siting opportunities; the high level of production (2 000 000 b.p.d.) brings rapidly increasing siting difficulties.
>
> Yet-to-be defined regulations, in their stringent forms, could change this finding. These regulations include visibility, short-term nitrogen oxide ambient standards, extension of prevention of significant deterioration (PSD) regulations, hazardous wastes standards, toxic product regulations, and occupational safety standards.

Because of the limited time available, and because it was anticipated that a large number of follow-on questions would be raised in Congress, a second, more detailed draft assessment (phase II) was planned to be completed within about six months. The phase I report was forwarded to the president as an appendix to the overall synfuels initiatives and was released for public review in July 1979. By early August the results of the study had been reported (sensationalized) in the press, and the need for a more detailed analysis to resolve new public concerns had become obvious.

Before describing the design and results of the detailed phase II report, it would be useful to discuss briefly how phase I was publicized (by others) and how it provided analytic information to the early congressional debate on synfuels and the environment.

After the *Washington Post* published an article on 5 August 1979 suggesting that the DOE assessment was actually a device to select specific counties for synfuels development, a period of sensationalized reporting and intense official inquiries into the purpose and accuracy of the study went on. The primary reaction of the public and state units was unhappiness, but the reasons for this were mixed:

- Environmentalist groups stated that the analysis should have been greater in depth, in order to identify more severe environmental impacts and constraints.
- Industry groups believed that the analysis included too many potential, but unlikely, problems, and that it was not sufficiently clearly stated that these were only potential problems.
- Western state officials were unhappy that the DOE had suggested so few constraints to synfuels developments in their states.
- Eastern state officials were unhappy that the DOE had suggested so many constraints to development in their states.

Therefore, the several opportunities that DOE officials had to testify to Congress on these subjects during the fall were welcomed since the purpose and scope of the report could be addressed and the more detailed follow-on studies could be publicized. In congressional testimony DOE officials were questioned, and their arguments were convincing. By midfall, synfuels development and the associated environmental impacts had changed from a topic of general apprehension to one that suggested that a phased development plan that included strict environmental monitoring had great merit. No area of the phase I findings was refuted; in most cases additional information from other groups and independent studies supported the general findings. By late November the congressional view was obvious — there would be a Synthetic Fuels Corporation similar to the presidential proposal. Based on the draft results, and recognizing the congressional change, the draft assessment was sent out for public review in January 1980. With minor changes, the final report was published in June 1980.

The Phase II Assessment

Because of the time constraints a number of limitations had been recognized and accepted in phase I that remained to be corrected in phase II. Because the congressional synfuels proposals were larger in scope than the original administration proposal — in terms of both the technological products and in the time frame of the application by the SFC — the phase II assessment was expanded. Also, the time frame of the national proposal was extended from 1990 to 1995, so that the number of eligible technologies that were likely to become commercial was greatly increased, thus introducing a much larger set of environmental concerns that would have to be considered. Also, new concerns included occupational safety risks and public exposure to hazardous products.

In regulatory analyses, one limitation often cited about the obsolescence of earlier studies are rapid changes in regulations promulgated or proposed. In the case of the two reports considered here, several major regulatory activities occurred between July 1979 and June 1980. These included changes in the regulations concerning air quality (PSD and visibility), hazardous wastes, surface mining, and water quality. It is interesting to note that the phase II report states that even though these regulatory actions were taken into account, the uncertainty of yet-to-be-defined regulations on slowing synfuels development was *greater* at the end of phase II than at the end of phase I.

The phase II study was designed in the two weeks following the publication of phase I. Because its primary purpose was to add detail in order to answer or clarify remaining questions, its general design was similar to that of phase I (see Figure 4.2). However, the level of detail was much greater, contained in 12 supporting studies (AMS 1979, BAH 1979a,b, Berkeley 1979, DOE 1979d, Flores and Appleman 1979, Hart 1979a,b,c, SRI 1980).

Some of the major limitations of phase I created by the time constraints were corrected as follows:

(1) *Environmental impacts considered*: Phase I included only air quality and water availability in the regional siting opportunity analysis, whereas phase II increased the analytic scope to consider water quality, federal land management, solid wastes management, transportation and mining impacts, and intrusions on wildlife habitats.

(2) *Level of detail of regional analysis*: Phase I considered regional data only on a county level; phase II used physical feature maps for the graphical analysis, thus allowing environmental impacts to be considered to a much finer degree. This is important, especially in the western resource areas where counties are often very large.

(3) *Quality of impact models used*: Aggregate models and stylized terrain were applied in phase I, whereas in phase II the level of models generally used for individual facility permitting decisions were applied to typify results for major subareas of regions.

(4) *Consideration of resource needs*: Phase I arbitrarily considered only one large facility size (output of 100 000 b.p.d.), did not recognize the ability of nearby counties to supply a large facility with energy feedstocks, and arbitrarily removed a county from siting consideration if it included a national park or if it did not include sufficient coal reserves for 20 years of operation. The use of more detailed models in phase II allowed these arbitrary limits to be removed, thus increasing the areas that could be included in detailed siting assessments.

As shown in Figure 4.2, the greatest area of expansion occurred in the third step, the regional assessment of potential siting opportunities (see below). The three other assessment areas were also expanded and updated in the following ways:

* *Regulatory analysis*: Because environmental regulations are continually modified and expanded, the limited set of existing and potential regulations explicitly considered in phase I were greatly increased. However, even in phase II no effort was made to consider state and local regulations/ordinances that could have a significant impact above the national provisions. On the positive side, in 1979–80 some major federal regulatory initiatives that would affect synfuels development did occur and were analyzed in phase II (visibility, air quality, and hazardous wastes management regulations). However, analyses of federal regulations continued to find that undefined future programs could constrain development more than existing ones — in other words, the unknown is a greater constraint than existing regulations in most corporate planning.
* *Technology assessment*: A primary change in this case was the inclusion of more technological devices and presentation of more detailed pollutant data, but because of several detailed technology/environment analyses prepared in 1977–79, little new work was necessary.
* *Permitting constraints assessment*: The states' permitting processes that were surveyed were expanded from one to eight primary coal-producing states. For each of the permitting flow charts, optimistic, pessimistic, and probable times were considered in drawing up schedules. However, due to the scope, the impacts of unscheduled litigation and lack of processing resources were not considered.

Phase II assessment methods

The topics considered as part of the regional analysis included an analysis of the fuel resource areas. Four such areas were selected for the regional environmental impact analysis, including counties with significant uncommitted coal and oil shale reserves. Counties close to these fuel-plenty areas were also considered to allow greater access to water and labor. The resource areas were (see Figure 4.3):

(1) Northern Great Plains (coal): eastern Montana, eastern Wyoming, and western North Dakota.
(2) Rocky Mountains (oil shale and coal): western Colorado, eastern Utah, northwestern New Mexico, southwestern Wyoming.
(3) Mideast (coal): Illinois, southwestern Indiana, western Kentucky.
(4) Appalachia (coal): West Virginia, eastern Kentucky, eastern Ohio, western Virginia, western Pennsylvania.

The choice of these resource areas was made according to coal and oil shale reserve data on a county basis. These data were then compared with the lifetime feedstocks needs of a synfuels plant. In recognition that a better site from an environmental perspective might be adjacent to, but not in, the resource area, a wider area that added about 100 miles in each direction around the mining areas was chosen to define the total regional dimension.

Primary Environmental Constraints

The first analysis done for the resource areas considered those environmental factors that could affect the location or size of a facility on a subregional (county) basis. The general analysis procedures chart is shown in Figure 4.4; the actual topic areas were:

Local air quality impacts. Because only one oil share resource area existed, the actual proposed facility locations and technologies were modeled to determine the limitations presented by national ambient air quality standards and PSD restrictions. The models used were those often applied in analyses to support actual permit applications. No air quality restrictions were predicted for oil shale deployments up to the expected size of the national program.

In coal resource areas, using similar models, there are some local constraints due to SO_2 concentration limits in national parks, but no significant constraint would exist for any of the liquefaction technologies in these areas. Greater constraints exist in the two eastern coal resource areas due to four factors:

(1) Eastern coal generally contains high levels of sulfur, so that emissions due to any liquefaction technology include more SO_2, the limiting air pollutant.
(2) The coal liquefaction technology assumed to be used in eastern areas was direct liquefaction, which has above-average SO_2 emission rates.

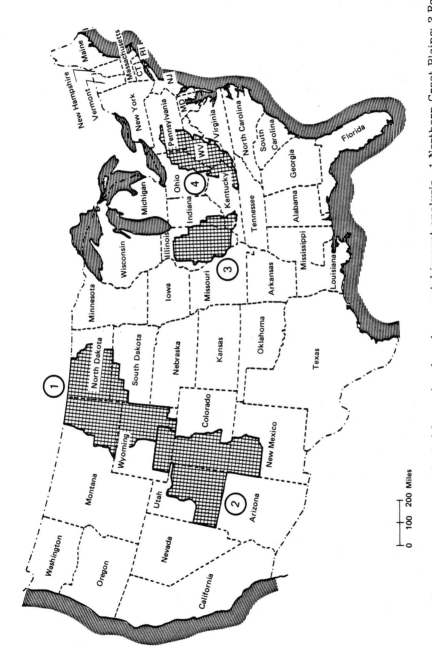

Figure 4.3. Fuel resource areas selected for regional environmental impact analysis. 1 Northern Great Plains; 2 Rocky Mountains; 3 Mideast; 4 Appalachia.

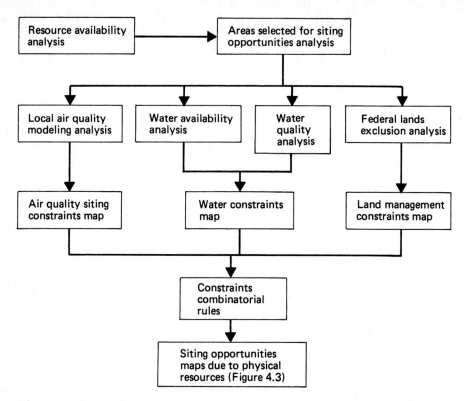

Figure 4.4. Phase II primary environmental constraints analysis steps.

(3) In the Mideast and northwestern Appalachian resource areas several areas presently have non-attainment status for SO_2, suggesting prohibitive costs for new industries in installing more stringent control technologies.

(4) The eastern two-thirds of Appalachia is mountainous, suggesting that any synfuels facility in this area is likely to be nonattainable solely because of emissions.

The assessment methods included operations of local air quality models in typical situations and for typical technologies for each resource area. Variations in terrain and emission stack parameters were considered (see Table 4.2), and where an air quality constraint was noted, redesigned emission streams were reviewed for feasibility. For areas such as the western shale and coal areas, where clusters of facilities are likely to be built, the air quality model was run to simulate synergistic impacts (see Figure 4.5).

Table 4.2. Model results from rough terrain (from the phase II report; DOE 1980).

Process	Capacity (10^3 b.p.d.)	Site (state)	Max. height of terrain above plant (m)	Emissions (g/s)		Model	Maximum concentrations ($\mu g/m^3$ – 24-hr ave.)	
				PM^a	SO$_2$		PM^a	SO$_2$
EDS	60	IL	43	6.4	217.0	CRSTER	2.5	42.4
		ND	53			VALLEY	3.0	139.0
		MN	101			VALLEY	166.0	5590.0
		WV	488			VALLEY		
MMG	45	ND	53	8.8	84.0	VALLEY	*	*
		MN	101			VALLEY	*	*
		WV	488			VALLEY	129.0	1230.0
FT	45	IL	43	56.5	115.0	CRSTER	24.0	2.3
		ND	53			VALLEY	11.0	*
		MN	101			VALLEY	*	*
		WV	488			VALLEY	1260.0	1740.0
Colony	50	CO	314	32.5	35.5	VALLEY	214.0	250.0
Union	50	CO	314	17.6	68.0	VALLEY	194.0	494.0
Ca-MIS	76	CO	314	79.5	76.5	VALLEY	200.0	180.0
Occ-MIS	57	CO	314	10.4	21.8	VALLEY	29.0	62.0
						PSD II increments	37	91

* Emissions do not impact nearby terrain.
^{a} PM = Particulate matter.

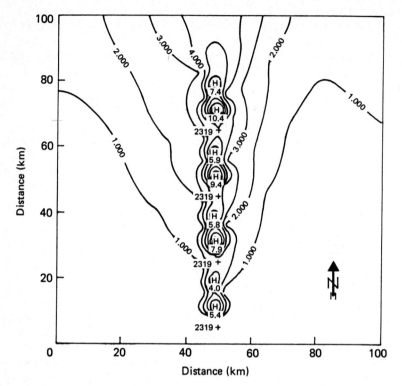

Figure 4.5. 24-hour worst-case SO_2 concentrations for four synfuels plants (in $\mu g/m^3$). PSD increment: class I, 91; class II, 5 (from SRI 1980).

Long-range transport air quality issues. Three long-range transport air quality issues were raised in the public debate that followed the phase I report. The phase II report demonstrated that for two of these issues (global CO_2 concentrations and acid rain), not only would synfuels development *not* cause discernible increases, but even its anticipated growth (given a highly successful initial deployment period) would make only minor contributions to the problem until well after the year 2000. This is not to say that the use of fossil fuels may not have large impacts in these two areas; only that synfuels combustion products would contribute an extremely small fraction of the total emissions.

The third long-range transport issue, visibility, had greater potential for limiting synfuels developments, since the visibility regulations had not been promulgated at the time of the assessment. Since 1980 regulations associated with plume blight visibility have been set and appear to have had only a minor effect in western areas; however, regional regulations on diffused pollutants have still not been set, leaving the private developer exposed to potential regulations that *might* require costly retrofitted controls on new facilities.

Estimates of emissions from new synfuels facilities and of overall regional and national emissions were made using the strategic environmental assessment system (SEAS) developed at the EPA and the DOE. SEAS is used on a two-year cycle to assess the environmental impacts of national energy policies, and also to estimate source emissions in interagency acid deposition research, so that the DOE analysis for synfuels is consistent with these other ongoing national policy efforts.

Water quality impacts. The primary impact on water quality is the discharge of mining or technology process liquid effluents to streams. For all western resource areas, the synfuels technologies are expected to have no discharges except to evaporation ponds; hence no effluents are discharged to the natural surface water system. In eastern coal regions some local problems could exist in areas with low-flow watercourses. While these problems can be managed, water availability (due to low flow) could also be a problem by compounding water-related environmental impacts.

Water availability impacts. Water availability in some areas is both a physical and an institutional constraint to developers. Because of the institutional aspect, ensuring access to water for energy developments can involve long delays prior to resolution at the facility level. The study findings, *at the regional level*, were generally optimistic and were based on detailed analyses by the appropriate regional water basin commissions (Colorado 1979, Missouri 1978). In the Northern Plains area, the greatest constraint was the smaller tributary water basins feeding into the Missouri River in the Dakotas; yet two reservoirs exist in the Dakotas (Sachakawea and Oahe) that will not be heavily drawn upon in the foreseeable future. The analyses of river basins done for the Northern Plains suggest that there is sufficient water to support the *total* national program; thus there is a safety factor to ensure that regional demand levels for synfuels can be met, once the institutional arrangements are set. In the Rocky Mountains region there are greater constraints due to present water storage and commitments. However, the detailed water basin study suggests that if reservoirs are developed as planned, the Colorado River could support a synfuels industry of over 2 million b.p.d., although some subregions within the basin could have water deficits, causing some facility relocations (Colorado 1979).

Solid and hazardous wastes imports. The only special regional problem associated with synfuels process wastes is that of the tremendous volumes of shale that must be processed in retorts. When this is done in surface retorts, the disposal areas that will require reclamation are immense; if *in situ* retorts are used, less waste will be produced, but the possibilities of groundwater contamination and occupational hazards are increased. Another hazardous waste produced in direct liquefaction is organics. Insufficient waste stream analysis has been done to determine the need for control measures, but the issue is primarily one of management economics.

Support industry impacts. The primary support industries for synfuels operations are resource mining and transportation. No specialized regional impacts were determined by the study; issues are associated with increased volumes of existing technologies except in the case of product transportation. Even here, the problems are not great since the products will probably be upgraded and refined within the area, thus minimizing unique transportation issues.

Phase II assessment results

The regional siting analysis provided a series of maps for air quality, water, and land use. A graphic combination of primary environmental impacts was then done for each resource area (see Figure 4.3), combining air and water constraints, plus federal land management considerations on composite maps. These were generally the equivalent of the absolute constraints determination of phase I. The results of phase II appear to be considerably less constraining than those of phase I.

In order to address the relative weighting problem, a combining rule was formulated for use in the preparation of composite ratings. This rule reflected the concern that a composite rating that simply averages individual ratings does not reflect the true difficulties that would be encountered in an area with one or more "low" siting ratings. Thus the combining rule for assigning composite ratings was as follows:

- If an area has been rated "low" for two or more factors (e.g., air quality, water), it receives a composite "low" rating.
- If an area has been rated "low" for any one factor, it receives a composite "medium-low" rating.
- Areas receiving no "low" ratings are assigned "medium-low", "medium", or "medium-high", based on rough averages of ratings for individual factors.
- If an area has nearly all "high" ratings, and no ratings lower than "medium", it receives an overall "high" rating.

In the Northern Plains area, over 80% of sites have medium-high siting ease or higher. In the actual coal resource areas, the only areas of moderate or severe siting constraints would be the air quality PSD I areas (e.g., the Northern Cheyenne Reservation and the Theodore Roosevelt National Monument). In the Rocky Mountain oil shale area, most areas have medium-high siting ease; Wyoming and central Utah coal areas medium-high; and other Four Corners/Rocky Mountain coal areas medium siting ease.

In the Mideast resource area, more than 50% of the area has low siting restrictions, and about 25% medium to medium-low. Thus although
much of the area is free of major constraints, some areas (south central
Illinois, urban locales) do have significant potential siting constraints.
Appalachia presents a less well defined picture, since its rough terrain,
when modeled on a site-specific basis, is often a significant constraint;
less than 20% of the area has high or medium-high siting ease. If rough
terrain does not generally have a major impact in later detailed modeling, up to 60% of the area would be of at least medium-high siting ease for
specific sites.

The phase II assessment of primary (or absolute) environmental
impacts was no more restrictive than that of phase I. The summary conclusion of the phase II report was therefore highly optimistic that deployments of synfuels plants, on a national basis, was quite feasible at the
projected and probably even higher levels.

Secondary Constraints Assessment

Two final topics were considered in the regional siting analyses: ecological and socioeconomic impacts of synfuels development. Because of
the poor quality of the data, however, these results could only be depicted
on a county basis. In the phase I report, following the direct environmental impacts analysis, lesser constraints were analyzed to determine
socioeconomic impacts and other competing demands for coal resources
and for air quality improvements. A number of ecological considerations
were listed, but no quantitative analysis was attempted. Phase II provided a more complex analysis of socioeconomic constraints, including an
innovative procedure for considering many ecological impacts. For each
general resource area, a set of maps was drawn up to combine the two
constraints using rules similar to those described for the environmental
impacts (see Figure 4.6).

It should be noted that the two constraints included submeasures
based, at least in part, on county population levels. Socioeconomic indicators were measured in order to identify counties with low siting ease
(21%) and high siting ease (2%). Measures of ecological susceptibility to
disturbance were based on the assumption that the lower the present disturbance, the higher the area's susceptibility to future development-
induced disturbance. Therefore, in the western areas comprising all low
siting ease counties (less than 40 000 population) for socioeconomic reasons the same counties tended to be judged to have low siting ease for
ecological sensitivity reasons. The same combining rules as used for primary constraints were used for these temporal secondary constraints
(see above). Substantial differences are noted and are discussed next.

Secondary socioeconomic and ecological constraints on siting may
cause delays in facility development, reductions in plant sizes, and may
be unable to satisfy environmental protection criteria in some locales.
Therefore, this second set of siting constraints could influence

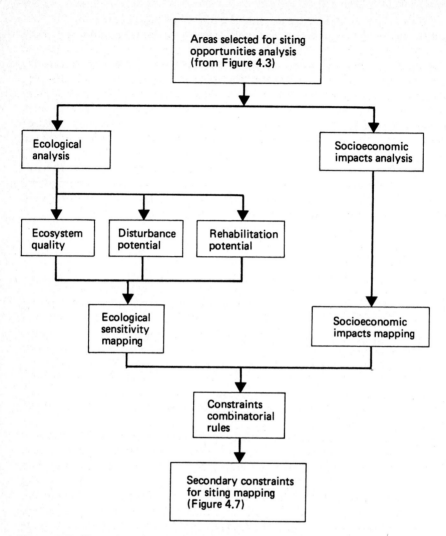

Figure 4.6. Procedure for considering ecological impacts.

development in areas that would appear suitable based on the first, more absolute siting criteria of primary environmental constraints. The diversity of factors that can impact a locale is impressive, and in many cases these are based on value judgments. Such judgments have led to the widespread use of environmental impact statements (EISs) and to the development of mechanisms for detailed public comment to ensure that such judgments are appropriately incorporated into industrial planning. In many cases, a collection of factors, rather than a single, overwhelming one, may affect the size or location of a planned facility.

Some factors that lead to delays can be widespread throughout an area, suggesting that a short relocation does not always solve the problem; this is evident in these analyses of western regions where the lack of urban socioeconomic infrastructure is a problem. The solution is (1) careful planning of the incidence and timing of impacts by extending and flattening the boom element of facility construction, and (2) strong planning of and financial support for small communities during the early growth period. In no locale was it judged that no measurable impact would occur. However, levels of impact may vary widely, especially within eastern resource areas, but industry could minimize impacts by judicious planning and by fully exercising the procedures and objectives of EISs and the NEPA process. It should be cautioned that a monolithic judgment for a region of probable causes of delays is unwise; detailed examinations for each locale, as is done for an EIS, are needed.

Uses of the phase II report

In one sense, the phase II report was unnecessary; when it was published in June 1980 the congressional debate on the SFC was over, and the Act was about to become law. Therefore, the final report did not support passage of the SFC proposal through the Congress, but drafts had been available, and had played a substantial role. Since the report had been produced, however, it did have a major impact on this process. Phase I had been accepted as a telling, positive statement that the environmental impacts of synfuels appeared to be manageable, but that too many details were still unanswered, and these would be furnished in the phase II report.

The first true products of phase II were specific special issue papers on congressional and public follow-on questions after they had read phase I. Several of these papers were published, but their true contribution had been made several months previously. Examples are the analyses of CO_2, acid rain, and water availability in western resource areas. When the technological analyses and detailed regional databases were completed, most of the final results had already been considered by several congressional committees and used in various hearings.

The draft report was widely distributed and review comments were requested. Over 75 written sets of comments and an equal number of telephone comments were received. In at least two states, officials distributed the report to affected locales to collect local comments. It was well received; the only changes made from the draft to the final report concerned updated factual information on recent events. Thus the progress of the *preparation* of the final report met its first objective well: it provided timely, amplified information to the Congress, states, and the public. However, secondary advantages could also reasonably be expected from such a process. The Administration's proposal stimulated an atmosphere for beginning and continuing private commercial development.

What happened after June 1980? The next section describes examples of subsequent (or contemporary) activities that illustrate how that initial momentum was continued.

Subsequent Activities

The DOE phase II report was well received by state authorities. Two eastern states performed similar studies for their resource areas to confirm that they contained acceptable sites, and one western state (at least) undertook a study of the carrying capacity of its resource areas using a similar methodology. The western states, as a unit, performed a series of similar regional environmental impact studies of synfuels and power plants. One western senator held a series of hearings in Colorado to increase public awareness of oil shale impacts to the year 2010 and to obtain opinions from the affected locales.

In almost every case the subsequent analyses have sought to extend the DOE study; for example,

- If the national program is realized by 1995, what will be the cumulative growth impact by 2000 — or by 2030?
- If surface water is a limiting resource constraint, what is the likely demand for groundwater supplies or for large reservoir development?
- If one region really is the primary locus for a large synfuels industry, what other levels of industry will co-locate, or will migrate to that region?

Such studies continue even as actual private development slows.

Another form of follow-on activity is perhaps of greater usefulness: the availability of critiques of the results and methods carried out by others. Three such critiques have been made of the DOE report to my knowledge. First, a government-selected environmental advisory committee to the DOE reviewed the draft phase II report (NPC 1981), including the public comments received, and issued a general statement of acceptability of the procedures and results, but unfortunately with no detailed critique. Secondly, the National Wildlife Federation used phase II to develop its own report (Masselli and Dean 1981), stating that the unquantifiable impacts should receive more attention; however, it did not argue with either the general findings nor any specific results.

The third detailed critique was produced by an industry-selected subcommittee of the National Petroleum Council (NPC 1982), who had some reservations as to the merit of the regional analyses:

> While an extensive literature search was conducted and other reports
> were evaluated [by NPC], none were found to have the depth and wide

coverage of the DOE report. The NPC recognizes that any report on a rapidly developing industry is quickly rendered out of date by changes in technology, regulations, and other factors. The Council believes, however, that a review and assessment of the DOE effort can identify areas of improvement in organization, data collection, and analysis that may be helpful in future assessments.

The following, more detailed comments were provided by NPC:

Certain subjects were omitted or insufficiently covered in the DOE report, including:

- the role of state and local governments;
- environmental research conducted by industrial laboratories;
- the comparative environmental impacts of synthetic fuels relative to the conventional petroleum industry and other industries;
- human health concerns and protective measures.

With respect to broad issues raised by the DOE report, the NPC concluded that:

- All synthetic fuel development is improperly divided into two time frames: research and development (R&D) from 1980 to 1985, and commercialization from 1985 to 1990. In fact, the timetable will vary widely among the various synfuel technologies [this is not a problem of the assessment method, but an artifact of the Administration's proposal].
- The report correctly states that first generation plants require close environmental scrutiny. However, this greater knowledge should be used not only to assure the adequacy of environmental controls, but also to avoid unnecessarily severe controls.
- The DOE report states that new major regulatory constraints are unlikely to emerge. While this may be true, the DOE report overlooks the cumulative effect of numerous small, site-specific constraints, which cause lengthy delays. The NPC believes that the DOE report's estimates of 24 to 36 months for permit acquisitions are overly optimistic.
- The DOE report implies that smaller plants are more advantageous than larger scale plants. This may not necessarily be true. There will be many case where large plants offer cost and control advantages over small plants.

This in-depth and substantive critique by the NPC, done about two years after the DOE phase II environmental assessment report was published, therefore serves as a good perspective on the merits and limitations of national policy assessments. It points out that results can date quickly, and that the purpose of the original product can be obscured. However, this report met its purpose — it provided an analytical basis for the belief that the new national policy was environmentally feasible. Further, as a compilation of data it continues to be used by other technical and development committees.

Large-Scale Energy Projects: Assessment of Regional Consequences
T.R. Lakshmanan and B. Johansson (Editors)
Elsevier Science Publishers B.V. (North-Holland)
© IIASA, 1985

CHAPTER 4

Synfuels Development in the USA: Case Studies of National Environmental Feasibility and Local Socioeconomic Impacts

4.2. The Cumulative Impacts Task Force Experience in Colorado

J.A. Chalmers

Introduction

The western slope of Colorado is a term used to refer to the 21 counties west of the Continental Divide. The economic base of the region has depended in the past on agriculture, mineral and fuel resources, and on tourism. Since 1970, energy-related development in the region has intensified, particularly in the northwest, as shown in Figure 4.7. There has also been significant oil and gas development, especially since the late 1970s, as well as increased exploitation of oil shale reserves.

In 1970 the population of the region was a little over 100000, but by 1980 it had grown to 158000, with about half in the Grand Junction area. The potential scale of oil shale development generated a widely recognized need for collective efforts by the public and private sectors to assess and plan for both the project-specific and the cumulative effects of existing and proposed developments. This led to the call in 1980 for the formation of a Cumulative Impacts Task Force (CITF); this paper describes the evolution of the CITF effort in 1980–82. Emphasis is on the methods adopted, their implementation, and on their relationship to the public policy process. Each of these emphases requires particular scrutiny in light of the rapid and unexpected cutback in oil shale developments in 1982.

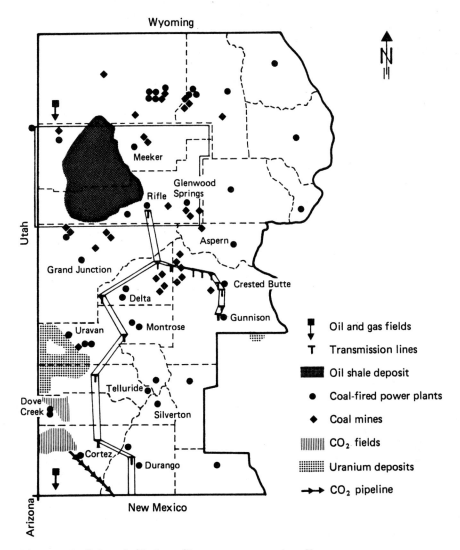

Figure 4.7. Colorado Western Slope energy area baseline map.

The Cumulative Impacts Task Force (CITF)

The purpose of the CITF is twofold: to prepare a cumulative assessment of the developments proposed for northwestern Colorado, and to provide planning tools that will be of continuing use to CITF participants. The dominant principle underlying the effort is that a shared view of the future, and shared methods of deriving that view, are essential for effective communication between private and public sectors. CITF has therefore proceeded by trying to establish a common base of understanding with respect to methodology, data, and assumptions through a high level of state, local, and industry participation, by reviewing all databases and assumptions, and by keeping procedures transparent and open.

Structure. The CITF is a joint undertaking of Colorado state government, northwestern Colorado local governments, and private industry. The task force meets monthly to make the policy decisions that have guided the work of CITF, which is organized around four work groups:

(1)   Work group 1 (projects): to develop and maintain a database on both existing and proposed projects.
(2)   Work group 2 (economics/demography): to develop a methodology for projecting employment, income, and population.
(3)   Work group 3 (public expenditure): to develop a methodology and data necessary for projections of public expenditure requirements associated with any population projection made by work group 2.
(4)   Work group 4 (public revenues and fiscal balance): to project public revenue flows from resource developments and the associated economic/demographic activity. These are then compared with the public expenditure projections of work group 3 to derive projections of net fiscal balance for the affected jurisdictions.

Each work group contains 25–35 members to develop methodology and assumptions, and to structure and oversee data collection efforts. The final structural element of the CITF is the consultancy firm of Mountain West Research, Southwest, Inc. (MWR), which was contracted in October 1981 to provide technical and support staff. Its principal responsibilities have been to implement work group decisions in the form of computer models and to document the results.

Motivation of the parties. The structure of the CITF implies, but does not make explicit, the very large number of individuals involved and their generally high level of public and private responsibility. Participants include oil shale company executives, and state and local government officials, and a total of 100 or more persons are regularly involved.

It is risky to generalize about party motivations, but some overview is necessary. State government and industry provided the momentum for the formation of CITF. State government's motivation lay in three areas: first, the state governor and his cabinet members wanted to be of service to the citizens and local governments of the area. In particular, since Colorado has no effective state siting legislation (most siting decisions are made at either the federal or local level), the state felt it appropriate to adopt a protective stance in relation to the oil shale industry. Second, CITF provided a vehicle for state involvement in an important set of analyses and policy decisions for which there is little legislative basis for state involvement. Given the excitement on the Western Slope in 1981, this may have been an influential motivation for many state agency personnel. Finally, many state planners and technicians were strongly committed to the perceived efficiencies that could be made using common tools and improved communications.

The motivations of industry were probably more uniform. The county in which a facility is to be located must grant a special-use permit. Application for, and granting of, such permits has become the forum for the negotiation of mitigation actions between developers and local government. The bargaining position of local government is very strong. Much of industry's support for CITF came from the effect they thought a "shared-view" of oil shale impacts could have on bounding the negotiating space with local government. At the same time, many industry planners were firmly committed to CITF because they felt communication with local governments would be enhanced and efficiencies would be achieved in their own planning and assessment efforts.

Local government had the least obvious motivation to support CITF. There was, to be sure, some genuine shared attempt to analyze and understand the implications of cumulative energy developments, and some important opinion leaders have strongly supported CITF from its inception. At the same time, there has been an ever-present wariness of the CITF process by local officials since they instinctively recognize its potential to reduce their autonomy.

But whatever the motivations of CITF participants, the organization's continued existence required that consensus be reached on (1) properties of the modeling system; (2) calibration and maintenance of input data; and (3) operating assumptions under which scenarios were generated.

The CITF Modeling System

Design criteria

In 1981–82 the CITF effort focused on six counties of northwestern Colorado, which comprise a total of 106 jurisdictions — counties, municipalities, school districts, and special districts. For each jurisdiction, expenditures by function and revenues by type are projected for 1981–2000.

CITF tools are best thought of as simulation rather than prediction tools; that is, they allow the user to examine the implications of different sets of assumptions about the future of the region. For example, the user can simulate the economic/demographic implications of a slow-down in coal development, a speed-up in oil shale development, or a changed location for a power plant. The tools are not designed to predict the future, nor to evaluate the likelihood of different resource development scenarios. The tools do not predict which level of shale oil development will occur; rather, they allow the implications of *assumed* levels of development to be projected.

The objectives of CITF and the setting suggested several design criteria for the models. First, there was little direct interest in economic variables; attention was focused on population, public expenditure requirements, and anticipated public revenues. Economic variables were important only as a means to project these variables.

Second, several levels of spatial disaggregation were needed. Analysis of the Grand Junction area and of the potential for purchases of materials and equipment in the area clearly required regional analysis. At the same time, jurisdiction-level analysis was necessary on both the expenditure and revenue sides, and required that various demand and revenue-determining variables be disaggregated to the jurisdiction level.

Third, since a principal objective of the process was to increase access to the analysis tools, it was essential that they be "user-friendly", and that the underlying structure and operating characteristics of the models be transparent to users. The fourth criterion centered on the issue of accountability. The models were developed to facilitate the planning that would be required by large-scale energy developments. Since implementation of these plans requires substantial resource commitments, the models' inputs and outputs must be able to be carefully monitored so that the models can be recalibrated or revised as necessary in the light of actual developments.

Finally, it was clear that the potential existed for major structural change in the region. Population could double or triple, a substantially wider variety of materials and equipment required by the oil shale industry could become available, and new trading patterns could emerge. CITF models thus had to be able to accommodate these kinds of structural change.

Overview of the CITF models

Work group 1 has been responsible for developing and maintaining a database on existing and proposed activities; these activities are contained in a basic activity system (BAS) database, which contains information on all parts of the economic base of the region. Work group 2 produces population and employment projections for any set of activities contained in the BAS, first at the county level, and then disaggregated to the subcounty level. The county-level analysis is carried out by the county projection module (CPM) and the spatial allocation by the subcounty allocation module (SAM). These three models are part of a larger system referred to as the Mountain West planning and assessment system (PAS), which was used to meet the requirements of work groups 1 and 2. Most of the discussion below is devoted to the structure and operating characteristics of PAS. Work groups 3 and 4 then require expenditure and revenue models, respectively.

The system PAS

PAS comprises three modules — the basic activity system,[1] the county projection module, and the subcounty allocation module — which are linked together in a database management and simulation system. Each component is designed to facilitate linking to additional modules such as those for facilities/services or fiscal analyses. Table 4.3 shows the three modules and their major functions and outputs.

Basic Activity System (BAS)

The BAS module stores information on basic economic activities within the region that introduces new income, thus stimulating new jobs and income in other sectors of the economy. It may be a single project, such as a power plant or a coal mine, or it may be the aggregation of several activities within a particular sector, e.g., agriculture or government. BAS was developed because of the complexity of planning problems faced by public and private decision makers, especially in those areas experiencing rapid growth due to energy developments. The problems often center on the large number of activities and their associated inherent uncertainties. It is thus important that the precise assumptions about each activity are known and that the information can be easily updated or modified as new developments occur.

BAS is linked with the PAS projection module. Individual activities can be added or deleted from the activity file and key information on each activity can be changed. The information stored for each activity can be divided into four components: activity descriptors, employment and income, composition and residential distribution of the workforce, and local purchases of materials and services.

All BAS activities are specified at the user's discretion. The user must then identify each activity as one of the following types:

(1)   aggregation of several basic activities in a single economic sector, e.g., basic agriculture;

(2)   operational and maintenance phase of a fixed-site project, e.g., a mine, power plant, or major manufacturing facility;

(3)   construction phase of a fixed-site project of the kind identified in (2).

---

[1] Basic economic activity is defined, within the structure of PAS, as that economic activity within the study area wholly determined by forces originating from outside the study area. This commonly includes activity associated with exported goods and services, but may also include tourist-related business and some government activity. Nonbasic (induced) activity is that economic activity determined by the level of economic activity within the general study area. In addition, when a county serves as a regional trade and service center, nonbasic employment in PAS includes that employment which is due to personal income in the counties in the center's market area.

Table 4.3. The three operating modules of the Mountain West planning and assessment system (PAS).

Basic activity system (BAS)	County projection module (CPM)	Subcounty allocation module (SAM)
Purpose: database manager for all basic activities.	Purpose: Project county-level economic and demographic conditions for assumed set of basic activities.	Purpose: subcounty allocation of county-level economic/demographic projections.
Data stored for each activity includes:	Outputs include:	*Allocation area component*
• Name and description of activity • Activity type • Time period • Employment levels by year • Residential allocation of the workforce • Average earnings per worker • Local purchases of materials and supplies	• Components of population change • Components of employment-related migration • Components of nonlocal construction workforce • Population by age and sex • Employment-related migration by age and sex • School-age population by age • Deaths by age and sex • Births by age of mother • Nonlocal population by age and sex • Total employment by sector • Basic employment by sector • Nonbasic employment by sector • Employment by type • Labor income by type • Personal income by component	Outputs include: • Components of population change • Employment-related migration by type • Components of nonlocal workforce • Population by age and sex • Employment-related migration by age/sex • School-age population by age • Deaths by age and sex • Births by age of mother • Nonlocal population by age and sex • Employment by type • Labor income by type • Households by age/sex • Housing by population type • Housing units by type *Jurisdiction component* Outputs include: • Age/sex-specific population • Housing by unit type • Personal income

County Projection Module (CPM)

The CPM has three major submodels — demographic, economic, and labor market — which produce county-level population, employment, and income projections for any set or subset of the basic activities contained in BAS. A total of 15 tables can be produced, as shown in the CPM column of Table 4.3. The impact of a given project, or set of projects, is assessed by comparing projections with and without the project or set of projects. The CPM can display the runs directly or display the differences between any two. The difference between a run with and without a project would be the measure of the impact of the project.

Subcounty Allocation Module (SAM)

The SAM disaggregates CPM outputs and assigns economic, demographic, and housing values to subcounty units. Two components of SAM are used, corresponding to two distinct levels of geographical disaggregation of interest to planners. The allocation area component facilitates projections of socioeconomic variables for subcounty areas which, in aggregate, total the county value. Thus the planner may analyze allocation area conditions that are quantitatively comparable and consistent with county projections.

The second component, jurisdiction, allows the user to quantify socioeconomic conditions and impacts at a level of detail consistent with the operational service provider's areas of service. The projections support the investigation of growth impacts upon municipalities, school districts, special jurisdictions, etc. Jurisdictions need not be exhaustive of the county and frequently overlap. Each component is supported by a distinct set of data and methodology.

Fiscal models

Work group 3 is responsible for projecting the public expenditure requirements associated with any project and economic/demographic scenario that a system user wishes to examine. The approach developed by work group 3 is best examined in terms of operating and maintenance expenditures and capital outlays.

The operating and maintenance budget of each jurisdiction is organized into a uniform set of functional categories for each type of jurisdiction. Per-capita expenditures in each category were then examined to see how they were affected by the size of the unit and by its recent growth experience. In order to increase the sample size, counties, school districts, and municipalities from outside the study area were included.

Projections of capital outlays are more difficult. To start with an inventory of public facilities in the study area and identification of new facilities or facility expansions for which commitments had already been made and funds in place, provided a basis for estimating the capacity of a jurisdiction to accommodate growth. Population projections are multiplied by physical standards that approximate the facility demand associated with a given population. The resulting demand is then compared with the estimated capacity to determine whether there are unmet facility needs. Demand and capacity are examined over a ten-year planning horizon although construction takes place twice during the period so that it can track unmet demand more closely.

Costs are assigned to facility construction based on a set of region-specific cost standards, which are modified so that they only reflect public costs. Once capital outlays are calculated, they are added to operating and maintenance costs to project total public expenditure.

Revenues and Fiscal Balance

Work group 4 is responsible for producing revenue projections and for comparing projected revenues and expenditures to get a measure of net fiscal balance. No attempt is made to force jurisdiction budgets to balance; rather, existing tax rates are extrapolated, subject to statutory limitations, and resulting estimates of revenue-generating capacity can be contrasted with expenditure requirements. The approach of work group 4 can best be discussed in terms of three categories of revenues — project-direct revenues, and indirect and induced revenues.

Project-direct revenues. Each project in the BAS file (type 2 or 3 activities) will generate revenues for local government jurisdictions (property tax, severance tax, royalties, and sales/use taxes). The revenue statutes as they apply to each type of project (e.g., coal or power plants) were examined, therefore, and the necessary input data were collected for each project to calculate direct revenues. Consequently, whenever a given set of activities is selected from the BAS file to create an employment and population scenario, direct revenue estimates are simultaneously developed for this same set of activities.

The same basic procedures are followed with respect to oil shale projects, except that a disclosure problem arose because of the detailed information required from the shale companies in order to calculate their tax liabilities. In particular, information is required on cost components of a project that the shale companies felt could not be shared in light of antitrust statutes. A plan was developed, therefore, that used a CPA firm to receive the detailed input data from each company. The data were then processed and aggregated up to a level where the shale companies were not disclosed. The aggregated data for each project were then passed to MWR and used to calculate the expected revenue stream from each project.

Indirect and induced revenues. Indirect and induced taxes refer to all sources of revenue other than those due directly to projects in the BAS file. The most important are sale, use, and property taxes. It is also necessary to project intergovernmental revenues, fees, fines, etc. Many of the relevant statutes are quite complicated in Colorado, and so significant effort was made to develop the projection procedure for each revenue source. These are explained in detail in MWR (1982).

Conclusions

It is premature to try to draw conclusions about the effects of oil shale development on northwestern Colorado or about the role of CITF in anticipating and mitigating those effects. It is clear, however, that the CITF effort has provided the decision-making structure with a new set of commonly understood concepts that are facilitating communication and understanding. There has been significant standardization of vocabulary: words like basic, indirect basic, or project-direct taxes have widespread and largely common usage in the region. Important theoretical notions such as changes in the central place hierarchy or import substitution are also increasingly well understood. Of perhaps even greater significance, there has been real progress toward the standardization of data formats; for example, different private developers are now using the same set of allocation areas to describe the geographical distribution of their employees. In sum, these results of the CITF process have had an unmistakable impact on the discussions between the public and private sectors. These better reflect many of the relevant technical issues, the parties are able to be more efficient in their communications with one another, and there is better appreciation of the fundamental issues about which the parties disagree.

Second, CITF has significantly increased the access of the public sector to the tools used by industry to prepare impact analyses. This has the very important implication of moving the public setor out of a reactive posture with respect to the presentation of industry and their consultants. Industry would have pursued planning and assessment studies similar to CITF whether CITF existed or not. The big difference for government is that these analyses are being carried out using a single modeling system to which they have access, which means that they can investigate their own version of industry impacts rather than being in the position of only being able to try to discredit industry's analysis. The result is a more balanced process in which all parties are able to participate and which promises more constructive planning and negotiation.

Finally, CITF has clearly established the case for an ongoing planning and assessment process that is able to respond to both the long-term policy issues and short-term crises attendant on large-scale energy developments. The implication is that the region must have tools and persons trained to use them on an ongoing basis. The value of any particular analysis is very difficult to anticipate given the vicissitudes of the energy industry. The value of the institutional capability to carry out analyses as they are needed is much more obvious. Emphasis must remain, therefore, on user-oriented systems that can be understood and applied by technicians in the region.

Large-Scale Energy Projects: Assessment of Regional Consequences
T.R. Lakshmanan and B. Johansson (Editors)
Elsevier Science Publishers B.V. (North-Holland)
© IIASA, 1985

CHAPTER 4

Synfuels Development in the USA: Case Studies of National Environmental Feasibility and Local Socioeconomic Impacts

4.3. Technical Review of the US Case Studies: I

William P. Anderson

Characterization of the Studies

In recent years, rapid increases in oil prices and disruptions in supplies have given impetus to the development of new technologies to produce direct oil substitutes from indigenous resources. Such technologies, known collectively as synfuels technologies, produce liquid fuels
from coal, oil shale, and agricultural biomass, all of which are relatively
abundant in the US. While the development of such technologies have
slowed recently due to the economic recession and depressed oil prices,
it is likely that they will play an important role in the energy future of
the US.

One impediment to the development of any new technology is the
lack of previous experience from which to draw expectations about its
environmental and socioeconomic implications. Before large-scale commercial application of synfuels technologies can take place, a number of
questions need to be resolved, which involve their ability to conform with
environmental regulations, their employment- and income-generating
potentials, and their effects on local government expenditures and revenues. Both studies employ techniques that may be classified generally as
impact analysis, but their overall objectives and the types of impacts
they examine are very different. The CITF study seeks to project the
demographic, economic, and fiscal outcomes associated with siting a

synfuels plant at a particular location. Neither environmental impacts nor resource constraints are considered. The DOE study combines a number of environmental impact and resource availability analyses in order to assess the feasibility of producing large quantities of synfuels, and thus could more accurately be described as a feasibility study rather than an impact analysis.

The DOE Study

The DOE's study of the US synfuels acceleration program was designed to answer the following question: Given existing technologies, the availability of the requisite resources, and existing environmental regulations, is it possible for a US synfuels industry to produce 1.5 million b.p.d. of oil equivalent by 1995? Two major points should be made at the outset. First, the question asks whether this much liquid fuel *can* be produced, not whether it *will* be produced. Therefore, questions of economic feasibility, opportunity cost, and oil price expectations are not relevant to this analysis. Second, while the question posed concerns a national aggregate, the constraints involved are largely site-specific. Therefore, the analysis must be largely regional in nature, essentially translating the question to read "are there a sufficient number of acceptable sites in the US to produce 1.5 million b.p.d.?"

Engineering data are used to create models of several representative technologies. These models relate inputs of coal, oil shale, and water to outputs of liquid fuels and pollutants. The study area is restricted to regions in which sufficient coal and/or oil shale is available and extractable at or below a pre-set maximum cost. The goal of the analysis is to classify all of the regions in the study area according to their "ease of siting" with respect to resource availability and environmental constraints. A two-step process of classification is undertaken. First, each region is classified with respect to four types of constraints: air quality, water quality, water availability, and land management. Given these classifications, an overall, or "combinational" classification is constructed.

This process of classification does not in any sense select the best sites for synfuels plants. For example, the classification of regions with respect to air and water quality does not seek to minimize environmental degradation, but rather to screen out sites where local conditions would make it impossible or improbable for such plants to comply with existing environmental regulations, such as prevention of significant deterioration (PSD) regulations. Therefore, in the jargon of mathematical programming, the classification is analogous to, but not as rigid as, the identification of a set of feasible locational—technological configurations given a constraint set. Selection of sites by optimization of an objective function is beyond the scope of this study.

The "primary constraints combination" represents an attempt to provide a measure of the overall ease of siting a synfuels plant in a particular location, combining information from air quality, water quality, water availability, and land management ease of siting ratings. Since these four ratings are based on noncommensurate criteria, the overall classification drawn from them should be interpreted with caution.

A number of approaches could be adopted in the design of this rating. The most obvious approach is to assign weights to the individual ratings and take the overall classification as a weighted average. The authors of the DOE study were wise to avoid such an approach for two reasons. First it implies a set of judgmental statements such as "air quality is 1.5 times as important as water quality". Also, a weighting system implies that a low classification in, say, water quality may be compensated for by a high classification in air quality in the same sense that goods may be substituted for one another in a neoclassical utility function. Since the elements being considered are constraints rather than goods or attributes, a noncompensatory approach is more appropriate.

The DOE opted for a set of simple decision rules such as "if an area has been rated 'low' for any one factor, it receives a composite 'medium-low' rating". While this approach avoids the judgmental statements implicit in a weighted average, it retains an element of compensation between, for example, the ease of siting with respect to air and water quality.

It is questionable whether this compensatory approach is appropriate. For example, a low ranking for water availability means that the required water supply will not be available more than 60% of the time and that conditions are not appropriate for empounding sufficient water to carry the plant over streamflow interruptions (DOE 1980, pp 5—51). This situation is in no way made less damning by the fact that air pollution does not pose a problem in the region in question. A case could therefore be made for changing the decision rule to "if any area has been rated low in any one factor, it receives a composite low rating".

This issue is of major importance since the results of the study are highly sensitive to such changes in decision rules. For example, at present, 90% of the area in the Four Corners/Rocky Mountain resource area are rated medium or better in overall ease of siting, even though more than half of this area is rated low based on water availability (DOE 1980, fig. 5—15). Therefore, if the change in decision rules suggested above were made, there would be a dramatic change in the overall ease of siting rating. In the light of this, it would probably be a constructive exercise to redetermine the composite ease of siting classifications under several sets of decision rules in order to assess how sensitive the generally optimistic conclusions of this research are to changes in the decision rules.

The CITF Study

The CITF model assumes that the driving forces in regional economic and demographic growth are activities (industries) producing goods and services for consumption in national rather than local markets. Growth in national market-oriented activities (basic activities) provides employment and income, which stimulate growth in local market-oriented activities (nonbasic activities). Therefore, the total contribution of a new basic activity to regional income will be greater than the sum of the wages paid to its employees. Thus the approach taken here is consistent with the well known economic base theory of economic growth. The model is flexible enough to include a wide range of basic activities, but synfuels industries are a basic activity that is of particular interest in the CITF study area.

Economic base theory is conceptually appealing because it makes explicit the relationship between the regional economy and the larger national economy. Also, it provides a simple format for assessing the economic impact of infusions of new basic activities into a region. However, economic base theory has come under a great deal of criticism as a basis for the design of operational models (see Tiebout 1956). One major criticism of this model is that it is difficult to draw a clear distinction between basic and nonbasic activities, although the large-scale energy projects that are of particular interest in the CITF study area are unambiguous examples of basic activities. Another major criticism of the economic base approach is that the value of employment multipliers associated with basic activities vary with the scale at which the local region is defined. The larger the area in question, the more likely it is that income derived from basic employment will be spent within it, thus generating local nonbasic employment. Recognizing this, the authors of the CITF study have taken great care to make adjustments for variations in county size. Also, it is often argued that the emphasis on basic activities as generators of economic growth may be misplaced because the likelihood of basic activities locating in a region depends first on the mix and quality of nonbasic activities available there. However, in the siting of large-scale energy facilities, it is likely that the availability of raw material inputs will outweigh such considerations. Therefore, the use of economic base theory as a guiding principle in model design seems appropriate in this instance.

The income-generating capacity of a basic activity depends on its employment requirements and wage levels, its local purchases of inputs and services, and the propensity of its employees to reside and spend their incomes locally. For each basic activity considered in the CITF study, a complex set of assumptions about these variables is made and stored in the basic activity system (BAS) database. A simple model called the county projection module (CPM) takes these quantitative assumptions as input data and projects the consequences of siting a particular type of basic activity in a particular location. Clearly, the BAS assumptions embody most of the analytical power of the CITF modeling system — that is, the projections can only be as good as these assumptions.

A wide range of available information, such as regional input–output coefficients and data from previous labor force studies, has been employed in determining these assumptions. Also, they are continually updated as new information becomes available. However, it would be prudent to test the model in such a way as to determine the sensitivity of the ultimate projections to changes in the initial assumption of the BAS.

It is not so much a criticism as an observation to point out that the CITF modeling system does not have the capacity to simulate any true market mechanisms. The underlying economic assumptions employed are the same as those of input–output analysis. In particular, all supply functions are infinitely inelastic and assume that there is sufficient excess capacity in the system to fill the requirements of growth in any particular sector. While this constitutes a significant weakness in the model, a specification consistent with economic theory would have two major drawbacks. First, the data requirements for estimating parameters constituting demand and supply elasticities for all sectors of the local economy would be prohibitive at this level of technological and regional specificity. Second, and equally important, one of the initial criteria for model design established by the CITF is "user-friendliness", which means that "the underlying structure and operating characteristics of the model should be transparent to the user" (see p 104). Integration of supply and demand effects would constitute a significant complication of the model's structure and thus render it less accessible to its users.

It may be possible to employ *ad hoc* techniques to partially integrate some market effects. For example, the labor market submodel of the CPM assumes that any shortfall in local labor supply is remedied by immigration from other regions. A more structural model would recognize that excess labor demand puts upward pressure on wages, and that increased wages attract migrants. This effect could be indirectly simulated within the structure of the CPM by assuming that immigration is accompanied by an increase in wages and therefore basic income. Schedules for such increases could be extrapolated from regions where basic activities have already been located.

Since the objective of the model is to simulate only the income, demographic, and fiscal impact of siting basic activities, the environmental impacts of these activities are not considered. However, environmental factors may be significant to these projections in cases where the impacts of one basic activity have a detrimental effect on another. For example, oil shale processing facilities and tourism facilities are both basic activities in the sense that they produce a product for consumption in the national market, but an oil shale facility has environmental consequences that are detrimental to tourism. Therefore, when assessing the impact on incomes and population of siting an oil shale facility in a region which also has a tourist industry, the possible reduction in income due to resultant contraction in the tourist industry should be taken into account. While it is probably unreasonable to expect that these effects be integrated directly into the CITF modeling system, they should be kept in mind when interpreting the results of its projections.

The economic component of the CPM is combined with an age/sex-specific demographic model to provide detailed demographic projections which take account of employment-induced immigration. These projections are distributed among public sector jurisdictions in order to project the fixed and variable costs of providing public services. Also, the direct and indirect public revenues from large-scale energy projects are calculated so that the net fiscal impact of a particular siting on political jurisdictions may be assessed. This information is especially valuable in rural areas where population influx would require large investments in public infrastructure.

Conclusions

In assessing the utility of the DOE and CITF studies, it is important to bear in mind the circumstances under which they were developed and the functions they were meant to serve. Many aspects of the CITF modeling system may seem a bit simplistic, depending more heavily on the assumptions embodied in the basic activities system (BAS) than on highly developed, theoretically consistent model specifications, but this simple structure is consistent with the stated objective of "user friendliness". This raises an interesting question concerning the design of models to provide information for policy makers. Adding complexity to a model's specification produces benefits by improving the accuracy of its projections. However, in some cases these benefits may be outweighed by the disadvantage of making the model's structure incomprehensible to the end users of the informatin it provides. The use of model validation techniques to measure the marginal benefit of added complexity in models of this type may be helpful in determining how complex the model's structure ought to be.

The DOE study was designed to assess the feasibility of a very specific program of development for synfuels industries proposed by the Carter administration. The scenario evaluated by the model was designed to be consistent with this proposed program. Naturally, this scenario may be altered in order to consider alternative development programs. However, the model is not intended to identify a single optimal development program.

While the specific points raised above deal only with issues of model design, the value of the databases constructed by both the DOE and CITF studies cannot be overemphasized. The DOE study, by bringing together data on water availability, fuels availability, and environmental conditions in a large number of regions, provides a set of constraints that may be used in assessing the feasibility of many alternative energy pro- positions. The CITF database (BAS) is certainly formidable, and should prove invaluable in simulating the effects of many types of industrial development in addition to synfuels.

Large-Scale Energy Projects: Assessment of Regional Consequences
T.R. Lakshmanan and B. Johansson (Editors)
Elsevier Science Publishers B.V. (North-Holland)
© IIASA, 1985

CHAPTER 4

Synfuels Development in the USA: Case Studies of National Environmental Feasibility and Local Socioeconomic Impacts

---

4.4. Technical Review of the US Case Studies: II

Leen Hordijk

Evaluation Criteria

This review of the two US case studies is based on criteria developed by Lakshmanan *et al.* (1982), and describes issues that should be contained in case study reports:

(1)   project history;
(2)   project development (especially techniques, methods, and data), interdisciplinary problems, and the problem of integrating techniques and designing the interactions between models and methods;
(3)   description of consequences for four broad areas: environmental, economic, social/institutional, and energy;
(4)   spatial and temporal dimensions of the models: study area, subcategories and spatial linkages; projection horizons and time dependence;
(5)   evaluation; and
(6)   policy analysis and the analyst—client interface.

The DOE Study

Comparing the report on the US synfuels acceleration program and the issues listed above, several remarks can be made. First, the paper does not contain much information about criterion (2) on techniques, methods, and data.[1] Secondly, approximately half of the paper deals with project history, while policy analysis and matters such as the influence of the press on congressional debates are only broadly commented on. Several important issues are not addressed; in particular, the models and methods used to assess regional and environmental impacts could have been described in more detail.

Environmental Impacts

In the phase II DOE assessment a wide range of regional environmental impacts was considered: air quality, water quality, water availability, land management, solid waste management, transportation, and intrusion on wildlife habitats. On the international level, the question arises as to whether the ambient air quality in some areas of Canada will be affected by large-scale US synfuels development in the Midwest and Appalachia.

There are strong interactions between water availability, demand, and environmental consequences. For example, a high level of water consumption can change an ecosystem completely, but this notion is not discussed. In addition, the impacts of solid and hazardous wastes from synfuels technologies, though produced in tremendous volumes, are not considered. These wastes deserve special attention, not only because of their volumes, but also because of their toxicities and possible carcinogenic effects.

Regulatory Analysis

The DOE assessment did not consider state and local regulations that could have significant impacts above the national provisions. Considering the emphasis given later in the report to factors that may cause delays to synfuels development, local regulations could play an important role in siting decisions.

Methods

Apart from some rough descriptions of the models used in air pollution transport the paper does not provide sufficient information on methods and models. An extensive discussion of methods of combining individual ratings is given, and I would like to raise the following points:

---

[1] One of the models in the study, SEAS, is described in Chapters 6 and 8 of this book.

(a)   The combining rule is sensitive to the number of factors taken into consideration. For example, the first decision rule assigns a "low" to an area that has been rated "low" for two or more factors. If there are more than three or four factors that matter, this decision rule becomes questionable.

(b)   The meanings of the ratings are not made clear. For example, what does it mean when air pollution is rated "low"? Is it low compared with existing emissions in the area?, or low compared with standards of ambient air quality?, or low compared with other areas?

(c)   The fact that ratings like "low", "medium", etc., could be assigned to factors could indicate that it is also possible to construct a (qualitative) project–effect matrix. If so, the use of multicriteria analysis seems possible.

The CITF Report

In accordance with the suggestions of Lakshmanan *et al.* (1982), the CITF report focuses on models, methodology, and data. Unfortunately, the CITF modeling exercise does not cover energy resource extraction and its corresponding environmental effects.

Energy and the Environment

Although the CITF was initiated to facilitate better planning for large-scale energy developments, the paper does not pay much attention to energy. It is only in the regional overview that the reader is briefly informed about the energy potential, the possible locations of power plants, coal mines, and oil shale extraction sites. I would have liked to have answers to questions such as:

(a)   In what way do the Colorado plans correspond with federal plans?

(b)   There are already many coal-fired power plants in the area, and an additional capacity of some 10 000 MW is proposed (see Figure 4.7). Will that lead to regional overcapacity and thus to electricity exports to neighboring states?

(c)   The BAS does not include data on energy, but it focuses entirely on the socioeconomic consequences of the developments, e.g., employment, income, taxation, etc. Why was this choice made?

Every use of energy produces environmental pollution of some kind, such as SO_2, oxides of nitrogen, particulates, solid wastes, or thermal pollution of water. The surrounding areas of mines usually bear a large part of the burden, and miners breathe polluted air. Oil shale projects deserve special attention in this respect for at least two reasons. First, this rather new technology has only been used in a few places, so that our knowledge of emissions is only partial. Secondly, the scale of operations will be larger than most other current energy utilization technologies.

Decisions on large-scale energy projects should be based not only on effects measured in monetary terms, but should take into consideration factors such as human health and effects on ecosystems. Two remarks can be made on this topic. First, the CITF is a joint undertaking of the Colorado state government, local governments, and private industry, so I assume that the public has been represented through local government participation. If not, how has the public been involved in the CITF activities? Secondly, the BAS contains data on activities, so that it should be possible to add environmental consequences of the activities, for example, using the SEAS databank.

Spatial Linkages

The PAS is essentially a top-down model containing three modules. At a (sub)regional level this approach is often unavoidable because of the large amounts of data necessary for a bottom-up approach. I wonder whether the top-down approach is necessary in PAS. Data in the BAS and CPM are apparently already available at the subcounty level. The projects registered in BAS are at fixed locations, so a bottom-up approach would be feasible. In CPM, basic employment is estimated as a function of personal income and, if the area is a trade and service one for other areas, on the personal income in its market area (MWR 1982). Apart from this the only spatial linkage discussed is migration. It seems that the small and open economy has been modeled using only these two spatial linkages. But interregional trade may also be important for the level of economic activity and employment.

These three spatial linkages (income spent in another region, migration, interregional trade) seem to indicate some kind of simultaneous interregional model, but it is not clear how the model deals with these features.

Methods

Considering the low level of spatial disaggregation, I expected that the models would be based on assumptions about producer and consumer behavior. The description of the models, however, leads me to the conclusion that they are rather mechanistic. For example:

(1) the propensity to consume does not vary with income;
(2) if unemployment rises above a certain level, people seem to migrate automatically to another county;
(3) nonbasic employment is directly related to personal income (through a coefficient).

The working of the model seems to be primarily one-way: BAS→CPM→SAM. In some places, feedbacks seem in order; for example, housing for immigrants is assumed to be available. If this is not so, the houses will be built and the BAS construction sector is affected.

Reflections on Some Details

(a) The CITF effort focused on six counties with a total of 106 jurisdictions. Was so much detail really necessary? How much of the final results of this disaggregation have actually been used by the authorities?

(b) CPM does not contain consumption variables, but instead uses personal income, even though consumption habits of locals and non-locals can vary widely and thus affect nonbasic activities.

(c) How many economic sectors are involved?

(d) Unemployed people are assumed to migrate out of the county, but how can you be sure that they do so? Are jobs available in adjacent counties?

(e) Iterations do not necessarily converge, e.g., personal income and nonbasic employment.

(f) The labor market submodel forces unemployment to an acceptable level, but this only shifts the burden elsewhere.

(g) Immigration occurs whenever labor shortages exist. The projects in BAS need people with certain skills, maybe different from those in surrounding areas.

(h) Is there any check on top-down/bottom-up consistency?

(i) The allocation area component of SAM produces figures on housing demand. Data on housing supply would also be interesting because of the effects on the construction sector.

(j) Which functional categories have been distinguished in the operating and maintenance budget?

Conclusions

This review deals with a complex system of models, and the critical remarks above should be read with this in mind. This (mathematics-oriented) reviewer would have preferred further detail on equations and results, which would help the reader to get more insights. I repeat my disappointment about the absence of consideration of environmental consequences of the projects and conclude with one final question. Chalmers states: "By mid-1982 all but one of these projects was indefinitely delayed, thousands of workers had lost jobs in the region, and there is no obvious source of major economic stimulus in the short term." To what extent can the models still be used in this situation, where not only have the parameters obviously changed, but structural changes have also occurred?

References

AMS (1979) *The Application of Interstate Compacts to Energy Facility Siting.* Draft Issue Paper (American Management Systems, Inc.).

BAH (1979a) *Environmental Regulatory Constraints Affecting Oil Shale Facility Siting and Operation — Perceptions of Industry and Potential Roles for the EMB.* Draft Working Paper (Booz, Allen, and Hamilton, Inc.).

BAH (1979b) *Impact of State Environmental Laws and Regulations on Emerging Energy Technologies.* Final Report (Booz, Allen, and Hamilton, Inc.).

Berkeley (1979) *Interstate Compacts to Address Multi-state Permitting and Regulatory Problems Associated with Synfuels Development.* Draft Working Paper (Berkeley Energy Facility Study).

Colorado (1979) *The Availability of Water for Oil Shale and Coal Gasification Development in the Upper Colorado River Basin.* Public review draft (Boulder, CO: Colorado Department of Natural Resources).

DOE (1979a) *Second National Energy Plan* (Washington, DC: Department of Energy).

DOE (1979b) *Environmental Analysis of Synthetic Liquid Fuels.* DOE/EV-0044 (Washington, DC: Department of Energy).

DOE (1979c) *Environmental Readiness Document: Oil Shale.* DOE/ERD-0016 (Washington, DC: Department of Energy).

DOE (1979d) *Carbon Dioxide Emissions from Synthetic Fuel Energy Sources* (Washington, DC: Department of Energy).

DOE (1980) *Synthetic Fuels and the Environment: An Environmental and Regulatory Impacts Analysis.* DOE/EV-0087 (Washington, DC: Department of Energy).

ERDA (1976) *Recommendations for a Synthetic Fuels Commercialization Program* (Washington, DC: Office of the President; Synfuels Task Force, Energy Research and Development Administration).

FEO (1974) *Final Report: Project Independence* (Washington, DC: Office of the President; Federal Energy Office).

Flores, C. and Appleman, J. (1979) *Analysis of Coal Electric Facility Permitting and Construction Timelines.* Draft (Levin and Associates, Inc.).

Hart (1979a) *Implications of the Designation of Energy-Related Waste as Special Wastes* (Fred C. Hart Associates, Inc.).

Hart (1979b) *The Impact of RCRA on Coal Gasification Wastes* (Fred C. Hart Associates, Inc.).

Hart (1979c) *An Analysis of the OSM Estimates of the Cost of Implementing SMRCA* (Fred C. Hart Associates, Inc.).

Hart (1979d) *Federal and State Environmental Regulatory Requirements Impacting Synthetic Fuels Development* (Fred C. Hart Associates, Inc.).

Lakshmanan, T.R., Ratick, S., and Johansson, B. (1982) *Assessing Regional Consequences of Large-Scale Energy Projects: An International Comparison of Experiences with Models and Methods. Project Definition* (mimeo). (Laxenburg, Austria: International Institute for Applied Systems Analysis).

Masselli, D.C. and Dean, N.L. Jr. (1981) *The Impacts of Synthetic Fuels Development* (Washington, DC: National Wildlife Federation).

Missouri (1978) *Upper Missouri River Basin — Water Availability Assessment for Coal Technology Requirements* (Missouri River Basin Commission).

MWR (1982) *CITF Technical Documentation and Summary.* Prepared for the Cumulative Impacts Task Force (CITF) (Denver, CO: Mountain West Research, Inc.).

NPC (1981) *Environmental Conservation* (Washington, DC: National Petroleum Council).

NPC (1982) *Environmental Conservation — The Oil and Gas Industries* (Washington, DC: National Petroleum Council).

SRI (1980) *Environmentally Based Siting Assessments for Synthetic Liquid Fuels Facilities.* Prepared for US Department of Energy DOE/EV-10287 (SRI, Inc.).

Tiebout, C.M. (1956) Exports and regional growth. *Journal of Political Economy* 64.

Large-Scale Energy Projects: Assessment of Regional Consequences
T.R. Lakshmanan and B. Johansson (Editors)
Elsevier Science Publishers B.V. (North-Holland)
© IIASA, 1985

CHAPTER 5

Conservation and Fuel Switching in Sweden

5.1. Large-Scale Introduction of Energy Supply Systems: Issues, Methods, and Models in Sweden

B. Johansson and F. Snickars

Reshaping the Energy System in Sweden

The 1970s was a period of serious discontinuity for Sweden in which many traditional characteristics were lost. Over a period of a hundred years the country had experienced a rate of economic growth that was never astonishingly high but, in an international perspective, remarkably steady; as well as a healthy balance of trade. The 1970s, however, brought economic stagnation, imbalances in foreign trade, and a severe energy policy conflict that cut across established political parties. These phenomena were marked by the defeat of the Social Democratic party in 1976 after 43 years in office, and by the nuclear power referendum in 1979.

In the mid-1970s the population of Sweden was 8.2 million, the GDP per capita was around US$8000, the trade volume exceeded 50% of the GDP, and the energy supply structure depended strongly on imported oil. Rising oil prices and the retardation of world trade hit the country like a cold wind.

Much attention was given to the energy situation, and a search for a new supply system was begun. Politicians began to emphasize adaptation and flexibility (based partly on diversification) as desirable. Several energy system assessments were carried out, but the notion of a system was partly lost. Forecasts and evaluations were made from sectoral and national perspectives, and alternative energy technologies were analyzed separately, without a thorough integration with the national system.

The outcome of several studies, together with assessments by commissions (see Figure 5.3), was a set of objectives for energy production and consumption, formulated in a national context and transformed into demanding and definite targets that the municipalities were expected to reach at particular times. The feasibility of these targets and associated recommendations were not assessed in a multiregional context, so that intricate problems of energy system combinations, characterized by interdependences and synergisms, were left to be solved through interactions between more than 270 politically independent municipalities.

We now outline some aspects of this fascinating story, and then examine the conditions they created for two energy assessment studies.

(1) The Commission on Consequences (COC) was set up to study the national consequences of abolishing nuclear power, and those of introducing alternative supplies. Within 3–4 months the Commission had to penetrate national and regional levels when evaluating the multidimensional consequences of the various options. The energy policy targets formulated before the referendum, and the constraints that followed from its outcome, created complicated and frustrating restrictions within which the municipalities had to find flexible and adaptive system solutions.

(2) The energy assessment studies carried out by the Regional Planning Office (RPO) for the Stockholm region reflected the uncertainties felt at the regional level. Many authorities, decision-making bodies, and local governments attempted to make their own assessments of the national and interregional consistency of various energy supply alternatives, and this led to strong conflicts. However, the RPO studies were more ambitious than many others undertaken, in that they aimed to integrate assessments for about 20 municipalities in the Stockholm region (see Figure 5.1).

Dimensions of energy system impacts

The two impact assessments described in this paper did not focus on the impacts of marginal supply changes. The COC had to assess the national effects of the closure of all nuclear power plants, as well as those of introducing alternative sources of supply. The RPO studies evaluated options for changing the whole energy supply system of the region. One option was to extend the district heating system and to build a large-scale hot-water tunnel from the Forsmark nuclear plant (Figure 5.1), which will continue to supply electricity until it is closed down in accordance with the referendum result. Another option was to construct a hot-water pipeline from the planned energy complex at Nynäshamn, to extend the district heating system, and to introduce a system of heat pumps into that system. There is no ready-made answer as to how impact analysis should be carried out in cases like this.

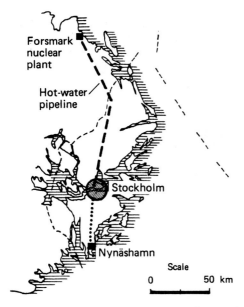

Figure 5.1. The Stockholm region (county), which contains one-fifth of Sweden's population, and one-quarter of the income.

In these two studies several complex interdependences may be identified, such as:

- those within the energy system itself, i.e., between components of the system;
- logistics of various parts of the system; and
- the interrelations between decision making at the planning and implementation stages.

These aspects are also interrelated in different ways in different time perspectives.

In this paper we adopt a philosophy of impact evaluation of large-scale energy projects outlined in Figure 5.2. We can identify three impact dimensions: spatial (the impacts on the geographical distribution of costs and benefits); sectoral (the impacts of various activities or resources directly or indirectly involved in energy development); and temporal (the impacts of a project in different time perspectives).

We stressed above the need for a non-marginal analysis in the context of new energy supply system components. Thus, when we speak of the introduction of alternative energy supply systems on a large scale, we basically mean the whole process, from research and development, through system design, to implementation. In the following we illustrate this view when presenting the main issues in Swedish energy planning,

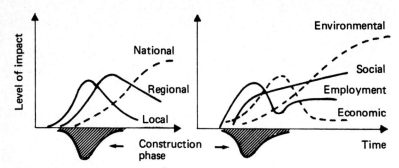

Figure 5.2. Impacts created by the introduction of large-scale energy supply systems: time profiles.

and specify the basic alternatives contemplated during the 1970s in the planning process.

Long-Term Energy Policies in Changing Perspectives

Changing national perspectives

The relationship between economic growth and energy use has changed over time. Per capita energy use in Sweden grew substantially more rapidly than the GNP per capita during the post-war period up to the end of the 1960s. Thereafter, the growth rate of energy use per capita has fallen steadily below the GNP per capita growth rate. At the same time, economic growth itself has slowed down for both structural and business cycle reasons, and in the early 1980s the Swedish GNP has tended to decrease.

Figure 5.3 illustrates how this process reveals itself in total energy demand forecasts. The figure shows that these forecasts have consistently overestimated the actual total energy demand. Over the short period 1970—81 the demand forecasts for 1990 have been reduced by more than 300 TWh/yr, or some 60% of the energy use in the mid-1970s.

There are at least three explanations for these observations and forecasts, which can be illustrated by distinguishing between a growth effect, a structural effect, and a technological effect. The first factor points to the stagnation of total economic growth as a moderation factor. We have already indicated that the growth of the Swedish economy was very sluggish in the 1970s.

The second factor stresses the explanation that structural change in the economy will result in altered energy use levels, even with a constant GNP. Such restructuring processes are evident in post-industrial society; for example, the composition of energy demand in Sweden since 1955 is

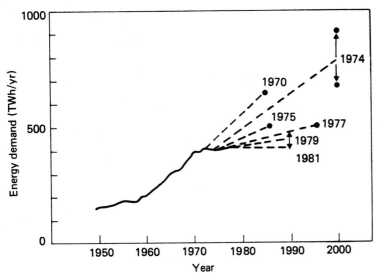

Figure 5.3. Forecasts of total energy demand in Sweden. The years indicate when the forecasts were published (from Steen *et al.* 1982).

Table 5.1. The development of energy demand in Sweden 1955–78.

	Demand (TWh/yr)			
	1955	1965	1978	Annual change 1955–78 (%)
Manufacturing	78	125	147	2.8
Transport	27	45	67	4.0
Other sectors	69	115	171	4.0
Total energy use	174	285	385	3.8
of which electricity	21	42	81	6.0
Population (thousands)	7262	7734	8276	0.6
Energy use per capita (kWh)	24000	37000	47000	2.9
Electricity use per capita	2900	5400	9800	5.5

shown in Table 5.1. Industrial energy demand has grown more slowly than total energy demand, while energy demand in the transportation and other service sectors has grown at a faster rate. Electricity use has grown much more rapidly than average energy use, especially since 1965. The electricity component is therefore the most important one to forecast; much of the debate on nuclear power has centered on the use of electricity.

The third and most difficult factor to discern behind the stagnation of energy demand is technological development, which may give rise to reduced total energy use even though the level of GNP and the mix of demand types remains unchanged. Technology is a strategic issue relating not only to cost-optimal substitution processes within industry, but also to changes in housing supply types and in human behavior. Technological change in the energy component of housing services is often termed energy conservation; this is always tied up with investment costs, however, so that there is always a technical change component. Current national policy in this respect is to reduce energy use in housing built before 1978 by 25–30% over a ten-year period, but this goal has been difficult to implement uniformly throughout Sweden. An estimated relationship between investment sacrifices and the level of gross energy consumption indicates exploding marginal conservation costs at an energy conservation level above 25 TWh/yr.

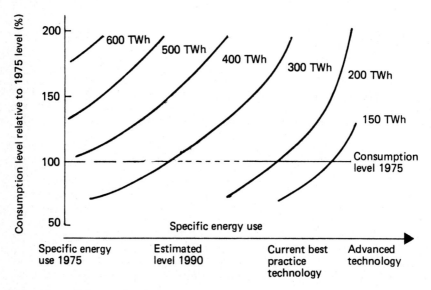

Figure 5.4. Relationship betwen consumption level, specific energy uses, and total energy use in Sweden (from Steen *et al.* 1982).

Technological change in the industrial sector relates to both capital embodied and disembodied processes. Machinery with low specific energy demand may be installed, production processes may be trimmed, and new plants may replace old ones, thus pushing towards the current best-practice technology. The speed of this substitution process is by no means independent of economic growth, even though technological change can also occur at zero growth. Figure 5.4 illustrates the considerable range of energy demand arising from the technological effect at constant GNP and economic structure, based on detailed studies of the least energy-intensive technologies (now) available. An introduction of the current best-practice technology would lead to a considerably lower energy demand level than that estimated for 1990. Figure 5.4 illustrates the large gap between technological feasibility and economic competitiveness, and points out the constructive role of planning in guiding Sweden's realization of a sustainable energy system faster than could be achieved by market forces alone.

Tables 5.2 and 5.3 show the 1980 reference scenario up to the year 2000, with regard to the combination of energy resources and the composition of the electricity supply subsystem, respectively. Both tables contain the nuclear power option since they do not go beyond the year 2000. Thus the long-term issue of phasing out nuclear capacity is not considered here.

Table 5.2. Gross supply of primary energy resources in a reference scenario of energy system development 1980–2000 (TWh/yr).

Energy resource	1980	1985	1990	2000
Oil, oil products, and methanol	313	266	225	179
Coal	3	21	40	83
Metallurgical coal	17	19	20	24
Hydropower	62	64	65	65
Wind	–	–	1	4
Solar	–	1	3	6
Back pressure	37	38	41	41
Wood, straw	3	13	25	37
Peat	–	1	4	20
Nuclear	23	47	58	58
Total	458	470	482	517

It is assumed that the goal of reducing the dependence on oil imports will be realized by increasing the use of coal and domestic renewable resources (wood, straw, and peat). The introduction of wind or solar power on a large scale is not realistic in Sweden in the time perspective adopted.

The electricity produced by the nuclear sector will exceed demand in the 1980s, if current trends continue (see Table 5.3). It is a major dilemma for Sweden that nuclear power is currently so competitive that only taxation can reduce its attractiveness. The most unusual feature of the energy supply system is the expansion of cogenerated heat and electricity for district heating systems, which will replace individual domestic boilers. Cogeneration is a technology that must be assessed in a local and regional context since remote heating systems are only viable in regions with a high energy density.

Table 5.3. The electricity supply subsystem in a reference scenario for 1980–2000.

Energy source	1980		1985		1990		2000	
	MW	TWh	MW	TWh	MW	TWh	MW	TWh
Hydropower	15000	62	15900	64	16200	65	16200	65
Nuclear power	3700	23	8400	47	9450	58	9450	58
Industrial back pressure	900	5	1000	5	1200	7	1500	9
Combined heat and power	2150	6	2450	4	2450	6	3750	15
Oil-based condensation	3100	4	3000	1	2500	1	800	–
Coal-based condensation	–	–	–	–	–	–	3000	3
Gas turbines	1800	–	1800	–	1800	–	1800	–
Wind power	–	–	–	–	(300)	1	(1300)	4
Heat pumps	–	–	–	–	–	–	500	–
Total	26650	100	32550	121	33600	138	37000	154
Final electricity use		91		110		125		140
Distribution losses		9		11		13		14

Formulating long-term energy policies

Prior to 1973 Swedish national energy policies were formulated in a context of continued growth in GNP, employment, and energy demand. Nuclear power was intimately associated with that growth philosophy, but its safety and long-term contribution to the energy system were already hot political issues. Energy planning in the 1960s had led to a massive expansion of the nuclear sector, at least in relation to the size of the economy. However, by the time of the first oil crisis in 1973 the public did not engage in an even stronger support of the nuclear option, but rather intensified the campaign against it. The energy issue was brought into the political limelight, resulting in continued surveillance of nuclear technology in the media. In fact, it was not until the nuclear referendum in 1979 that the political debate settled down. The oil crises, and the Three Mile Island incident, had an enormous impact on energy policy formulation in Sweden.

Figure 5.5 highlights the official investigations into the energy issue and their accompanying government propositions. The 1970 Energy Committee assumed that energy demand would continue to grow at a faster rate than the GNP and that an expansion of the electricity supply was necessary. In particular, hydroelectric peak-load stations were planned to be complemented by nuclear rather than oil-based condensation plants to meet baseload demand.

The 1973 oil crisis precipitated a new set of energy demand forecasts in 1974–75, based on an extensive energy study that was eventually used

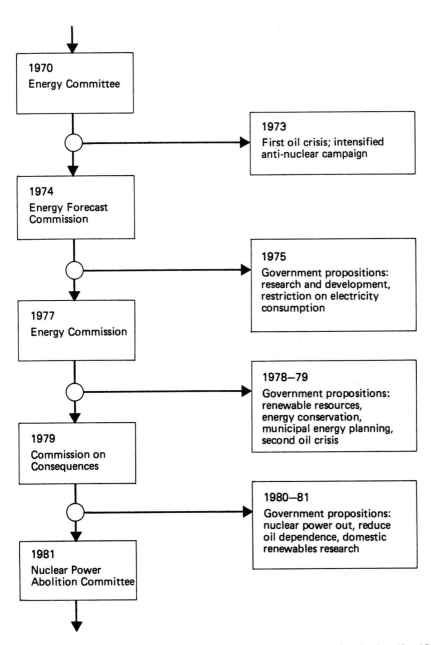

Figure 5.5. The process of formulating Swedish energy policies during the 1970s.

to support a government proposal in 1975 to start a massive R&D program focusing on new technological options. Forecasts indicated that restrictions on electricity consumption would be needed, and speculations were made about a situation with zero growth in energy use in the 1990s, without any substantial underpinning.

R&D activities were undertaken on a broad scale and several energy research coordination bodies were set up, although none paid much attention to regional and conservation issues. A major investigation was made by the Swedish Energy Commission, which led to a new government proposal stressing the role of conservation, and substantially increased responsibilities for energy planning were devolved to the municipalities. At the same time, the debate on nuclear versus renewable resources led to a political crisis on top of the second oil price shock.

A referendum on nuclear power emerged as the only viable alternative in view of the political stalemate, and this finally led to a narrowing of Swedish energy policy options. The COC prepared the background material for that referendum during the fall of 1979. The majority that voted to keep nuclear power during the 25-year lifetime of existing plants, including those under construction, was as slim as 58%. Following the referendum, the government set up a committee to prepare for the phasing out of nuclear technology, and stressed the necessity to reduce the dependence on oil, even at the cost of substituting imported coal. Research into domestic renewable resources was intensified. During this period, strategic decisions on energy system investments were postponed, even though in many regions such as Stockholm such decisions were badly needed.

Regional implementation of national policies

Long-term national goals for the Swedish energy system stress flexibility rather than efficiency, in order ultimately to arrive at a sustainable and differentiated system based on domestic renewable resources. The latest government proposals have given greater emphasis to the goal of reducing the use of oil, whereas earlier policies aimed to decentralize energy planning to the municipal level. Many municipalities thus see the reduction in the dependence on oil as the major objective, and this has resulted in a loss of competence in the field of comprehensive energy planning. Also, regional planners have experienced increasing uncertainties about the implications of national policies for their particular regions, since uncoordinated decisions by individual municipalities can easily create undesirable solutions.

This regional/national predicament can be illustrated by three separate alternatives: combined heat and power plants; gas pipelines; and peat processing. The potential of peat processing has a spurious relevance for municipal and regional energy planning because the competition between the potential sources and systems has not been spelled out, even at the national level, and also because local variations in costs and resource availability are uncertain. Thus, even though such inventories are useful as a starting point for national/regional energy policy considerations, they are by no means sufficient. Such questions will have to be resolved by special energy studies that distinguish between national, regional, and local systems. Regional studies have been started since the completion of the COC studies, such as those for the Stockholm region described below. However, the national/regional perspective of the COC studies[1] is still unique.

Impact Assessment Methodology used by the COC

Alternatives investigated

The basic methodological problem faced by the COC was how to generate and compare a set of alternative energy supply scenarios. The line of attack chosen was to elaborate a reference scenario, in line with current economic development trends *and* the nuclear power program, and then to specify alternative scenarios for the period 1980–2000, assuming that the nuclear sector would be phased out before 1990.

Since nuclear power is used primarily to produce electricity (no nuclear waste heat is yet used in remote heating systems), alternative energy systems may be compared by describing electricity production subsystems and by assessing the structure of electricity demand, at equilibrium, in various cases.

The *reference* case assumes that existing plans will be put into effect to produce 91 TWh/yr of electricity in 1980 and 125 TWh in 1990. Twelve nuclear power plants will be in operation for their service lives, but no longer. In 1990 nuclear power will provide 58 TWh of electricity, more than double the 1980 level. The structure of electricity consumption will change to a more intensive use in the "miscellaneous" sector; a considerable proportion of this increase relates to the expansion of domestic and industrial heating by electricity.

The *abolition* alternative has two variants for 1990, one yielding 105 TWh of electricity, and the other 95 TWh. The total consumption is lower in both of these in 1990 and 2000 than in the reference case, stemming from the difficulties in completely replacing nuclear power within ten years.

The 105 TWh level may be attainable by 1990, but it presupposes a rapid expansion of coal-fired power production, and there may be difficulties in building and commissioning the necessary new plants with sufficient speed. No expansion of domestic electric heating will be

---

[1] A summary of the Commission study in English is given in Guteland (1980).

allowed. The 95 TWh level represents a situation in which increases in electricity consumption are heavily restricted, and presupposes a particularly strong emphasis on energy saving in the miscellaneous sector. This alternative has been advocated by those who desire the rapid closure of the nuclear sector.

The abolition of nuclear power will mean that resources will have to be applied to the expansion of other electricity production systems and to energy conservation. More coal and oil will have to be imported, which sooner or later will have to be paid for in terms of lower living standards than in the reference case. The COC assumed that the cost of abolition would be met from private consumption because even in the reference case public sector growth is kept quite low. Another conceivable recourse would be to reduce other investments or to increase international borrowing, thus deferring some of the costs until a later date.

The main finding of the COC was that the total cost to Swedish society of abolishing nuclear power would correspond to 2–3% lower private consumption in 1990 than if it were retained; i.e., a capital loss of 20000 Swedish crowns (US$3800 in 1980) per worker for the period 1980–2000. Another important result was that if labor market policies to achieve full employment are implemented, no drastic effects on production can be isolated. The case of electricity price increases for industry at the 95 TWh level is an exception, with strong negative effects in the pulp and paper industry. Price increases on the order of 50% for households and 30% for industry were deemed necessary to keep aggregate electricity demand at the required level during the nuclear power replacement phase (1980s).

Organization

The COC worked under heavy time constraints so that no major model development work was attempted. Instead, the work was divided among several groups, who used suitable existing models and methods in order to assess the magnitude of the consequences of abolishing nuclear power. But a serious problem arose because of this organizational framework: how were the analyses of the several work groups to be integrated?

In Figure 5.6 an outline of the links between work groups is given. The division may be seen as concomitant with a division of the systems analytic problem of developing a set of models and techniques to cope with the complex problem of assessing effects in an interdependent system. The Commission provides a good example of an organizational as well as a factual problem solution.

In the same way that a decomposition approach to mathematical programming consists in isolating subsystems, the internal workings of which need not be fully considered at the superordinate level, so it was *not* necessary for each work group to deliver to all the other groups all its information, but only those items of central importance. The idea was that a number of iterations of this information would lead to a fully

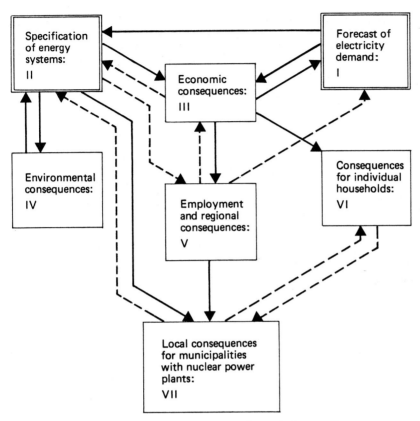

Figure 5.6. Work group organization in the Commission on Consequences.

consistent impact analysis, but the time constraints meant that such an overall consistency could not quite be achieved.

The iteration began with a forecast of electricity demand development (group I) that was consistent with earlier forecasts, although the total demand level of 125 TWh in 1990 implied a lowering of earlier results. This forecast was conveyed to groups II (energy systems) and III (economic consequences). The next step was the specification of energy systems capable of producing the energy demanded at minimum cost, under environmental, regional, and other external constraints. The results of the group II analysis were then reported to groups III (investment costs, composition of primary energy supply), IV (sizes and locations of projects), V (sizes and locations of facilities), and VI (locations of new plants at former nuclear power plant sites).

Information from groups I and II was pooled into an overall analysis of economic consequences in group III, where the total costs of the transition to a new energy system were evaluated in several time

perspectives. The costs were measured in terms of the private consumption levels that could be attained for various demand levels and production systems. The results of these analyses were reported back to groups
I (scarcity prices, production structure, etc.), V (production structure), VI
(level of public and private consumption), and VII (local impacts).

The results from the environmental, regional, and household groups
were then analyzed. A strong feedback was exerted from the environmental to the energy systems group. Criteria were applied to see whether the
energy production scenarios were environmentally acceptable. Information on the level of regional efficiency and welfare goals was also fed back
from the employment and regional group to groups II and III. An example
of such a feedback was the cost—benefit analysis of alternative locations
in northern Sweden for a coal-fired condensation plant.

This organizational framework was actually used in the investigation, with explicit deadlines for the reports of external information
between the groups. It is fair to say that some integration was achieved
in this way, although complete consistency was not possible mainly due
to time constraints, but institutional frictions also played a part.

The models

The above description of the work group organization does not reveal
the extent to which the groups used quantitative models or other analytical techniques. Quantitative analyses were used by all the work groups,
but at very different levels of sophistication. The methods used by groups
IV, VI, and VII were quite rudimentary from a mathematical point of view,
amounting to a more or less systematic application of various types of
multipliers and ratios. They were not necessarily internally or externally
consistent. For example, group II used models to find efficient ways of
using renewable, domestic primary energy resources in industrial
processes. Local biofuel sources such as peat were considered as alternatives to coal and oil in combined heat and power production facilities.

By far the most sophisticated set of models was used in the
economic analyses. This included the use of both medium- and long-term
economic forecasting models of the Swedish Ministry of Economic Affairs.
The medium-term model was an input—output Keynesian type, with consumption and import functions, but with exogenous investment variables.
The long-term model was a variant of multisectoral growth models with
linear energy demand and export/import functions. The core model (the
general equilibrium model of Bergman and Por 1980; see also Bergman
1981) was chosen because it simulates long-term substitution possibilities in an open economy when the energy production factor becomes
more expensive in real terms.

The economic models used were almost an order of magnitude more
complex than the regional breakdown models, at least with respect to
their applicability to assessing the impacts of alternative energy

scenarios. The result of the general equilibrium model is a balanced situation in the national economy. Production factors are used such that there is no excess supply or demand; this state is of course attainable only in the long term, especially if the starting period is characterized by severe economic imbalances.

The idea behind the COC's national-level economic model exercises is simply to compare equilibrium states in terms of private consumption and the equilibrium economic structures for the energy scenarios. The impact of the abolition of nuclear power is simulated by a higher capital depreciation rate in the nuclear sector. The model outputs contain both factor inputs, production levels, capital stocks, foreign trade data, and employment (measured in terms of the work-hours needed in the various sectors).

The breakdown model transforms results into forecasts of the total number of persons needed to perform the necessary work-hours. Furthermore, these figures are disaggregated to the regional level in order to outline the consequences of alternative national energy scenarios with respect to total employment (or, rather, total demand for labor) at the regional level.

(a) How will the total regional labor demand be affected by changing equilibrium patterns of production and employment by sector at the national level?

(b) What are the direct (and subsequent indirect) effects of reducing regional production in individual sectors, such as energy?

In these exercises, the breakdown model was used in conjunction with medium- and long-term economic forecasts for Sweden (Snickars 1979). Judgments were also made about regional labor supply trends; since this is assumed to be independent of the energy system, the current application amounts to a comparison of labor demand scenarios.

An aggregated breakdown model of the type described above is too coarse to identify all the regional labor demand consequences, even though it is theoretically possible to build in a submodel for each sector in which more details are included. In the nuclear power application, a significant result was that scarcity prices had to be used to keep down electricity demand, implying that a closer investigation should be made of the electricity dependence of energy-intensive industries at the regional level. Such an analysis is especially applicable in a country such as Sweden, with its low population density and many small towns and villages that are often dependent on one dominant industrial enterprise, particularly in northern and central areas. A complicating factor is that these enterprises are most common in energy-intensive sectors, where economies of scale have led to concentrated production centers (e.g., pulp and paper, metallurgy, and chemicals).

A special study was performed by the COC to assess the effects of a 50% electricity price increase on energy-intensive industries. The results showed that scrap iron works would be the most seriously affected branch of the steel sector; some 1200 jobs would be lost within five years (although in the reference case some of these jobs were also likely to disappear). This illustrates the basic methodological problem in performing an impact analysis without a comprehensive modeling framework within which to evaluate in a consistent way various direct and indirect effects.

It should be strongly emphasized that the studies of energy-intensive sectors were regarded as a useful complement to the macro breakdown model exercises. Since one central result of the economic analyses was that only small effects on the sectoral structure of the whole of Sweden could be expected (assuming full employment), the regional effects were also rather small. At least this was true for large regions and for the total labor demand. The micro-oriented sectoral studies indicated a considerable negative effect on the local scale in certain industrial sectors.

Since these results are presented at different levels of aggregation, it is not possible to ascertain immediately whether or not they are consistent. The fact that micro analyses are rather short term also makes them less comparable with medium-term micro analyses. In an attempt to reconcile the two approaches, interregional input—output analysis was applied to estimate the total indirect employment effects in the regional production system of the loss of jobs in energy-intensive industries.

It is clear that an integrated regional analysis of national energy scenarios would be useful. Sweden has considerable renewable energy resources, but these are unevenly distributed. It also has a regionally varying production structure, which means that the regional impacts of national and regional energy policies should vary, at least if the effects are evaluated in terms other than employment. Naturally, this problem is related to one of the most frequent criticisms of the results of this study: it does not investigate and assess the process of regional adjustments.

Regional Implementation of National Energy Policies: The Stockholm Region

One may regard the above process as one of formulating targets and restrictions for local energy decision making. For the 1980s the overall national target for oil consumption specifies a reduction in the current annual volume of imported oil (27 million tonnes) by 45%. It has been assumed that this can be achieved through conservation (covering 25% of the reduction), and through the substitution of oil by other fuels (including domestic solid fuel), the introduction of heat pumps, district heating, etc.

The Stockholm region comprises 20 municipalities, each of which has to carry out energy planning in accordance with government guidelines. With regard to studies that require competent systems analysis,

these municipalities rely to a large extent on two basic studies by the
RPO: (i) the long-term study REGI; and (ii) RPO's assessment of a study
made by the utility company STOSEB, and two other studies conducted
during 1979–82. In all these studies the national targets are binding in
character. RPO (1982) summarized the most important national restrictions as follows:

- The energy used for heating existing buildings should be reduced by
  30% before 1990.
- Oil consumption must be reduced as described above.
- All nuclear power plants will be closed down before 2010.

Since the output of electricity generated from nuclear power is still
increasing, one can foresee a potential excess capacity that will later
become a shortage. It has been taken as a constraint that the Stockholm
region will maintain its share of electricity consumption over the next
ten years.

Energy supply and regional development

The Stockholm region (county of Stockholm) contains around 20% of
the Swedish population and its share of the total national income is
almost 25%. More than 25% of all jobs in the service, trade, communications, and transportation sectors are located in the region. Despite having the largest regional manufacturing sector, Stockholm employs little
more than 10% of the national labor force in this sector. During 1975–80
the following sectors showed strong expansion: social services and health
care, consulting, education and research, and cultural activities. The
number of jobs in almost all manufacturing sectors declined during the
1970s.

Figure 5.7 gives a summary description of a reference scenario for
population change in the region. The total population increases from 1.5
million in 1980 to 1.6 million in the year 2000, implying a slowly growing
and at the same time ageing population. Moreover, the corresponding
labor force will grow at an annual rate of 0.5–1.0%. In the scenario the
number of one- and two-person households increases, particularly in central Stockholm. The urban structure of the Stockholm region is illustrated in Figure 5.8, which shows that the numbers employed in different
sectors fall, and that the number of dwellings increases, as a function of
distance from the city center.

In the late 1970s almost 90% of the heating system used oil as an
input, of which 33% was used in individual domestic boilers. Moreover,
the district heating system, which was expanded rapidly in the 1970s,
uses mainly oil. Table 5.4 describes the structure of oil consumption, and
Table 5.5 shows the distribution of different techniques used in the existing heating system of the region.

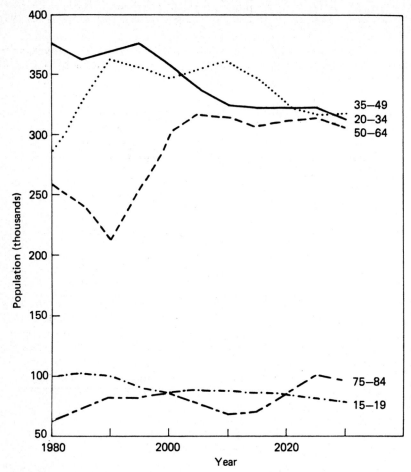

Figure 5.7. Reference scenario for population development in the Stockholm region for five age groups.

Table 5.4. The uses of oil products in the Stockholm region: distribution over sectors, 1980.

Sector	Proportion (%)
Single-family dwellings	7.9
Industry	10.5
Multi-family dwellings	15.8
Power and heat generation plants	18.4
Private and public services	21.1
Transportation and communications	26.3
Total	100.0

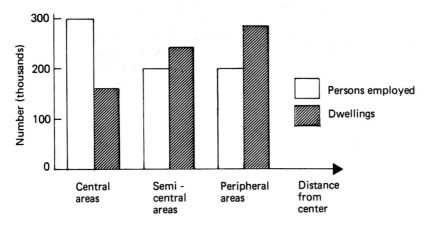

Figure 5.8. Distribution of jobs and dwellings over areas in Stockholm county, 1975.

Table 5.5. The distribution of heating techniques in the Stockholm region.

	Dwellings	Workplaces	Total
Individual boilers	32	42	35
Electric heating	11	3	8
District heating	38	44	39
Small-scale district heating	19	11	18
Total	100	100	100

Table 5.6. Extension of the district heating system in the Stockholm region, 1975–80 (TWh/yr).

	1975	1980
Housing	2.8	4.5
Workplaces	1.4	2.4
Total	4.2	6.9

As a result of the increased supply of electricity and its associated low relative price, its use for domestic heating has increased since 1965 by 20% per annum in Sweden as a whole, and the process was accelerated in the 1970s as a result of the nuclear power program. In the Stockholm region there has also been a rapid expansion of the district heating network (see Table 5.6).

Organization and coordination of energy studies

Over the last ten years energy-related planning requirements have increased in a stepwise manner, but the adaptation to these new requirements has gradually resulted in a less well structured planning system. An overview of the participating planning and negotiating bodies in 1978–82 is given in Table 5.7.

Table 5.7. Organizations invovled in energy planning for the Stockholm region.

Organization and its role	The "objectives" of the organization as perceived by the authors
RPO: Overall regional planning (all municipalities)	To coordinate assessment and planning efforts. To provide solutions that reflect (or balance) different interests.
STOSEB: Design and operation of supply system (company owned by 15 municipalities)	To find solutions with "good economy" for the company and for 15 municipalities. Made suggestions in favor of Forsmark.
Nynäs energy complex (joint venture dominated by private interests)	To find solutions for the energy complex that fit into all different energy system options for the Stockholm region.
Vattenfall: National independent (authority) company, multiregional electricity supply (hydro- and nuclear power, etc.)	To sell expected overcapacity of electricity production; to economize its operation of the Forsmark nuclear plant.
Municipalities	Diversified, partly opposing interests. Demand for systems with "certain" (= known) features, simple solutions.

Electricity supply is planned at a national (multiregional) level by the national utility company Vattenfall, which has proposed a large-scale hot-water pipeline system from the Forsmark nuclear power plant and the coal-fired plant that Vattenfall has planned to build at Forsmark when the nuclear plant is closed down. The energy complex option has been designed by the Nynäs research group in such a way that it may be included in all alternative proposals.

Four basic alternative energy systems were proposed by STOSEB, all of which involve large-scale district heating systems that will cover around 80% of demand. These alternatives are: (i) the use of hot water from the existing Forsmark nuclear power plant; (ii) a decentralized coal-fired power generating system; (iii) a centralized system of the same type; and (iv) a heat pump system using the atmosphere, lakes, and wastewater as energy sources.

The utility company STOSEB has tried to integrate the research and planning efforts of the various municipal energy authorities, the Swedish Industrial Board of the Ministry of Industry (SIND), and the Nynäs group. The STOSEB planning area comprises 15 municipalities, while that of the RPO covers all 20 municipalities in its long-term land-use planning (building, transportation, energy supply and demand). The research activities of RPO cover broader aspects of the energy policy options than those of STOSEB and focus in particular on dynamic, long-term issues. In addition, RPO has been responsible for a long-term research project, REGI, initiated and financed by the Swedish Council for Building Research and RPO.

As part of its ongoing activities RPO has made a comprehensive evaluation of the STOSEB studies. Below we discuss two aspects of RPO activities:

- the assessments of the STOSEB studies, including the Nynäs group report; and
- the ongoing long-term study of the interdependence of energy planning and general regional development planning (the REGI project).

Methods and Problems in RPO's Activities

Regional implementation of national energy policy

The implementation of national energy policy described above will require a complete restructuring of the energy supply system in the Stockholm region. This presupposes a systems analytical approach, which recognizes that (i) the region is an integral part of the national energy system and shares its dependence on imported oil; (ii) the number of potential technical solutions is large; and (iii) the effects of technical and economic investments will be long-lasting, and will restrict some other developments. Such changes will have environmental effects that will need detailed control in such a densely populated region. However, the durability and large scale of the investments, together with the associated environmental impacts, may create conflicts of interests and opinion between various groups. In order to analyze such problems, the energy system must be specified in a well structured way; Figure 5.9 illustrates how this was done.

Methodological approach of the REGI project

The standard case of an impact analysis may be outlined as follows: (i) a given project is characterized over time; and (ii) thereafter the multidimensional consequences are derived or traced over space and time. The Stockholm studies do not fit this standard form, for several

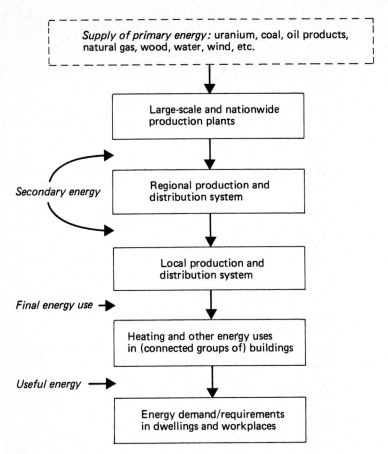

Figure 5.9. The structure of the energy supply system in the Stockholm region.

reasons. First, they include a comparison and evaluation of many alternative (competing) large-scale projects, and second, they are also searching for future regional spatial structures that are compatible with certain energy system alternatives. The determination of policy decisions to ensure that a desirable future structure is obtained implies that the impacts of these decisions are crucial. The complex structure of this approach can be decomposed into a sequence of subsystem analyses, as illustrated in Figure 5.10. These interlinked "subsystems" can then be analyzed sequentially as follows:

I   National sectoral development scenarios can be obtained by means of dynamic multisectoral nonlinear input—output models. Two equilibrium models of this type are available.

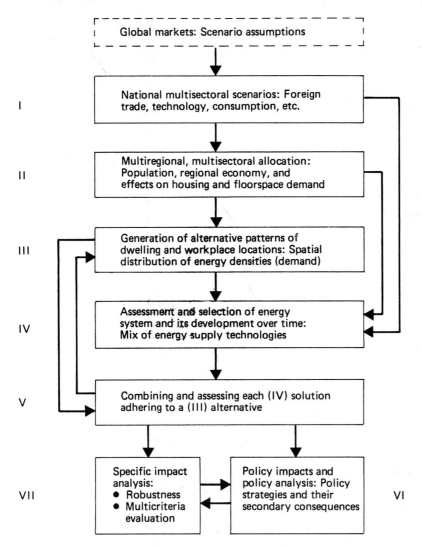

Figure 5.10. Scheme describing impact analysis, scenario assessment, and planning aspects of the REGI project.

II   National scenarios provide constraints on the analysis of multiregional development. At this stage, energy demand and supply are regionally distributed with the help of two multisectoral programming models.

III   The analysis of general regional development includes distribution of
       activities (housing, production, transportation, etc.) over subareas,
       changes in end-use energy technologies and consumption levels, and
       the associated pattern of energy densities, so that alternative
       development paths can be generated.
IV   The analysis of energy system development has to be based on infor-
       mation from I, II, and III on relative prices (including energy prices)
       and energy densities in subareas of the region.
V   In step V configurations of buildings and activities are combined with
       associated "optimal" energy system solutions into consistent pairs.
VI   A given development of subsystem III can, to a certain degree, be
       stimulated and enforced with regional policy instruments such as
       land-use policies, etc. In this sense a particular alternative in V
       implies a certain set of policy measures that is an impact in itself.
       Moreover, each set of policy instruments itself has regional and
       national impacts, so that the final assessment has to be analyzed in
       step VII.
VII   The final evaluation uses information from step V and interacts with
       the policy impact analysis in VI, based on a multidimensional com-
       parison of generated combinations of (i) an energy system solution,
       (ii) a regional development scenario, (iii) the associated policy mea-
       sures, and (iv) the specific impacts of (i)–(iii).

The time scale for the model system is a sequence of periods starting in
1980 and ending in 2020–25. The length of time periods is varied so as to
match already (nationally or technically) determined times at which certain strategic decisions must be made. The multiregional models operate
with a subdivision of the country into 6, 8, or 20–25 regions. With regard
to the specification of areas within Stockholm, varying degrees of spatial
disaggregation have been utilized, ranging from around 105 up to about
1000.

     In order to illustrate further the philosophy behind REGI we now
present an example of one recommendation generated by REGI. This
option is chosen on the basis of robustness criteria (Lundqvist 1982).

*   Reduce oil dependence by 65% over ten years.
*   The share of district heating should not be greater than 75%.
*   Use Forsmark for electricity production, but with no hot-water pipe-
    line system.
*   Develop the energy complex at Nynäshamn.
*   A gas system has no cost advantages.
*   Electricity for heating should not exceed 5 TWh.
*   The use of coal should not exceed 5 TWh before the year 2000.
*   Reduce primary energy consumption by 15–20% over the next ten
    years.

The basic models of REGI

This section presents a general description of the network of REGI models. In principle, this model system was also used for RPO's assessment of the STOSEB study.

Multisector, Multiregional Scenarios

The two multisectoral input—output models have a set of common features: they both apply export and import functions to each commodity group, which use the ratio between the domestic and the world market prices as an argument. Private consumption functions are derived from a linear expenditure system. For both models the development of world market prices is given by exogenous scenarios.

One of the models, the Bergman model, falls into the class of MSG models (Johansen 1974).[2] An early version of this model was used in the studies of nuclear abolition mentioned above (see Bergman 1981), in which the unit cost level of each sector was derived from a nested Cobb—Douglas/CES production function with electricity, fuels, labor, and aggregate capital as inputs. The model is a static equilibrium model and the impacts of variations in exogenous factors (such as world market prices of primary energy) are defined in terms of differences between equilibrium allocations of capital and labor over sectors and the associated activity levels. The nature of the model prohibits an analysis of the adjustment process over time; instead it generates a terminal point solution 10—20 years ahead. The model is primarily based on information from the Swedish Central Bureau of Statistics.

The second national multisectoral model, MACROINVEST (see Persson and Johansson 1982), is like the Bergman model in that it has general equilibrium properties; in particular, relative prices are determined endogenously. It allows for a study of adjustment processes such as the introduction and removal of production capacities and associated employment changes. It recognizes a distribution of production techniques in each sector, where each technique displays a constant elasticity of scale within the capacity limit of the technique, while the aggregate technique of a sector exhibits variable elasticity of scale. The removal/introduction of new capacity is determined by the endogenously given (i) profits of each technique, (ii) investment costs, and (iii) demand for total production capacity. For each sector a unit of investment has a distinct commodity composition. The model is designed to generate a sequence of five-year solutions, connected with an annually updated information system that contains data on production techniques. These data also have a location index (see Johansson and Strömqvist 1981). The outputs from the national models contain sector allocations of

---

[2] This model, in combination with MORSE, will probably be used to generate the final scenarios for REGI.

employment, production, investment, shut-down, energy use, etc. This type of information provides an input to the following multiregional linear programming (LP) models:

• MORSE is a multiregional, multisectoral model (Lundqvist 1981); its basic structure is obtained through a breakdown technique applied to national-level input—output information, together with various regional-level constraints (Snickars 1978). MORSE is dynamic and has been applied to generate results in five-year periods. It has eight regions, and the economy of each region is divided into nine sectors. A bottom-up approach is used with regard to consumption and to the majority of production sectors, whereas a top-down relation is used for energy consumption, capital formation, and international trade. In the REGI project, the model is used to assess the impacts of energy supply systems and oil price increases. In particular, the impacts may be generated in the form of trade-offs between various criteria.

• PROMISE is a multiregional model containing 19 industrial sectors with a potential disaggregation to around 100 (Johansson and Strömqvist 1981, Førsund et al. 1982). With regard to industrial statistics, the model uses the same information as MACROINVEST. PROMISE was developed using an information system for the manufacturing and mining industries, and contains data on production techniques for around 1500 groups of production units (establishments) between 1968—80. It includes estimates of removal and introduction of new techniques (this information is also included in MACROINVEST) and recognizes inputs of electricity and liquid fuels for each available (existing and potential) technique.

PROMISE is based on a vintage-type production theory and combines production efficiency criteria with (i) regional constraints, and (ii) national scenario inputs from national models of the type described above. Potentially, an interactive approach may be used. The model contains six regions, for which the analysis can be disaggregated to the county level in a second step. Energy impacts are generated in the form of energy composition and ability to cover energy costs over techniques in each sector in each region, as described in Figure 5.11.

Analysis of Regional Supply and Demand

The regional analysis has two system components: supply and demand. For each given spatial configuration of energy demand, the supply analysis provides a cost-minimizing solution over time, so that it is important to generate a set of alternative, internally consistent scenarios of the spatial distribution of activities and associated energy densities. One may thus generate "optimal" pairs of combined supply—demand solutions. One may also search for a supply solution that is robust with regard to variations in the spatial demand for energy over time. For each solution there is a need to examine the consistency between

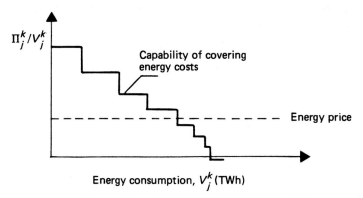

Figure 5.11. Energy impacts in PROMISE, distributed over production technologies in industrial sector j. Π_j^k = gross profit of technology k, before energy costs have been deducted; observe that Π_j^k is determined as an explicit function of prices and wages, and that V_j^k is specified both for electricity and liquid fuels.

intraregional/regional and multiregional/national levels. Repercussions of this kind have not been analyzed with formal models.

The objective of the intraregional analysis in the model system is to derive spatial and temporal distributions of useful energy demand for heating by specifying energy densities in about 100 areas of the region at different points in time (1980–2020). This is done by analyzing and putting together three components in consistent development paths:

- development of population, household formation, and housing demand;
- development of building structure (housing, workplaces, transportation); and
- land-use planning and siting decisions.

The model of household formation and housing demand uses as inputs population scenarios generated by a multiregional demographic model that may be described as a Markov-type transition model. Apart from standard demographic change probabilities, it also includes interregional and international migration, and uses a set of alternative estimates of transition structures, each of which refers to a socioeconomic situation. Therefore, the population scenario selected can be contingent on the desired overall economic development path (see Andersson and Holmberg 1980).

The population analysis is connected with household/housing analysis, as indicated in Figure 5.12. Household formation is analyzed by means of a transition model based on five-year population censuses, while the housing demand model has the form of a logit model. Market analyses can be carried out with two models using similar information: an

LP model that maximizes consumer surplus, and a constrained entropy type of model (see Härsman 1981).

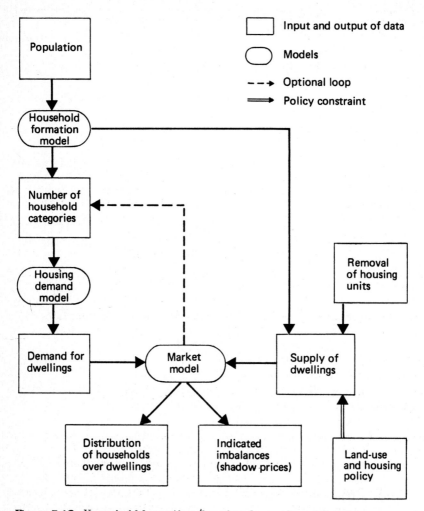

Figure 5.12. Household formation/housing demand model system.

The building structure forecast has two components. Stock reduction is projected via an age-dependent removal rate for various types of buildings (including dwellings), and the erection of new buildings on the basis of projections of activities and associated employment. In particular, these building projections have to be allocated over the set of subareas of the region. This analysis combines traditional land-use planning and two supplementary models: BOLOK (Lundqvist and Mattson

Table 5.8. Four alternative structures of the region.

Housing and workplaces *central* and *dense*	Housing and workplaces *peripheral* and *dense*
• Many multi-family dwellings and offices	• Many multi-family dwellings and many offices
• Increased public transport with a small number of cross-city trips	• Increased share of public transport and cross-city trips
• Large district heating system	• Smaller district heating system
• Balance between north and south, between dwellings and workplaces	• Balance between housing and workplaces for individual sectors
• Economy of use of the existing infrastructure	• Requires infrastructure investments
Housing and workplaces *peripheral* and *non-dense*	**Housing *peripheral* and *non-dense*, workplaces *central* and *dense***
• Smaller number of multi-family dwellings	• Smaller number of multi-family dwellings and offices
• More industry	
• Large share of private transport	• Large share of private transport
• Increased commuting	• District heating in the center and new energy technologies at the periphery
• Many options as regards alternative "energy technologies"	
• Balance between housing and workplaces for individual sectors	• No balance between housing and workplaces
• Requires infrastructure investments	• Requires infrastructure investments

1982) and ISP (Roy and Snickars 1982). ISP is a land allocation system that can be used interactively within traditional planning frames. Given scenarios that form constraints on future land-use patterns, ISP provides an allocation that minimizes structural change, based on a minimum information principle. The model is designed to allow for a fine subdivision of geographical area and simultaneously to recognize sectoral disaggregation.

Table 5.8 describes four alternative physical structures for which associated energy system solutions were designed. ISP can be used to generate this type of solution in such a form that performance indicators are defined to measure the multidimensional impacts of each specific

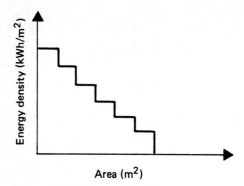

Figure 5.13. Energy densities in subareas (useful energy for heating).

solution. The models and techniques for land-use planning can be used to generate a sequence of 5–10 year solutions in the form of development paths. The outcome of the analysis is twofold: (*a*) it provides alternative restrictions for energy system analysis; and (*b*) it generates information for the evaluation/assessment analysis in terms of welfare and performance criteria. With regard to energy system analysis the outcome has the form of a calculated distribution of energy densities of regional subareas, as indicated in Figure 5.13.

Energy System Model

The assessment of energy system solutions has been constrained by several factors such as oil import reduction plans, national electricity demand, the existence of the Forsmark nuclear power plant, and the planned Nynäs energy complex. Since electricity generation will increase over the next 15 years, there is a short-term problem as to the most economical use of the excess supply. In the long term, the closure of nuclear plants may instead result in a shortage of electricity. This defines a truly dynamic national problem that will be affected by the decisions for the Stockholm region. A reduction of oil imports implies that coal will be used to provide energy for heating. This may include large-scale pipelines to deliver hot water from the Forsmark nuclear plant in the short term and from coal-fired plants in the long term. Another option includes hot-water pipelines from Nynäs, combined with decentralized hot-water production and heat pumps.

The model used to evaluate feasible solutions was based on energy system modeling at IIASA, and is called MESSAGE II or METRO MESSAGE (Energy Systems Group 1982). This is a dynamic LP model that reflects the essential stages in the energy chain from primary energy supply to final energy requirements (see Figure 5.9). An essential part of the model specification is the formulation of relevant constraints on the speed of structural change, the availability of new technologies, and energy import ceilings. A basic constraint is that model solutions must conform to the existing energy system at the outset. The environmental effects of each technology are considered as constraints, so that the final evaluation of environmental impacts is restrained within a bounded set of impacts.

The basic set of available technologies considered in the study so far contains almost 100 distinct technologies, more than a third of which refer to end-use technologies. The model changes and adjusts useful energy consumption over time according to endogenously calculated final energy supply costs, so that the model switches from one heating technology to another when energy supply costs vary. Conservation is included in the models in the form of a "supply technology" (e.g., insulation).

The model also allows for the treatment of mixed-integer problems, and generates cost-minimizing solutions within certain constraints (e.g., operating and capital costs). The basic model outputs are investment decisions over time and the associated costs. The time horizon of 1980–2020 is divided into seven periods of different lengths, determined on the basis of gestation lags for certain large investments, and the times at which nuclear capacity will be reduced. For a distinct technology in the chain from primary to final energy use the time path of the introduction and closure of production capacity may have the form indicated in Figure 5.14. Hence the time scale is long enough to allow for technologies introduced early, scrapped in a later phase, to be reintroduced in the future.

One should observe that the energy system analysis in fact operates on two time scales. For each period the model has to select technologies that combine into a system that can match seasonal variations in demand. This is illustrated in Figure 5.15, which shows the effect of heat pumps that will be fully introduced in 1988. Data were obtained from STOSEB, the Nynäs research group, and overall regional planning and technical information from various European sources.

The Nynäs Energy Complex

The Nynäs research group report does not contain detailed or formal descriptions of the methods used, but Figure 5.16 gives an outline of the necessary systems analysis carried out. Three inputs are considered (coal, waste oil, biomass). The output markets are transportation, chemical processing, and heating. The basic impacts on these markets are analyzed in terms of cost effects, as well as the effects on the balance of trade and the long-term positive influence of the project on the Swedish chemical industry. For example, methanol production requires significant amounts of cooling water, and this forms the connection between the Nynäs project and the Stockholm energy system — the latter will simply function as the cooling system of the complex.

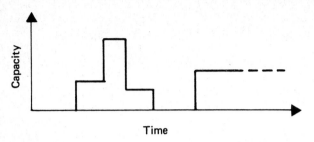

Figure 5.14. Introduction and removal of capacities of a given technology.

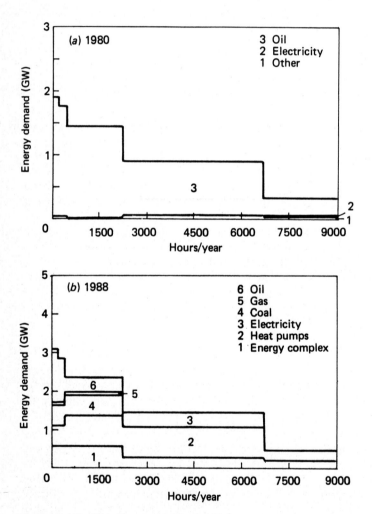

Figure 5.15. FE – Forsmark electricity scenarios: district heat production load curves for (a) 1980, and (b) 1988.

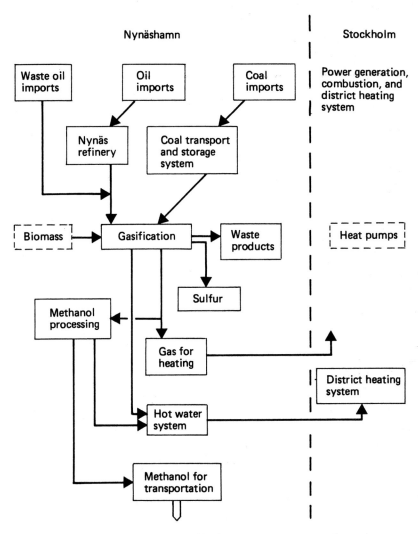

Figure 5.16. Components of the Nynäs energy complex. Dashed boxes denote system components that are external to the Nynäs energy complex.

The Nynäs project will help reduce oil imports, but it must be complemented by national decisions that will guarantee the methanol market in Sweden. Such a market is ensured if the government demands that gasoline be mixed with methanol (as suggested by the Oil Reduction Committee). The environmental impacts of the Nynäs project have been analyzed on the basis of detailed knowledge of the processes involved, and the location is regarded as suitable for this type of development in national land-use plans.

RPO's assessment of the STOSEB study

An important part of RPO's activities deals with the evaluation of policy alternatives for the region. Therefore, when STOSEB presented its final report *STOSEB 80*, RPO had to turn from its more research-oriented and systematic schedule of the REGI project in order to provide an assessment of *STOSEB 80*. One conclusion of RPO's assessment was that the Forsmark option could not be accepted without a more detailed analysis.

The RPO analysis focused on several weak points in *STOSEB 80*, such as (i) projections of future world market prices of primary energy; (ii) the analysis of electricity demand; (iii) population, household, housing, and workplace scenarios; and (iv) associated distributions of energy demand and energy densities. The basic methodology of the STOSEB study was criticized on the grounds that it was based on comparative cost analyses of various energy options, but that the comparisons were not made simultaneously for the whole energy system. The study compares "components" one by one, eliminating marginally costlier options; such an approach does not recognize that options eliminated in this way could become attractive when the whole energy system of the region is considered. The RPO evaluation was based on:

• National scenarios of economic development and long-term national energy policy. To a large extent RPO achieved this by collecting existing scenarios and energy policy analyses.

• Projections of changes in the stock of housing and workplaces. RPO made use of the population model described above, and relied partly on existing model system applications for household formation, housing demand, etc. Less sophisticated methods were used to obtain workplace projections, and a housing removal model was used to generate potential removals that could be counteracted either by renewal of ageing dwellings or by the construction of new ones (see Figure 5.17).

• Land-use planning. RPO prepared four alternative land-use structures as inputs to the energy system analysis (see Table 5.8).

• Economic evaluation of STOSEB's alternatives using an existing LP model (Bergman 1976), and a cost—benefit approach. This study included a discussion of impacts with regard to (i) the regional energy, labor, and housing markets; (ii) national markets for electricity and fuel for transportation and heating; and (iii) national capital market and the balance of trade. Each energy system option requires investments totalling more than half of the total annual industrial investment in Sweden.

• Labor market effects. STOSEB's time profiles of labor market impacts were calculated on the basis of detailed project descriptions. A similar calculation was made for the Nynäs project. Although the effects vary considerably over time, they are small in relation to the regional labor market.

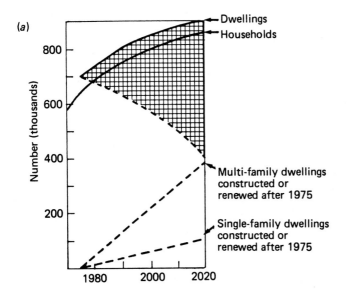

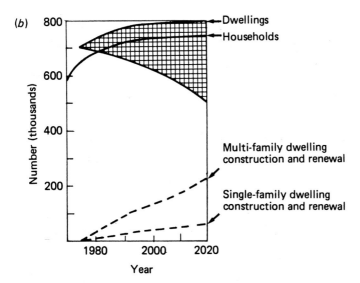

Figure 5.17. Development of households and dwellings assuming (*a*) high population growth and a high rate of renewal; and (*b*) unchanged population and a low rate of renewal. The shading denotes housing stock built before 1975.

• Heat pump technologies. RPO initiated a set of studies to investigate the potential of heat pump systems to utilize the water systems in the region. Two smaller studies focused on the use of solar and wind power, which provided inputs to the energy system analysis as well as to the overall regional analysis.

• The Nynäs energy complex. RPO's assessment of the Nynäs group study referred to in *STOSEB 80* concentrated on the economic risks associated with the project, using a risk chart technique (see Figure 5.18), and concluded that the project was not robust with regard to variations in the assumptions about future markets.

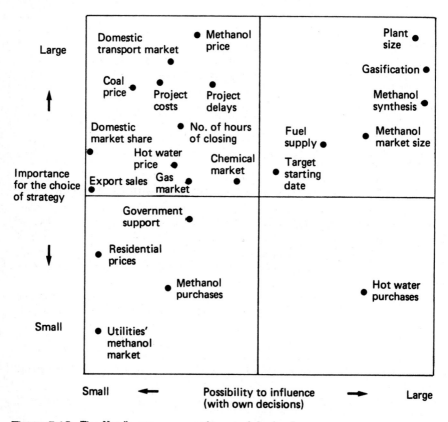

Figure 5.18. The Nynäs energy complex: a risk chart.

• Environmental effects. *STOSEB 80* contained diffusion studies of air pollution from coal processing, but RPO specified a broad set of environmental effects that were not considered in the STOSEB and the Nynäs group studies. The need for basic research in this area was also demonstrated: e.g., the effects of heat pumps on the water system, coal combustion (sulfur and metals), and storage of waste products from coal gasification, etc.

• Energy systems analysis with MESSAGE II. The STOSEB study alternatives were re-examined with the help of a comprehensive model using data from the IIASA study. This part of the assessment formed a summary evaluation of *STOSEB 80* by incorporating results from other parts of the RPO study. At this stage, the advantages of RPO's systems analytical approach became obvious.

The overall assessment implied that the Forsmark alternative could be considered inferior to all alternatives examined in terms of both cost/efficiency and flexibility/robustness in view of the uncertainties. Combinations of alternatives including heat pumps came out better. Differences in terms of uncertainties were generally greater than cost differences.

In terms of the chart in Figure 5.10 one may conclude that RPO's assessment ended in part V of the REGI project scheme. The final impact analyses and the selection of techniques for this remain to be solved in the REGI project.

Concluding Remarks

The COC and RPO studies were both initiated with the clear objective of being used as guidelines in political decisions. With strict time constraints this necessarily meant that certain ambitions had to be sacrificed. Such ambitions may be defined as the striving for models and methods that satisfy the demand for better (theoretical) understanding and more reliable forecasts, together with comprehensiveness and consistency.

The trade-off between the above objectives and policy relevance may be made explicit by recognizing policy relevance as the degree to which the results

(*a*) provide answers to the questions posed by the clients;
(*b*) increase the understanding of the problem, irrespective of the initial questions;
(*c*) are transferred and translated properly to different users in society; and
(*d*) are actually, used in decision making.

One important effect of the not always successful but ambitious efforts of the COC study was that new insights were acquired by both researchers and clients. The necessity of as well as the difficulties in applying a systems analytical approach were clearly observed. They also became aware of the failures (in the study) to obtain multiregional consistency. Finally, it was observed that the analytical approach was insufficient in that it did not treat the specific effects and disturbances caused by policy measures that have to be exercised in order to create stimuli, incentives, and regulations that will bring about the desired system changes.

One basic impact of the COC work was the initiation of new follow-up research projects. New research-financing organizations were formed, and existing ones were encouraged to give a higher priority to energy-related studies. A marked example is provided by the Swedish Council for Building Research, which started to allocate half of its total budget to energy-related studies such as the REGI project.

One may also observe how the researchers who participated in the COC studies have continued to refine their old models and to develop new ones in directions that have been influenced by experiences from the initial research efforts. Several of the models and ideas behind the REGI project have exactly this background.

A peculiar element of the Stockholm studies is that they were integral parts of an ongoing energy system investment process. The analyses were not simply elements of an outline structure plan but decision support documents. In this context one would like to see a further extension so that design instruments can be combined with tools for regular monitoring of change and impact.

Large-Scale Energy Projects: Assessment of Regional Consequences
T.R. Lakshmanan and B. Johansson (Editors)
Elsevier Science Publishers B.V. (North-Holland)
© IIASA, 1985

CHAPTER 5

Conservation and Fuel Switching in Sweden

5.2. Review of the Swedish Case Study

Roger Bolton

Introduction

Johansson and Snickars' review of a Swedish assessment of the national/regional effects of energy developments and policies succeeds in showing the great range of modeling problems that national and regional planners need to address, if only to try to approach the Swedish standard. The effects range from changes in cost and demand conditions in national industries, to feedbacks from the Stockholm region's adjustment to the national economy in a "bottom-up" fashion, to manifestations of the region's adjustment in its fine-grained structure, as in building types and densities, and commuting patterns.

The paper is challenging, but also sobering. It indicates high ambitions, but also the degree to which state of the art planning and research, even in Sweden, can fall short of what we academic observers might specify as ideal! In this review I first summarize Johansson and Snickars' (hereafter JS) basic outline, sometimes indicating what I think are gaps in the study. Whether those are gaps in Swedish planning and research, or gaps in the authors' reporting, I cannot always say. I then characterize a few essential needs of regional planning in a context such as this, and comment on how well the modeling and planning research efforts meet those needs.

Summary of the Case Study

The national frame

JS begin with the national frame for the Stockholm region, which translates some national goals into quantitative terms. They then describe the Stockholm region's economic and demographic structure, its present and possible future energy supply systems, and a "reference scenario" of population change. Presumably this was defined as what would happen *without* the drastic energy policies, but I do not have detailed knowledge of the assumptions on which it was based. The precise assumptions (did the regional planners make them all that precise?) are important, because the reference scenario may describe some long-term trends in Swedish society that planners will find difficult to slow or reverse.

An interesting question is whether certain trends in the reference scenario will survive the effects of the major restructuring of the energy system. Take, for example, the decline in the average size of households. Will that trend continue, in spite of the energy changes? The energy changes imply changes in the "urban design" — the physical structural features like residential densities, sizes and privacy of housing units, commuting patterns, etc. — and those are part and parcel of the decline in the size of households. Perhaps there will be pressures to change the average size; if there are economies of household scale in energy consumption, the average size of household might be an important variable in planning.

The question is at bottom one of how firmly Swedish society is committed to a decline in the average size of households. The decline is a feature of many industrial countries, and it is an expression in the form of residential living patterns of basic changes in relationships between successive generations, of changing attitudes toward the permanence of marriage, and of other fundamental social changes. An important consideration is how firmly this and various other characteristics of Swedish "lifestyle" will be held on to as planners directly or indirectly try to change them.

JS report a spatial pattern of housing and nonresidential buildings that is typical of Western cities (see Figure 5.8). The governments of the region are also fragmented in a typical way. JS express well how important it is to know the institutional and political details of the regional planning system, since it is complicated by the combination of the spatial pattern and governmental fragmentation. The fragmentation seems especially challenging to the planner. For example, the planning agency RPO includes all 20-plus municipalities, but STOSEB, an energy supply enterprise, serves only 15 of them. The planner must consider carefully *which* 15 it includes. Are they disproportionately representative of the primarily residential parts of the region, or of the mixed residential–industrial–commercial parts? There may be potential energy supply and distribution schemes that would require more than the 15 areas to achieve certain economies — of scale, or of scope, or of spatial configuration. The STOSEB municipalities might be able to exercise some collective monopoly power. Alternatively, the *other* municipalities might have some power; if they are not subject to STOSEB's energy price and service policies, but are crucially located, one can imagine unfortunate competition for industry and resulting political pressures by members of STOSEB to be allowed to "opt out" of its uniform policies.

The distribution of powers among the various actors — RPO, STOSEB, Vattenfall, individual municipalities, national government — is important. It is not necessary *only* for a complete picture of the local scene; it is also necessary to appreciate what is possible in planning: what incentives and constraints are there to make each public actor go along with regional schemes? It is a crucial aspect of policy implementation, but it also helps us to understand how to go about modeling the effects of policies.

Neither planning nor modeling can be effective without an appreciation of what I would call the "political economy" of the region and its planning system. JS hint of "conflicting interests", but we do not really get much sense of the relative "interests", public and private, that will tug and pull against each other in Stockholm in the next 30 years. It is essential to understand the political economy, both for purposes of evaluating the planning process *and* for purposes of building useful models.

REGI: The main components

A long review of RPO's REGI project is given, plus a report on RPO's somewhat separate but complementary evaluation of STOSEB's proposals. JS give convincing reasons why the usual "impact analysis" methods are not adequate in this case and why a more comprehensive systems analysis is necessary: the usual methods focus on one project at a time, and hold too many things constant each time. The problem in the present case is precisely that so many projects are possible, they have so many interdependences, and they impact on so many aspects of the regional economy simultaneously, that one needs a much more complicated model. In other words, typical impact analyses are partial equilibrium approaches, while obviously what is needed here is a (very) general equilibrium model. In one way or another, the authors do give us a sense of the many different aspects of the regional economy that *should* be taken into account.

Given this background, JS review a variety of models that are used as separate components of the REGI system. Each model is necessarily complicated and their simultaneous use is no less so, and JS do manage to convey the impression that the models are reasonable, and indeed are somewhat "standard" as far as modern energy and urban development modeling is concerned. What is not standard, indeed is truly sophisticated, is the comprehensiveness of the combination. One suspects that whatever their shortcomings, the combined models encompass at least as wide an array of policy concerns as the policy makers are in fact able and willing to cope with at one time in their own minds! Taken together, the models cover the macro detail of the national economy, the multiregional distribution of crucial variables, and also the micro detail of the region, such as the physical characteristics of its housing and other structures and their location and the resulting patterns of "energy density".

REGI integrates the socioeconomic and urban design models with an "energy system model", which is a model of physical characteristics: energy flows; conversion and transportation losses; size, fuel, and technology of electricity and hot-water generating stations; and residential heating technology. This energy system component seems quite detailed and sophisticated. REGI aims at constructing a variety of alternative *consistent* solutions to the regional planning problem, consistent in the sense of describing simultaneously national and regional economies, the physical energy supply system, and the "built environment". In other words, the various models together produce energy demand and supply projections that are consistent with all of the following:

- where people live, in the sense of how many live in each "zone" of the region and the population density gradients; JS indicate that the intraregional population and land-use submodels distinguish about 100 separate zones, which is impressive;
- what sorts of residential structures they live in — single- or multi-family, typical lot sizes, etc.;
- where the jobs are, again in the sense of distribution by zone, and what that implies for commuting patterns and modes;
- how much energy is used in each zone, as determined by the population, density, and industrial and commercial enterprises in each one;
- the energy production and transmission facilities needed to produce and deliver the energy used in those zones (the electricity and hot-water generating plants, their fuels and technologies, the cables and pipelines connecting them to users), and all this allows for transmission losses, which of course are affected by density and the type of transmission.

The first three items in this list essentially add up to a goal by RPO that REGI produce a comprehensive "land-use map" of the entire region. All in all, it is a very ambitious effort. I will probably appear to cavil if I call attention to some modeling capabilities that seem not to be present, and I will mention only a few omissions — and do no more than mention them.

REGI: Capabilities not present

I realize that the REGI analysts have so far produced consistent solutions to the planning problem, as shown in box V of Figure 5.10, but have
not yet proceeded to the impact analyses and sensitivity analyses in
boxes VI and VII. My comments are based on the report of what REGI will
eventually be capable of modeling.

There appears to be no attempt to model the detailed impact on the
size distribution of income by household, such as might be accomplished
by a microsimulation model of the kind sometimes used in the US (see
Bolton 1982a, reporting on Golladay and Haveman 1977, on SWRI 1981, and
on other more recent proposals for new models in the US). I presume
that REGI *will* be able to simulate the change in average household
income in each zone in Stockholm, so RPO can say something about the
intraregional distribution of income (results for different zones of the
Philadelphia city region are an especially useful output of the Lower
Delaware Valley economy—ecology model; see Russell and Spofford 1977,
Kneese and Bower 1979).

I will also add that it is a mystery to me how REGI models the implications of different financing methods. We are told in passing that the
energy supply investments amount to an enormous share of total Swedish
national investment, but are not told how those investments, or the
investments in new housing, business plant and equipment, and public
infrastructure that will be required by the spatial restructuring of the
region, will be financed. The planners will have to treat the *public*
finances explicitly or implicitly if they do want to assess the impact on
each zone, because local government fiscal adjustments will affect household real income in each zone. The resolution of such financing details is
an essential part of the "political economy" of a region.

Planning might be illuminated by showing graphically some "trade-
off" curves or surfaces that plot the necessary inverse relationships
between two or three goal variables under an assumption of efficient allocation. These would be "efficiency frontiers". For example, interesting
trade-offs would be:

- between average temperatures permitted in typical dwellings and
  the payment by a typical household for residential heat;
- between average household temperatures and the average land
  space per housing unit;
- between the ISP model's "performance indicators" in two different
  zones (these indicators sum up in a single number all the characteristics of the physical structure described in Table 5.8 (for examples of trade-off curves, see Dorfman and Jacoby 1977, Snickars and
  Granholm 1981).

I also note that the demographic model is said to be a Markov-type transition model, even as far as interregional and international migration are

concerned. Of course, the analyst can specify the transition probabilities on her own and need not rest on historical observations. She can in fact select the transition structure to be consistent with Sweden's overall economic development path. However, it appears that while migration flows are endogenous, the transition structure — the matrix of migration probabilities — remains fundamentally exogenous to the model, rather than being endogenously determined by a model of migration incentives run in tandem with the other economic models in the system.

REGI shows its potential value: The evaluation of STOSEB

JS report on RPO's assessment of STOSEB's alternative supply systems. Although this RPO effort was in a sense a diversion from the systematic pursuit of the REGI research plan, the results must have been significant and heartening in showing the value of REGI over a more traditional partial equilibrium approach. STOSEB's more traditional approach could be criticized for not being sufficiently systems-oriented because it compared supply alternatives one by one. STOSEB also did not consider a broad enough set of environmental effects, and, at least on the Nynäs energy complex, did not do adequate sensitivity analysis. JS remark: "At this stage the gains from RPO's systems analytical approach became obvious"; while the remark is specifically about the energy system analysis with MESSAGE II, one gathers they mean it to refer to RPO's assessment of STOSEB's plans more generally.

Crisis as the spur to research

JS also assess planning more generally in Sweden, including the research done for the Commission on Consequences (COC), which had a national focus. JS conclude that pressing national needs spurred enough progress so as to increase *both* research-scientific ambitions *and* policy relevance. This progress occurred between the time of research for the COC and the completion of the REGI system. The conclusion is significant, for surely it *might have* turned out that work which met research and scientific ambition had to come at the expense of some immediate policy relevance. JS conclude that things did *not* turn out that way. That doesn't mean there was X-inefficiency in the old system, by the way! It merely suggests that the crisis raised the relative price commanded by good research, and the suppliers responded admirably.

Four Essential Planning Problems

How can we best describe the problems faced by national and regional planners in a case like the Swedish one? In particular, how can we characterize them given that the system is a mixed market planning system? I suggest that we put major emphasis on four concepts from some rather traditional economic and planning theory: adjustment costs, externalities, regional—national feedbacks, and insurance against risk. In this section, I shall develop these four concepts further and give my own outsider's assessment of how well the Stockholm research and planning efforts deal with them.

Adjustment costs

Through a combination of markets and planning, the Stockholm region must make a gradual adjustment from one situation to another, with the new situation characterized by a different energy regime and likely different economic and urban design regimes as well. It probably does not do great harm to refer loosely to those situations as the "old equilibrium" and the "new equilibrium", although of course a model which recognizes that they are not strictly equilibrium situations has some great advantages. The process of adjusting to the new equilibrium imposes costs on some people and generates gains for others; there is a redistribution of existing rents and also the generation of new rents and the destruction of old ones.

What is the role of planning in this process? Planning should aim to minimize the adjustment effects above and beyond those necessary to effect the transition, and it should aim to distribute them fairly. At a minimum, it should be concerned with the adjustment *costs* of individuals. Policy-relevant modeling, therefore, should ideally include the capability to delineate those costs, their sensitivity to different energy scenarios, and their distribution. Adjustment analysis is an essential supplement to the capability to do comparative static analysis.

JS make it clear that the early research, in the COC stage, did not emphasize adjustment processes sufficiently. It is not clear to me whether the newer REGI system contains such capability or not. One of the two national models, the Bergman model, definitely does not predict adjustment paths, a shortcoming Bergman himself emphasized (Bergman 1981). The other, MACROINVEST, is said to allow a study of "adjustment processes", but we have no details on how well it can do that. It generates a sequence of five-year solutions, which does suggest some capability of the kind I am talking about. On the other hand, it is conceivable that the sequence is merely one of comparative static results as a function of a sequence of exogenous variables.

It is also not clear whether the multiregional and intraregional models allow one to analyze adjustment processes and their costs. Again, there is some language about sequences, and the Markov demographic model sounds like it qualifies, but one cannot tell about the other models or the system as a whole. One important consideration is whether the logit model of housing demand includes independent variables that reflect partial adjustment.

It is important to be explicit about all this. In the real world, the most significant costs that many people bear are temporary ones during the adjustment process. The difference in their welfare between one equilibrium position and another may be rather small for many people, particularly in the present value sense because any losses under a new equilibrium come only after some period of time. But the adjustment costs are often large, they start to hurt immediately, and they loom particularly large in the political process. They show up as unemployment, underemployment, losses of housing value, or as temporary curtailment of public services. Thus, a capability to model adjustment processes, especially when combined with a household microsimulation model and also with good models of public sector finances, can add a lot to a rational but politically sensitive planning process.

This is not to say that adjustment costs are necessarily a large part of the total costs in every single case. Bergman, in fact, guessed intuitively that the adjustment costs in the Swedish case were not a big proportion of total costs, although when he made that guess he was considering only adjustments in the national totals of use of capital and labor in each industrial sector. He did not look at regional changes in residential use, housing markets, and commuting patterns (Bergman 1981). It is possible, and indeed some of JS's comments suggest, that significant adjustment problems would appear on a more micro scale.

Environmental externalities

Energy conversion and transportation can create many environmental externalities. The energy changes in the Stockholm region might increase or decrease the remaining marginal externalities, and also change their interregional distribution (Stockholm versus the world) and the intraregional distribution (within Stockholm). Furthermore, the changes in the location of *non*-energy industries, which are expected in response to energy developments and policies, can also affect the distributions of environmental quality. Often governments themselves are the actors that especially bear watching! That seems especially true in the Stockholm region, with its 20-plus municipalities. Planning should attempt to internalize the externalities; modeling should help various levels of governments to measure the externalities and the consequences of various methods of internalizing.

Regional—national feedbacks

There are potentially very great feedbacks from the Stockholm region to the nation as a whole, because the region is large and has a large share of many important Swedish industries. Externalities are important examples, but there are others, which are transmitted through market forces. Even if a well functioning price system could internalize all the relevant national effects of Stockholm's regional economy, national policy makers would still need to predict and anticipate them.

For example, one national effect bound to be important in Sweden is the balance of payments. National decision makers will want to know the feedback effects from Stockholm's planning, energy pricing, and regulations to the international competitiveness of exporting and import-competing industries. In some industries, the plants in Stockholm collectively have some monopoly (and monopsony) power in their national or international markets. If a regional policy raises the costs of all of them uniformly, then they might be able to shift some of the costs forward or backward on to the rest of Sweden and the world. But such shifting affects their international competitiveness. Thus national planners need to know what will happen in Stockholm in order to develop anticipatory international trade and monetary policies, and, if they think it is in the national interest, to constrain Stockholm in certain ways and/or to subsidize its industries.

That is just one example. The feedbacks in terms of energy supply and demand are more obvious. In general, we have come to refer to the set of such feedback effects as "bottom-up" effects in recent years, but of course we worried about feedbacks of the kind we are discussing long before "bottom-up" entered the modeling lexicon. We have long known that in modeling a region as large and as important as Stockholm, we had to be wary of holding national variables constant even as we simulated significant changes in the region's variables. The same considerations enter here as they would in the US, for example, in modeling California or the entire Midwest, or as they would in the UK in modeling the London region.

Regional–national feedbacks may explain why there are bothersome inconsistencies between national and regional projections in the work of the COC. Without knowing more about the models used, we cannot say whether the inconsistencies should have been resolved by accepting the national projections, or the regional ones, or something in between, such as splitting the difference!

The REGI system has substantial feedback modeling capability, but exactly how much is again not clear. One of the multiregional models, MORSE, is bottom-up for consumption and the majority of production sectors, but it is top-down for energy consumption, capital formation, and international trade, meaning that national totals are *not* sensitive to policies and developments in Stockholm. This appears odd unless the top-down constraints are explicit expressions of exogenous policy targets, and I assume that is the case. That would be realistic if the national government decided in advance on planning targets for those variables, and then committed itself to forcing the total of the regions to fit the target — by aggressive intervention in markets for credit, materials and fuels, and foreign exchange. In extreme cases, such intervention would have to take the form of direct controls and allocations.

If there were not that policy stance, however, the projections of investment, energy, and exports and imports should be modeled on a bottom-up basis. The level of investment depends on the spatial distribution of the demand for output relative to the spatial distribution of existing capacity. One spatial distribution of output might require new capacity and another not, even if they have the same national totals. The national total of energy use also clearly depends on the sectoral composition of output and on its spatial distribution. And exports and imports seem to be bottom-up variables on the argument made above.

Insurance against risk

The protection of individuals against risk is not necessarily a separate concern from those mentioned above, but rather a dimension of all of them. What I mean is that in thinking about adjustment costs, externalities, and feedbacks, planners should think in terms of probability distributions of real income faced by individuals. And, they should be concerned not just with the expected values of the distributions but also with the variance and other parameters that describe risk.

Often, the endogenous variables generated in planning exercises are by definition expected values, and as such do not capture all the essential characteristics of a probability distribution as they are perceived by a risk-averse population. In a situation like this, a microsimulation model of the labor market may capture some of the legitimate concerns.

It may also be helpful to think of the real income of the whole population of a region as coming from a "portfolio" of assets owned by the region's residents (for a full development of the approach, see Bolton 1982b,c). Ideally, the assets should be broadly enough defined to include environmental resources and public capital which produce nonpecuniary income, but that does complicate the analysis immensely. In a simplified portfolio approach, the measure of risk is the variance of income from the entire portfolio, and effective diversification is accomplished by reducing the variance. A crucial concept of portfolio analysis is that the contribution of one asset to risk is not the variance of the asset's own income, but rather the effect it has on the entire portfolio's income. Even if its own income is highly variable, it might actually reduce the variance of total income if it has low or even negative covariance with other assets. Or, it might actually increase risk even if its own income is only moderately variable (see my discussion of regional cost–benefit analysis as an analysis of adding a new "asset" in Bolton 1982b).

Consideration of portfolio variance is helpful even when energy projects are evaluated one at a time. It is even more helpful when, as the Swedes have learned to do, planners do a genuine systems analysis and evaluate whole clusters of projects with due regard to their interdependences. Indeed, I was reminded of the utility of the portfolio approach precisely because JS note, in their discussion of STOSEB's inadequate approach of comparing energy alternatives one at a time, that "Such an approach does not recognize that options eliminated in this way may become attractive when the whole energy system of the region is considered". They did not have portfolio risk analysis in mind, but it struck me that in a planning agency that is so alert to interdependences anyway, my suggestion that it extend its analysis to covariances might be well received.

It would also appear especially attractive to keep the portfolio approach in mind in Sweden, where, we are told, planners strive for adaptability and flexibility. Of course, my suggestion can be followed only imperfectly: it would be an inevitably imperfect extension of existing imperfect planning techniques. We are admittedly a long way from incorporating this idea in modeling and planning; so far, our notions of risk are more intuitive, and our concepts of diversification in regional analysis tend to be based more on ideas of "diversity" than on the concept of portfolio diversification developed in financial and capital market theory. The distinction is this: "diversity" is the distribution of a total sum over a large number of different components, such as industries or markets; "diversification" is the reduction in the variance of the total sum that is achieved by combining components with low covariances, and it does not depend only on the number of components or the "evenness" of their shares (for a review of the small amount of regional literature which uses the portfolio diversification approach, see Bolton 1982b).

REGI does not estimate explicit probability distributions of real income and does not routinely produce risk measures by which one could evaluate policies. REGI does feature sensitivity analysis, of course, but I don't think sensitivity analysis in itself fully qualifies. It often varies only a few parameters or control variables in order to test sensitivity; it often concentrates on extremes rather than a more representative set of points on the probability distribution; and it often does not produce explicit quantitative measures of risk.

Because RPO is as ambitious as it is, I need not hesitate to suggest that extension of REGI in the direction of portfolio risk assessment would be a highly useful innovation.

Concluding Remarks

A summary of what is largely a summary would be tedious. I want to close by saying that it must be an occupational hazard, and frustration, of regional planners and modelers to be told that they are doing a good job but there are still some things left undone! I have tried to indicate some desirable additions to the REGI effort and to Johansson and Snickars' report on it, but I don't want that to conceal my admiration for a perceptive report on what must be one of the more sophisticated operational planning efforts in the world today.

Large-Scale Energy Projects: Assessment of Regional Consequences
T.R. Lakshmanan and B. Johansson (Editors)
Elsevier Science Publishers B.V. (North-Holland)
© IIASA, 1985

CHAPTER 5

Conservation and Fuel Switching in Sweden

5.3. The Swedish Case Study Compared with Experiences in the USA and Japan[1]

T. Takayama

National and International Background

Since the 1973 crude oil price increases, stagflation and recessions have spread, resulting in reduced oil demand. This process has stimulated several ideas on possible large-scale alternative energy supply systems in many countries.

Before 1973 the nuclear power plant signified a large-scale energy system. Even though many issues related to such systems were not fully evaluated until after the Three Mile Island incident of 1978, the major economic issues (cost of electricity, employment, and the environment) were carefully examined before permits were ever granted for a proposed nuclear plant. One of the most controversial issues has been the need for power. In a rapidly growing country such as Japan, in 1965–73 the need for power was obviously urgent, but only secondary to that of what industries were needed, of what size, and where. However, since 1973 the fuel choice has narrowed and the use of oil-fired power plants has been avoided. This is both a private and a national choice, and represents a substantial change in fuel choice behavior in the USA, if not so much in Japan.

---

[1] The views expressed in this paper are those of the author, and do not necessarily reflect those of the World Bank. The author is at present Professor of Japanese Studies, Economics Department, University of Western Australia, WA 6009, Australia.

In the case of Sweden, the closure of existing nuclear power plants is a major concern that almost inevitably touches on the larger issues mentioned above. These issues and the Swedish models that dealt with them are discussed in reference to those in the USA and Japan.

Issues

The short-term issue with regard to energy in Sweden is the overburdening budgetary drain of current levels of oil imports, and the long-term issue is how to provide energy after the abolition of nuclear power. Short-term objectives for 1980–90 specify a 45% cut in current oil use through (i) energy conservation efforts contributing to a 25% reduction, and (ii) the substitution of oil by other fuels such as domestic solid fuel and the introduction of heat pumps, district heating, etc.

The long-term issues are much more difficult to deal with than short-term ones. These require (tentative) information on (1) future domestic and foreign demand for Swedish goods; (2) future sectoral structure and development of the Swedish economy; and (3) the accompanying fuel use technologies. In planning the energy future of the Stockholm region, Johansson and Snickars (JS) are well aware of the fact that regional energy planning is conditioned by national economic development/energy planning, and *not* vice versa. Thus the RPO summarized the most important national restrictions as follows:

- the energy used for heating existing buildings should be reduced by 30% before 1990;
- oil consumption must be reduced to 45% from the present level by 1990;
- all nuclear power plants will be closed down before 2010.

The first restriction seems to be more severe than the nationwide conservation savings of 25%. It is one thing to establish a target, but quite another to realize it within a given time frame. The second restriction is also undesirable, but the question is whether the target is realizable under a business-as-usual scenario, or conceivable only in the upper range of the business environment. The third condition may or may not stick, but let us assume that this may remain unchangeable for some time.

It is well known to economic planners that there are two ways of generating numbers: by a "top-down" or by a "bottom-up" method. JS describe seven steps used to generate regional and subarea economic activities and energy (use) densities in a consistent, top-down framework. Thus national energy policies may never be tested for their feasibility or realizability simply because the interactions between the national policies and individual agents' behavior in implementing them are not clearly delineated. More explicitly, the issues identified here are those related to (1) the future demand for Swedish goods, and (2) the future sectoral structure and development of the economy. Based on tentative answers to these issues, one can develop rational energy policies. JS do *not* identify and penetrate national economy-wide issues, which gives the impression that the paper is simply a report of model system exercises applied to the Swedish energy sector, especially in the Stockholm region.

Methods for National and Regional Studies

Methods: The national level

Given the top-down approach, JS naturally start with national energy policies, discuss national policies related to regional ones, and finally reach the local level. Obviously, throughout the process the consistency of policies at all spatial levels has to be kept in perspective.

It is difficult to forecast the future energy demand in Sweden (or any other country for that matter); in fact, forecasts have had to be continually reduced, even to a no-growth scenario in the 1981 forecast (see Figure 5.3). JS recognize that in evaluating future energy demand one has to consider carefully three factors: (i) the state of the economy; (ii) the changing economic (sectoral) structure; and (iii) the changing technological bases of sectoral energy use. These factors are explained, but not in sufficient detail to help identify future economic development patterns. Instead, the report steps straight into the work of the Commission on Consequences (COC; see Guteland 1980), leading into national issues, and finally to the Stockholm region case study.

The work of the COC has been carried out in seven steps (iteratively, if necessary): (1) forecasts of future energy demand; (2) specification of energy systems capable of meeting that demand at minimum cost under environmental and other regional or local constraints; (3) investment cost calculations, individual fuel specification and evaluation; (4) environmental impact evaluation; (5) employment and regional impact evaluation; (6) evaluation of private and public energy consumption; and (7) evaluation of local impacts of nuclear power and alternative subsystems. At all of these steps, models of various levels of sophistication were employed. For instance, steps (4), (6), and (7) used models that "were quite rudimentary from a mathematical point of view, amounting to a more or less systematic application of various types of multipliers and ratios. They were not necessarily internally or externally consistent". In step (2), on the other hand, some optimization models were employed. The methods used in step (1) must have been extrapolations with some price and income elasticity adjustments. Step (5) used some top-down, shift-share type breakdown models. The most sophisticated modeling was performed in step (3), where the Bergman general equilibrium model was used to calcualte output and factor substitutions "over the long term in an open economy".

Why was this modeling approach selected to analyze the inherently dynamic future energy—economy interactions? Did the COC expect that the Swedish economy in 1980—2000 would be static, with no structural changes or technological innovations? This is a hard question to answer, but since the COC did not raise it at the outset, it may not be possible at this stage to find out one way or the other.

Because it is a national aggregate model, regional analyses of factor (re)allocation, sector development, prices, etc., cannot be carried out on the basis of model results. A further breakdown of the results can be done using another top-down regionalization method, as described in Snickars (1978, 1979).

Where is the connecting link between step (3) and the Stockholm study? Essentially, there is none except that the RPO accepted similar types of national scenarios as its planning constraints.

Methods: The Stockholm region

The methodology used to study the Stockholm region seems to be simpler and more firmly grounded on observation than that used for the nation as a whole. The RPO is responsible for long-term energy planning, and STOSEB formulated the regional energy plan for 15 municipalities. A slight complication arises, however, in terms of energy planning since the Nynäs energy complex does its own planning.

An outstanding anomaly in the REGI approach from a standard impact analysis viewpoint is the fact that it starts with a proposed (or already completed) project, and its spatial and temporal consequences are derived or traced. Very little is reported about STOSEB, Nynäs, and other related studies; what were the methodologies and the results of these studies? JS concentrate on the RPO studies, and the others are only reflected through the RPO activity. Since the RPO analysis is an offshoot of the REGI project, the authors address the methods and model structure of REGI.

The administrative responsibilities of RPO, STOSEB, Nynäs, Vattenfall, etc., are explained in Table 5.7, but the role of REGI in relation to the other studies and the Stockholm energy plans remains rather dubious. JS review the REGI approach and then report how the REGI analysis was used to assess the STOSEB study, but the framework and the accompanying models of the *ideal* REGI approach do not seem to be finalized.

REGI-based evaluations of the STOSEB study

Global and/or national energy studies carried out in the 1970s have certain common features: the models used were incomplete or inadequate, or data were inaccurate, imperfect, or lacking. The STOSEB study seems to share some of these problems, so that the RPO assessment focused on them. The RPO also stressed the crucial point that the study was "...based on comparative cost analyses of various energy options, but that the comparisons were not made simultaneously for the whole energy system. The [STOSEB] study compares 'components' one by one, eliminating marginally costlier options; such an approach does not recognize that options eliminated in this way may become attractive when the whole energy system of the region is considered" (p 156). In this context, the integrated systems approach such as PROMISE or PILOT (planning investment levels over time; Dantzig *et al.* 1980), could be quite effective.

As a result of the application of the REGI project methods to the Stockholm region (together with the assessment of *STOSEB 80*), one clear conclusion emerged "that the Forsmark option could not be accepted without a more detailed anlaysis". It is therefore clear that a regional or subregional analysis cannot be complete until it is properly and strategically integrated into a system that contains subregions. This also demonstrates the necessity of an integrated systems approach in energy planning that incorporates national (or international), regional, and subregional systems, in order to produce an effective energy-related analysis or policy evaluation.

The final, but not insignificant problem related to diverse data sources must also be mentioned. The inconsistency of data from different countries, ministries, companies, etc., often restricts its availability for use in modeling and analysis. In the REGI project, technical information was obtained from various European sources. Local adaptation of these sources may actually force some changes in the input combinations from the originals, and eventually the future technology choice may differ from those chosen through optimization.

Comparative Review: Sweden, the USA, and Japan

In the following I review briefly a US government approach to the subject and one outstanding example of a regional energy system study, in order to draw some comparisons with the Swedish approach.

The first example is a modeling effort by the US DOE's Office of Conservation and Solar Energy (OCSE; ORNL 1980) to evaluate the energy-saving impacts of the OCSE program. The individual programs do not constitute "large-scale energy projects", but in aggregate they represented a $1 billion government investment in 1980. Naturally, Congress was not comfortable with this rapidly expanding budget item and requested the DOE to perform a cost–benefit analysis. The DOE reported as follows:

> The ORNL/MITRE[2] approach consisted of estimating energy saving impacts for all analyzed program elements under a common set of energy prices and economic growth assumptions. A three-step

---

[2] Oak Ridge National Laboratory (ORNL) and MITRE were contractors to this project.

estimation procedure (for 1980–2000) was followed: (1) development of energy consumption projections under the baseline scenario; (2) element by element estimation of energy saving impacts for each program; and (3) development of energy consumption projections under the program impact analysis scenarios (PIAS) that incorporate into the baseline analysis the changes due to program effects.

The baseline analysis provides a best estimate of the energy use in the presence of existing legislation, but without the programs. Assumptions concerning key demographic variables (such as population and labor force), macroeconomic variables (such as gross national product and disposable income), and energy variables (such as fuel prices, including the price of imported oil) formed a common set of inputs of this exercise. These data were developed by BNL (Brookhaven National Laboratory) and Dale Jorgensen Associates (DJA). DOE's fiscal and policy guidelines provided assumptions concerning oil import prices. ...Using BNL's TESOM model [see Chapter 6] with these fuel prices (generated using imported oil prices and appropriate markups), domestic energy production and consumption were projected. Economic growth projections were made using DJA's LITM model. In these computations the characterization of energy use is highly aggregated; it is based on historical data in LITM and on exogenously specified elasticities in TESOM.

Here, TESOM is very much like MACROINVEST in structure and function, and LITM is similar to the Bergman model. These projections of the baseline scenario driving variables were then used in regionalized (usually ten DOE regions) computer models for sectoral projection of energy use. Some of the models were: ORNL (residential, commercial, and industrial sector models), a gasoline demand model, as well as Jack Faucett Associates' transport energy conservation (TEC) model, the Federal Aviation Agency's jet fuel consumption model, and finally the MITRE Corporation's SPURR model for solar energy penetration exercises. These models were run independently to generate energy demand and solar use baseline projections for 1980–2000. Next, OCSE programs were introduced to compute the alternative energy demand, savings, and solar penetration. Finally, the scenarios were compared to derive the energy-saving impacts of the OCSE programs in 1980–2000.

Obviously, the first step in which all these models were run independently for each and all sectors appears to have been at fault because it ignores sectoral interdependence and market interactions of demand and supply. However, given the time constraints of less than one year in which to complete the project, this approach may have been the only one feasible, but was subjected to criticism similar to that faced by the STOSEB study with regard to its technology choice method. This was a typical top-down approach and, as such, constraints are imposed without employing iterative convergence between the "top" and the aggregated "down" calculations. The approach ignored the impact of uncertainty in the baseline scenarios and the alternative cases with the OCSE programs. As far as I know, this aspect has been commonly ignored in most large-scale energy-related modeling.

State of the art (untested) model-based (SPURR) market penetration prediction methods are weak. Also, throughout the model system treatment of cost was criticized as "weak". This was not typical of US energy impact evaluation projects; usually, health and environmental impact evaluations are attached to the project such as above. Until 1980 the DOE used a large-scale regionalized model SEAS (strategic environmental assessment system) to evaluate environmental impacts, which was usually run using solutions of some large-scale energy model such as the DOE MEFS (mid-term energy forecasting system) model, and the second-generation PIES (Project Independence evaluation system) model (see CEQ 1980). All of these DOE economy-wide (regional) models employ the top-down approach, and are not suitable for state- or substate-level energy impact analyses.

It was made clear to modelers both within and outside the DOE that the energy-related data were scarce, incomplete, or inadequate for their purposes. In this sense, it gave those involved in or concerned about these modeling exercises the distinct impression that the data could be blamed for any shortcomings in the analyses. In 1980 an energy consumption survey including all demand sectors was proposed in the DOE at a cost of $35 million, but this never materialized.

The first lesson from these massive modeling exercises during 1974–80 in the US is that the most effective policy analysis using a modeling approach should be based on existing, readily available data. Second, due to the very nature of factors of production and consumption, any successful energy policy modeling requires close and efficient collaboration between policy makers, economists, engineers, and operations researchers. A successful model is one that can be used easily by any class of professionals. In this sense, national/regional energy modeling in the US has been inspiring, but not altogether successful.

Another modeling exercise that I would like to discuss in relation to the Swedish case study is the Japanese local energy systems research project, an offshoot of the so-called Partnership Program of the Osaka and Tokyo Science and Technology Centers, IBM Japan Ltd, and Osaka University, under the auspices of the Kansai Electric Power Company and the Osaka Gas Company. The purpose of the study was as follows:

> In each region there is a need for a comprehensive investigation of energy demand–supply systems to forecast future energy demands — especially the growth of energy demand in the private sector — and to study changes in the structure of energy supplies. Also, as part of this study of long-term energy demand-supplies, it is necessary to investigate the feasibilities of use of alternatives to petroleum through a critical examination of the degree of economic and social changes to be brought about by new technologies. (*Local Energy Systems Research Focusing on the Kansai Region, Definition Report*, July 1982, p 2).

An outstanding feature of this project was that both energy demand and supply information came from local survey data and companies' billing and operation records. Comprehensive socioeconomic data were also collected from and analyzed for each 1 km^2 grid of the whole region. Using detailed energy consumption data by sector and fuel and energy supply technologies, the aim was to establish an operational dynamic model that optimally determines regional (and subregional) allocation of private housing, industrial locations and activity levels, transport energy needs, and location, composition, and size of power generating plants in the region.

One sizable problem is how to handle the tremendous amounts of available data, and inconsistencies in socioeconomic survey data and companies' billing records have to be resolved. In the US, for example, this could create serious problems in relation to the Protection of Privacy Act. Once the data are cleaned up for consistency and errors, however, this project will provide a great opportunity for experimentation with the whole system for a wide spectrum of energy policy exercises.

Conclusions

Sweden, with the moratorium on nuclear power in effect, will face a sizable fuel-switching problem in the coming decades, but the case study here does not deal squarely with this problem. Instead, a large part is devoted to methodological and modeling issues related to the REGI project. There are wide areas of commonality among various models used by many government agencies, research institutes (including university research groups, companies, and private researchers) throughout the world. For instance, MACROINVEST is very similar to LEAP used by the DOE; PROMISE resembles Dantzig's PILOT or BNL's TESOM; the Bergman model is very much like the five-sector version of the Hudson—Jorgenson model; and the household energy consumption modeling scheme could use the DOE Hirst model, etc. Thus, as far as the modeling is concerned, I feel that a compendium of models should be made available to the international energy modeling community with the specific purpose of helping future modelers in their choice of models for adaptation to their specific environment and data availability.

There must be official views or projections of (1) the Swedish economy (domestic as well as international trade perspectives); (2) the future sectoral structure (changes) needed to meet the projections; and (3) accompanying energy use technologies, before one can proceed effectively with an analysis of national consequences discussed in the case study. This report, like many others in the field, by not presenting these critical prerequisites, falls short of being comprehensive and convincing that the approaches used are necessary or sufficient for the effective implementation of Swedish national energy policies.

The above discussion of modeling approaches applies equally to those of the DOE up to 1980, maybe because they use a top-down approach. Top-down modeling lacks support from the bottom-up process. In political and administrative processes, I feel that there must be one additional mechanism through which top-down results can communicate with bottom-up views, opinions, or consensus of society and industry representatives, for the necessary scenario corrections and compromises. The Japanese example cited above could serve this purpose.

JS do not present a model for environmental impact evaluation. The DOE and others use several models for this purpose, and these may prove useful for Sweden. One important (and historical) footnote in using these models is that the national environmental standards must be firmly established (if possible) before the models are ever put to use.

These observations lead me to the conclusion that the Swedish (as any other country's) energy policies must be pursued on the basis of national consensus, based on close interactions between government, industry, and private consumers at all spatial levels. From the modeling point of view, top-down models must communicate with bottom-up models. Models are not an end in themselves; they are a means of providing better understanding of energy/economy issues, and of forming a better set of national, regional, and community energy/economic policies. In this context, I sincerely hope that the JS report and this review will serve to clarify these fundamental issues to the common benefit of the Swedish people as well as those of the rest of the world.

References

Andersson, Å.E. and Holmberg, I. (1980) *Migration and Settlement 3: Sweden.* Research Report RR-80-5 (Laxenburg, Austria: International Institute for Applied Systems Analysis).

Bergman, L. (1976) *A Model of the Swedish Residential Heating Sector.* Document D,4:1976 (Stockholm: Swedish Council for Building Research).

Bergman, L. (1981) The impact of nuclear power discontinuation in Sweden: A general equilibrium analysis. *Regional Science and Urban Economics* 11(3):269–86.

Bergman, L. and Por, A. (1980) *A Quantitative General Equilibrium Model of the Swedish Economy.* Working Paper WP-80-4 (Laxenburg, Austria: International Institute for Applied Systems Analysis).

Bolton, R. (1982a) The development of multiregional economic modeling in North America: Multiregional models in transition for economies in transition, in B. Issaev, P. Nijkamp, and P. Rietveld (Eds) *Multiregional Economic Modeling: Practice and Prospect* (Amsterdam: North-Holland) pp 157–70.

Bolton, R. (1982b,c) *An Expanded Portfolio Analysis of Regional Diversification.* Paper presented at meetings of Regional Science Association, Pittsburgh, PA; November; revised December 1982.

CEQ (1980) *Environmental Quality.* 11th Annual Report (Council on Environmental Quality).

Dantzig, G.B., Avi-Itzhak, B., Connoly, T.J., and Winkler, W.D. (1980) *Pilot-1980 Energy—Economic Model* Research Project 652-1 (Stanford University: Department of Optimization Laboratory).

Dorfman, R. and Jacoby, H. (1977) A public-decision model applied to a local pollution problem, in R. Dorfman and N. Dorfman (Eds) *Economics of the Environment*, 2nd edn (New York: W.W. Norton) pp 260–304.

Energy Systems Group (1982) *Long-Term Energy Supply Strategies for Stockholm County* (Mimeo) (Laxenburg, Austria: International Institute for Applied Systems Analysis).

Førsund, F., Karlqvist, A. and Strömqvist, U. (1982) *Structural Change and Regional Development — A Study of Swedish Manufacturing Industry During the Eighties* (unpublished).

Golladay, R. and Haveman, R. (1977) *The Economic Impact of Tax-Transfer Policy: Regional and Distribution Effects* (New York: Academic Press).

Guteland, G. (1980) *Suppose we go Non-nuclear? Summary of the Work of the Government Commission on the Consequences for Sweden Abolishing Nuclear Power* (Stockholm: Swedish Ministry of Industry).

Hårsman, B. (1981) *Housing Demand Models and Housing Market Models for Regional and Local Planning.* Document D13:1981 (Stockholm: Swedish Council for Building Research).

Johansen, L. (1974) *A Multi-Sectoral Study of Economic Growth,* 2nd edn (Amsterdam: North-Holland).

Johansson, B. and Strömqvist, U. (1981) Regional rigidities in the process of economic structural development. *Regional Science and Urban Economics* 11:363–75.

Kneese, A. and Bower, B. (1979) *Environmental Quality and Residuals Management* (Baltimore, MD: Johns Hopkins University Press).

Lundqvist, L. (1981) *A Dynamic Multiregional Input—Output Model for Analyzing Regional Development, Employment and Energy Use.* Paper presented at the European Congress of the Regional Science Association, Munich, 1980. TRITA-MAT-1980-20 (Stockholm: Royal Institute of Technology).

Lundqvist, L. (1982) *Systems Analysis and Perspective Planning, Plan 5,* Stockholm (in Swedish).

Lundqvist, L. and Mattson, L.G. (1982) *Transportation Systems and Residential Location.* TRITA-MAT-1982-5 (Stockholm: Royal Institute of Technology).

ORNL (1980) *Energy Saving Impacts of DOE's Conservation and Solar Program* Vols 1,2 (Oak Ridge, TN: Oak Ridge National Laboratory).

Persson, H. and Johansson, B. (1982) *A Dynamic Multisector Model with Endogenous Formation of Capacities and Equilibrium Prices: An Application to the Swedish Economy.* Professional Paper PP-82-9 (Laxenburg, Austria: International Institute for Applied Systems Analysis).

Roy, G.G. and Snickars, F. (1982) *An Introduction to the "ISP" System for Land Use Planning.* Working Paper WP-82-70 (Laxenburg, Austria: International Institute for Applied Systems Analysis).

RPO (1982) *Supplementary Analysis of the Region's Energy System.* Appendices to the Assessment of *STOSEB 80* (Stockholm Läns Landsting, Regionplanekontoret) (in Swedish).

Russell, C. and Spofford, W. (1977) A regional environmental quality management model: An assessment. *Journal of Environmental Economics and Management* 4:89–110.

Snickars, F. (1978) Estimation of interregional input—output tables by efficient information adding, in C. Bartels and R. Kethellapper (Eds) *Exploratory and Explanatory Analysis of Spatial Data* (Leiden: Martinus Nijhoff).

Snickars, F. (1979) *Regional Breakdown of Forecast National Demand for Labor* (Stockholm: Swedish Ministry of Industry) (in Swedish).

Snickars, F. and Granholm, A. (1981) A multiregional planning and forecasting model with special regard to the public sector. *Regional Science and Urban Economics* 11(3):377–404.

Steen, P., Johansson, T.B., Fredriksson, R. and Brogren, E. (1982) *Energy – For What and How Much* (Stockholm: Liber) (in Swedish).

SWRI (1980) *MRPIS: A Research Strategy* (Newton, MA: Boston College, Social Welfare Research Institute).

PART II

Review of Assessment Models
and Methods

In Part I a variety of models is presented from a contextual point of view. The review sections in Chapters 3–5 also reveal a high degree of similarity between various models developed and used in different parts of the world. In particular, the case studies reveal that the character of an assessment study, to a large extent, is determined by how different models (economic, demographic, environmental, etc.) have been put together. In other words, the architecture of the interlinkages between models and methods seems to be a factor that depends strongly upon the institutional and contextual conditions.

In Part II, models referring to different aspects are reviewed. Models, approaches to scenario generation, methods of impact analysis, and overall design of assessment studies, are examined with regard to four aspects or fields. Chapter 6 presents and characterizes national and regional models for economic assessment, and points out that time dimensions, adjustment processes, multiregional interactions, and consistency are crucial factors in studies of non-marginal energy supply investments and supply system design. Chapter 7 provides a review of energy-related boom town models. The boom town phenomenon is recognized as a dramatic dynamic process affecting settlements in resource frontiers such as Colorado, Alberta, and Western Siberia, but also in European regions around the North Sea in Norway and Scotland.

Chapter 8 classifies the fundamental dimensions of environmental consequences of energy supply investments, and approaches to their assessment. It characterizes the institutional and legal frameworks for environmental assessment in the USA, the USSR, Canada, and Sweden.

Finally, Chapter 9 deals with regional information systems designed for impact analyses, and makes a distinction between *ex ante* and *ex post* assessments. An attempt is also made to identify the type of information needed for large-scale energy projects and energy supply system investments.

Large-Scale Energy Projects: Assessment of Regional Consequences
T.R. Lakshmanan and B. Johansson (Editors)
Elsevier Science Publishers B.V. (North-Holland)
© IIASA, 1985

CHAPTER 6

National and Regional Models for Economic Assessment of Energy Projects

T.R. Lakshmanan

Introduction

The sharp increases in the price of oil in the early 1970s confronted many nations, particularly importers, with unprecedented economic challenges for which they were ill-prepared. The economies of the less affluent oil importers in the developing world were severely distorted, and even in the more affluent industrialized countries in the costs of adjustment to higher energy prices — in terms of higher overall price levels, unemployment, industrial restructuring, quality of public services, adverse distributional effects, and environmental quality — have been dramatic.

As a consequence, a two-pronged strategy of promoting energy conservation and large-scale development of new energy sources has been pursued in many countries. New energy sources include not only new fuels (from coal and oil shale and renewables), but also the mining and supply of conventional energy sources to new markets, and large-scale switching from one set of fuels to another.

When there is a sizeable change in a national energy sytem, three classes of economic impacts ensue. First, changes occur within the energy sector itself, which comprises an integrated set of activities operating within a complex private and governmental/institutional framework. These changes result from the supply–demand interactions of many energy products and technologies, and from regulatory mechanisms (e.g., taxes, price controls, average pricing schemes), which lead in turn to shifts in prices, quantities, and mix of primary, secondary, and final energy.

Second, changes in the price of energy affect prices and costs throughout the economy. The resulting demand for energy and the substitution possibilities between energy and other factors of production present economic impacts at the national and regional levels, which in turn affect employment, income, and consumption at both levels.

The third class of economic impacts is felt in the macroeconomic structure, in terms of investment, consumption, government spending, international trade, inflation, unemployment, asset markets, interest rates, etc.

The importance and relevance of these three classes of economic impacts has led to the development of economy–energy models in North America, Europe, the USSR, and Japan, which are capable of assessing the wide range of impacts of large-scale energy developments. We begin with a brief specification of the major interactions between the energy sector and the rest of the economy and sketch the evolution of economy–energy models as they have been used to tackle a variety of analytical issues. We identify the major methods used in these models and review briefly a few examples of the first-generation models of this type.

We then suggest that integrated models, which relate energy supply and demand, the energy sector, and the rest of the economy, are essential for a complete economic assessment of large-scale energy projects. We review the scope and structure of four such models (two of which are used in the US and Swedish case studies) and their application to the assessment of energy technologies. We conclude with a discussion of still unresolved analytical issues in this area and some directions for future work.

Modeling Economy–Energy Interactions: A Review of Research Directions

A simple model of economy–energy interactions

Since energy is used in the production and consumption of a wide variety of goods and services, significant changes in the energy system — in the form of higher prices or increases in supply — will affect energy demand, production processes, the sectoral composition of final demand, and output at the level of GNP. The major pathways of such effects are identified in Figure 6.1.

Changes in the energy sector in the form of higher prices or increased supplies affect national and regional economies in complex and interactive ways. For instance, the direct result of an increase or decrease in energy prices is a change in the structure of relative input prices. In the face of this shifting cost structure, producers move away from high-priced, energy-intensive inputs and processes, thereby reducing energy use. In this process, the substitution of other inputs such as capital, labor, or materials alters the pattern of production inputs.

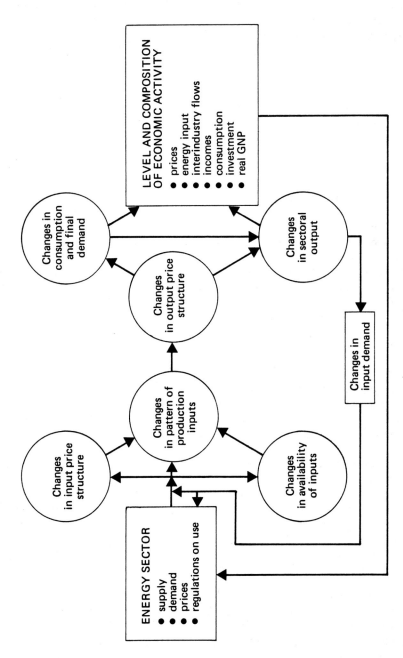

Figure 6.1. Pathways of interaction between the energy system and the rest of the economy.

Changes in the availability of inputs also affect such changes in the production input pattern.

Adjustments in input prices in turn cause changes in both the level and pattern of output prices, which then render goods and services relatively more expensive, particularly in energy-intensive manufacturing and transportation sectors. Less energy-intensive sectors such as light manufacturing, services, communications, or trade show only small price increases. Consumers respond to price changes by reducing their use of high-priced energy. Since their demand for energy is derived from the use of energy-using capital stock (e.g., heating equipment, cars, household appliances, etc.), over time they shift towards less energy-intensive equipment. Similar shifts in other components of final demand (investments, exports, and government purchases) lead to changes in sectoral output. Further, they reinforce changes in the supply side and cause further reductions in energy consumption. All of this affects interindustrial flows and, in turn, the level and composition of economic activity, and a variety of macroeconomic variables. Finally, the feedback effects of energy prices on capital investment are uncertain, depending upon whether capital and energy are viewed as complements or substitutes.

The purpose of this discussion of economy–energy interactions is to identify the analytical agenda for, and a basis for comparison of, models designed to assess the economic impacts of energy projects. The foregoing suggests that such models should contain components that represent the structures of the energy sector, the regional/national economy, and the macroeconomy.

The energy sector comprises the extraction of primary energy resources and the conversion and distribution of energy (e.g., refining and distribution, electric utilities, liquefaction, and solar). The analytical issues in energy sector modeling pertain to specification of costs and capital requirements, energy products and their prices, and interfuel substitutions. Since energy demand is derived as an intermediate demand, the representation of the regional/national economy requires considerable sectoral detail in the specification of both energy and non-energy sectors; hence the frequent use of input–output (I–O) model structures and nonlinear production functions. The substitution possibilities between production factors are of major analytical interest here.

Finally, the links to the macroeconomic structure are relevant in tracing the effects on aggregate prices, interest rates, growth, employment, etc. Models emphasize various aspects of the analytical continuum from the energy sector to the economy (Figure 6.1). The differences among them pertain to:

- Sectoral detail.
- Substitution and technology: this includes interfuel and factor substitution, as well as substitution of processes.

- Geographic detail.
- Dynamic adjustments: different parts of a system adjust at different speeds.
- Balancing mechanisms: the models use either a positive or a normative objective for this purpose. The former case corresponds to a market equilibrium, and the second refers to imposed (often aggregate) behavioral activities.

Evolution of economy–energy modeling

Prior to the early 1970s, there was a "top-down" linkage between economic and energy modeling. Macroeconomic models were used as a source of exogenous forecasts of aggregate economic variables such as aggregate and sectoral output. The latter were then utilized to devise growth rates for the energy sector.

The first phase of economy–energy modeling was predictably associated with the 1973 energy crisis and higher prices, which (given the historically similar growth rates of the economy and energy demand) generated fears for economic growth. The Hudson–Jorgenson (1974) study was the first to attack this "tight-fit" hypothesis between economic growth and energy, and identified the considerable substitution potential between energy input and other production factors. Hudson and Jorgenson use a four-factor — capital (K), labor (L), energy (E), and materials (M) — production function, specified by a translog that places no *a priori* restrictions on the elasticities of substitution. If input prices and output levels are exogenous, such a production structure can be equivalently described by a cost function C:

$$\ln C = \alpha_0 + \alpha_y \ln Y + \sum_i \alpha_i \ln P_i + \tfrac{1}{2} \beta_{yy} (\ln Y)^2$$

$$+ \tfrac{1}{2} \sum_i \sum_j \beta_{ij} \ln P_i \ln P_j + \sum_i \beta_{yi} \ln Y \ln P_i \ , \tag{6.1}$$

where $i, j = K, L, E, M$; P_i = factor prices; and Y = output. If (6.1) is differentiated with respect to input prices logarithmically, the derived demand equations can be obtained:

$$\partial \ln C / \partial \ln P_i = (\partial C / \partial P_i) P_i / C$$

$$= \alpha_i + \sum_j \beta_i \ln P_j + \beta_{yi} \ln Y \ . \tag{6.2}$$

From Shepard's lemma, $\partial C / \partial P_i = X_i$ is the cost-minimizing quantity of input i. Since the cost function is linearly homogeneous in prices, $C = \sum_i P_i X_i$. Substituting gives

$$\partial \ln C / \partial \ln P_i = P_i X_i / \sum_i P_i X_i = S_i \tag{6.3}$$

or

$$S_i = \alpha_i + \sum_j \beta_{ij} \ln P_j + \beta_{yi} \ln Y \ ,$$

where S_i is the cost share of factor i.

Of particular interest are the Allen elasticities of substitution, which can be defined as

$$\sigma_{ij} = \varepsilon_{ij} / S_j \quad , \tag{6.4}$$

where ε_{ij} is the common price elasticity.

From an empirical analysis of this model it has been clearly shown that the economy—energy linkage is a loose one. The substitution potential between energy and other factors of production is considerable, though it varies with sector and region (see Table 6.1).

The second phase of economy—energy modeling was exemplified by intermediate-term energy sector models such as the US Project Independence evaluation system (PIES). Comprising an energy demand model, a collection of supply models, and an integrating model, PIES projects energy prices and quantities. PIES can handle a variety of regulatory functions in the energy sector, and estimates the consequences of various policies such as import tariffs, import quotas, conservation measures, etc. However, structurally the PIES model accepts the macroeconomic model's projections of GNP, consumer price index, and other macro-indicators.

The third phase was characterized by a developing capability for technology assessment, as illustrated by the Brookhaven energy system optimization model (BESOM), the SRI-Gulf model (US), and the Siberian Power Institute model (USSR). The importance of analyzing engineering processes and interfuel substitution are evident.

The next phase was characterized by attention to environmental effects of energy technologies, so that economy—energy—environment interaction modeling was considered. The strategic environmental assessment system (SEAS) model was the first in the area, although environmental assessment capability has been added to a variety of economy—energy models. Table 6.2 provides brief descriptions of some of the major models (SEAS is described in detail below).

Methods used

The need to integrate economic and physical processes in economy—energy modeling has drawn analysts from many disciplines — economics, engineering, operations research, physical sciences and technology — into the field. Consequently, a variety of methods abound, including traditional fixed-coefficient input—output (I—O) models, variable-coefficient models and translog models, linear programming (LP), nonlinear optimization, and systems dynamics.

A useful way to distinguish between methods is to identify how they represent the energy sector, the economic structure, and the macroeconomy. The energy sector is represented by depicting in some form the energy reference system and using optimization routines for solving

Table 6.1. Substitution possibilities between energy and non-energy inputs: some empirical findings.

Study	Empirical context	Methods used	Findings
(1) Berndt and Wood (1975)	US; manufacturing 1947–71	KLEM model; translog iterative 3-stage LS	E and K complementary E and L substitutes E and M substitutes
(2) Griffin and Gregory (1978)	Nine OECD countries; manufacturing 1955, '60, '65, '69	KLE model; translog iterative Zellner	E and K substitutes E and L substitutes
(3) Pindyck (1979)	Ten OECD countries; manufacturing 1959–74	KLE model; translog iterative Zellner	E and K substitutes E and L substitutes
(4) Fuss (1977)	Canada; manufacturing 1961–71	KLEM 2-level model; translog	E and L substitutes E and M substitutes
(5) Fields and Grabenstein (1980)	US; manufacturing 1971	L, E, K (working and physical) translog	E and L substitutes
(6) Lakshmanan *et al.* (1980, 1981)	US; 19 manufacturing sectors 1971, '74, '75, '76	L, E, working K, physical K; two-level (different fuels) model; translog iterative Zellner	1. E and L substitutes 2. E and working K substitutes 3. E and physical capital substitutes in some 2-digit sectors, and complementary in others 4. Most of the above broadly variant regionally.

Table 6.2. A survey of selected energy policy models.

Model, author, etc.	Model type and systems described	Technological change, substitution	Model inputs	Model uses
(1) PIES (Project Independence evaluation system) model of DOE; a regional US model; 5–15 year horizon (Hogan 1975)	Energy demand model, collection of supply models, and an integrating model using an interactive LP approximation to a fixed-point algorithm for economic equilibrium. Requires tie-in to a macro model.	Own and cross-price elasticities of demand; interfuel substitution on the supply side.	Very large database required.	Estimates consequences of policies, e.g., import tariffs, quotas, price changes, conservation measures, electricity load management, etc.
(2) Hudson–Jorgenson model of the US; 25-year horizon (Hudson and Jorgenson 1974)	Interindustry model with energy sector detail; model of consumer demand driven by an overall macro economic growth model.	Productivity trends; variable elasticities of substitutions for energy (translog) price; variable I–O coefficients.	Labor force, population, government expenditures, unemployment, etc.	Analysis of the "fit" between economic growth and energy use.
(3) Wharton model of the US; 15-year horizon (Klein and Finan 1976)	A 59-sector I–O model with satellite models for energy-using industries (e.g., iron and steel, cement, aluminum, etc.).	Same as (2), except a CES function is used. Process models for key energy sectors capture energy and interfuel substitution. Column coefficients responsive to price.	Population, labor force, world trade policy; monetary and tax policies	Provides detailed sectoral impact of various energy, tax, price, and supply policies.

(4) Brookhaven energy system optimization model (BESOM) of the US: single-year model; 25-year horizon (Hoffman 1972)	LP model structured around "reference energy system" to minimize cost of meeting end-use energy demands from resource extraction through conversion, distribution, and end use. Needs a macro model.	Any new technologies can be considered; interfuel substitution considered.	Energy conversion efficiencies, annual cost for all technologies; end-use demands, environmental emissions.	Useful for assessing energy technologies. Impact of different energy policies on the energy system.
(5) Stanford Research Institute–Gulf model (SRI–Gulf) of the US: 50-year horizon (Cazalet 1977, 1978)	A regional dynamic "generalized equilibrium model". Representation of process technologies and market adjustment process by linking a network of submodels. Requires a macro model.	Flexible in the consideration of any technology, interfuel substitution, price elasticities of end-use demand.	Technological and cost data; market penetration data; demographic trends.	Used in the economic analysis of Western US energy resources development; also used by Gulf Oil to assess synfuel strategy.
(8) Helliwell, energy model for Canada; 5-region model; 15-year horizon (Helliwell *et al.* 1976, Helliwell 1979)	An econometric model of the energy sector with links to the Canadian econometric model RDX$_2$.	Synthetic crude oil tar sands technology; regionally variant interfuel substitution.	World crude oil prices; Canadian energy prices, tax, royalty rates.	Can be used to analyze a wide variety of energy price, taxation, trade, and development policies; used to show that high-priced Arctic gas is not needed until the 1990s.

Table 8.2. (continued).

Model, author, etc.	Model type and systems described	Technological change, substitution	Model inputs	Model uses
(7) Khazzom, model for Canada; 10-region; 25-year horizon (Khazzom 1975)	A nonlinear econometric specification of energy demand by fuel. Additional macro model needed.	Time-phased price elasticity of demand, based on "free" and "captive" demand estimates; interfuel substitution.	Demographic trends, personal incomes, prices of energy.	Useful for assessing energy conservation likely to result from price increases.
(8) The long-term energy demand model for Japan (Institute of Energy Economics 1973)	A systems dynamics model including I–O analysis of three subsystems – the economy, energy demand and supply, and the environment. Requires a macro model.		Demographic variables; private investment growth.	Useful for estimating energy demand levels by sector, but not for assessing the effect of prices on national economy.
(9) The Siberian Power Institute model of USSR; 15-year horizon (Kononov 1976)	A dynamic I–O model describing the external production relations of the energy supply system (ESS). Can account for investment lags.	Many new technologies can be considered.	Outputs of various energy resources and new capacities in the ESS and transportation types and capacities.	To study the effect of large-scale changes in ESS on other economic sectors in terms of investment, labor, and material implications.

a set of cost-minimizing energy flows. The structure of the economy can be described either via an I–O table or by an aggregate production function. While both describe the technological relationships between inputs and outputs, the I–O usually provides more structural detail and the aggregate production function permits analyses of substitution among inputs, technical change, economies of scale, investment, etc. Most economy–energy models, following the Hudson–Jorgenson work, combine both I–O components and nonlinear production functions.

Since I–O models underlie most economy–energy models, the methods can be categorized as follows (Griffin and Gregory 1976, PLANCO 1979):

- fixed-coefficient I–O analysis;
- fixed coefficient with LP optimization;
- variable coefficients based upon econometric or process analysis.

The major example of fixed-coefficient I–O analysis is the 367-sector model of the Illinois Center for Automated Computation (CAC), in which the coefficients are in BTU terms. While this model is used for estimating the direct and indirect energy costs of transportation alternatives and various government programs, it suffers from extreme rigidity. The fixed coefficients do not permit interfuel or factor substitution, thus limiting its usefulness for intermediate or long-term projections.

LP and I–O models can be coupled in various ways. In PILOT (Dantzig and Parikh 1976) an LP drives the overall model by minimizing total costs while maximizing final demand. The LP technique can also help to modify the production process implied by the I–O table. The solution values of BESOM (where the cost of meeting energy demand is minimized; see Table 6.2) can be used to compute the technical coefficients of the energy sectors in the CAC I–O model. In all these cases, the LP comprises four elements: technology, fuels in specific locations, demand, and supply. Although the technologies are linear, the inclusion of several processes for the same product provides substitution. Given a set of costs for various technologies, constraints on supply, demand, and material balances, the LP minimizes the total costs of energy provision.

The coefficients in the I–O model can be modified econometrically using translog results described above (Hudson and Jorgenson 1974). The Wharton model uses flexible I–O coefficients, based on estimates from a CES production function and a time trend. The time trend makes it possible to assume partial adjustment to changes in factor prices. The Wharton approach also uses process analysis to derive some of the I–O coefficients.[1]

---

[1] First, an LP model is used to generate optimal combinations of inputs for different sets of assumed input prices. From the "pseudodata" of these input prices and corresponding input quantities, a statistical cost function is estimated with which the production function can be recovered and the I–O coefficients calculated.

Most of these economy—energy models have existed for less than a decade and evidence problems of infancy. Often they rely on one or two methodologies, such as econometrics based on pre-1973 time series data. Some models escape this limitation by using optimization techniques with I—O analysis, in which case the limitations of I—O analysis emerge. Further, any assessment of energy technology or R&D issues requires engineering process analysis.

The major limitation of this generation of models is their focus on one or two policy issues. Such individual issues may pertain either to economy—energy growth linkages or to energy supply sector responses to prices or regulations, or technology or environmental assessment. Yet a complete assessment of major policy choices such as the scale, composition, location, and timing of large-scale energy developments requires an understanding of all of the above changes in the energy sector (in terms of demand—supply and technological process analyses), changes in regional and national production and consumption structures, and the environmental impacts of energy projects.

What is needed, therefore, is an integrated model that does justice to these interdependences by tracing the economic pathways from projects to changes in the energy sector in regional/national structures, and in the macroeconomy. In the last few years a few such models have been developed by linking many of the models described above. Thus econometric, optimization engineering processes, and environmental models have been linked to varying degrees, depending upon the policy context. We now provide a description of such integrated economy—energy models, which can be used to assess the economic impacts of large-scale energy projects.

Integrated Models for Assessing the Economic Effects of Energy Projects

The simple model of economy—energy interactions depicted in Figure 6.1 is aspatial and does not capture the multilevel interactive linkages in the case of large-scale energy projects whose economic impacts are localized, but are felt at the local, regional, national, and even international levels. While this model is useful for typical partial equilibrium impact analyses, it fails to do justice to the complex interdependences in a case study of a large-scale energy project. Where energy projects are undertaken in densely populated areas or in resource frontiers, alternatives are possible, each of which has not only multiregional and national economic effects, but also complex interactions with the regional built environment giving rise to adjustments in the latter. Thus, non-marginal, system-wide effects will result.

Given these multidimensional and simultaneous interdependences in an economic system, the economic impact model must incorporate and link several subsystems — the national economy, a multiregional economic system linked interactively with the national system, the energy system specified in some spatial detail, the regional built environment, etc. What is needed, therefore, is to step beyond the economy—energy modeling traditions developed in the last decade to develop more complex modeling systems. Such efforts appear to have taken the form of drawing models from different analytical traditions (e.g., energy system modeling, national and multiregional modeling, local public finance modeling, urban housing and infrastructure modeling, etc.), and linking them in the form of integrated impact models.

These models share some common features: they all have some version of a macroeconomic model, and they represent, to varying degrees, production and consumption. They attempt multiregional analyses, although they usually fail to incorporate regional—national feedbacks. They contain a reference energy supply system and depict energy technologies, demand, and prices. Finally, there are clear linkages between the energy sector and the rest of the economy.

Since these models are usually designed by linking existing models, their variations lie in the degree to which the component models differ in:

- sectoral detail in energy and non-energy sectors;
- the incorporation of energy technologies and factor substitution;
- specification of regional economies and the regional built environment (variations that affect energy demand); and
- specification of dynamic adjustments.

We review here four such integrated models, and identify their strengths and their degree of coverage of crucial analytical issues:

(*a*) the Hudson—Jorgenson (HJ)—BESOM model
(*b*) the IIASA energy models
(*c*) the strategic environmental assessment system (SEAS) model
(*d*) the Swedish regional—national economy—energy models.

The first two were designed for broad technology assessment purposes and contain components that are incorporated in the latter two. The structures of the last two, however, are more appropriate for our purposes and were used in the US and Swedish case studies.

The Hudson—Jorgenson (HJ)—BESOM model

The HJ and BESOM models (models 2 and 4 in Table 6.2) were integrated in order to assess the impacts of research, development, and demonstration policies on the energy sector (typical of BESOM) as well as the impacts of these policies on the entire economy (typical of HJ). The integration was based on an expanded version of the HJ interindustry accounts system. The five energy sectors of HJ are broken down to 11 primary energy sectors, 20 energy conversion processes, and 16 secondary energy forms and energy products sectors corresponding to the detail in BESOM.[2]

BESOM focuses on the technical, economic, and environmental characteristics of energy conversion, delivery, and utilization processes that comprise the total energy system. It is structured around a reference energy system (RES) that displays the flow of energy from a resource to the end-use point. The specialized format of RES indicates the detailed technological structure of the energy system, together with coefficients to characterize technical efficiency and emissions from the various energy supply processes. BESOM can be used in either the optimization or simulation mode (Kydes *et al.* 1979). In the former, when constraints on resource availability, market penetration of various technologies, and electricity generating capacity are specified, BESOM calculates the optimal supply–demand configuration. In the simulation mode, the model is constrained so as to duplicate desired supply–demand system and to estimate the corresponding total system costs and environmental impacts. BESOM has been used to assess the contribution of clean, renewable resources (e.g., solar or wind power) and their related impacts on costs, social concerns, etc.

While BESOM provides a "snapshot" of energy system configurations, it has two variants: TESOM (time-stepped energy system optimization model) and MARKAL (market allocation model) that permit, respectively, a simulation capability and a long time perspective on the evolution of the energy system over time. TESOM can be viewed as a "present trends", time-phased model in that the optimal levels of decision variables in a time period are determined entirely from: (1) the optimal levels of decision variables in the *previous* period; (2) assumptions of average lifetimes, retirement rates of "old" stock with associated costs; and (3) current period assumptions on energy-related economic and technological factors. Mathematically, the time-stepped model is formulated as a sequence of *expanded* LP problems representing national energy systems (one for each time period). TESOM was used to explore the implications of the *Coal in Transition: 1980–2000* assumptions on the demand side (Ahn *et al.* 1977).

MARKAL is a hybrid model developed by international cooperation and is a demand-driven, time-phased LP model designed to analyze the evolution of the energy system (within a particular R&D strategy). Given information on resource availability, technological characterization, and energy use, MARKAL selects an optimum energy system trajectory over a given time period.

---

[2] In one version, HJ–BESOM is combined with the 110-sector Brookhaven–Illinois I–O model. Further detail in terms of energy technology was expected in later versions. In recent versions, HJ–BESOM has become DJA–BESOM (DJA is Dale Jorgenson Associates).

BESOM and HJ are linked through a multistep, iterative procedure. HJ–BESOM is of interest here because it was one of the earliest attempts to integrate models. Its strength lies in its incorporation of technological detail and factor and fuel substitution. However, it is seriously deficient in two aspects: (i) it does not represent the regional economic structure — a serious deficiency in a study that focuses on regional consequences — as do other models; and (ii) adjustment processes are poorly specified, with the assumption of instantaneous adjustment of all factors to price changes in the static translog case.

The IIASA model system

The Energy Systems Program of the International Institute for Applied Systems Analysis (IIASA) developed a set of models in relation to a study of the transition from cheap fossil fuels to a long-term (15–50 years) energy future characterized by energy security, acceptable environmental quality, and higher energy prices (Häfele 1981). The objectives of the study were to assess the global implications of long-term regional and national energy policies and to evaluate alternative energy strategies (physical and technological), including their economic and environmental impacts.

The IIASA system comprises four component models (Figure 6.2). The macroeconomic (MACRO) component is a very aggregate representation designed to assess the potential difficulties of meeting the capital investment and manpower requirements of various energy strategies and the more general impacts of such strategies on growth rates of GNP and private consumption. The energy demand model, MEDEE-2, accepts the output of MACRO and a variety of assumptions about lifestyles (e.g., per capita housing), technical efficiencies (e.g., automobile fuel efficiency), and producers' energy demand scenarios. These are converted into secondary energy demand scenarios using assumptions on the allocation of demand for substitutable fuels to various fuel types.

The energy supply model MESSAGE attempts to balance the demand for energy and the supply of primary energy resources from various technologies. Technological relationships, build-up rates, and the availability of resources govern this process. MESSAGE was derived from MARKAL, and is a dynamic LP model that minimizes the total discounted costs of energy supplies over a given time horizon (Schrattenholzer 1981). The model output comprises physical flows of energy from primary to end use as characterized by demand data, shadow prices of supply, and environmental impacts along supply paths.

IMPACT is an extension of the Irkutsk model (Siberian Power Institute model; see Table 6.2). The time horizon is extended to 50 years; newer energy technologies and additional energy-related sectors are included; and the capability to assess the direct and indirect expenditures on water, energy, land, materials, and manpower, as well as

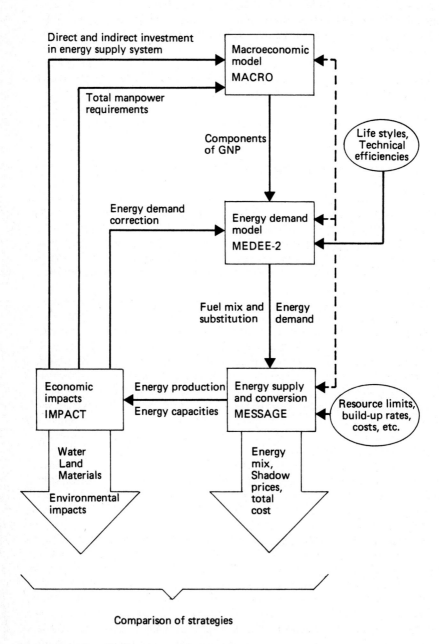

Figure 6.2. The IIASA energy model system.

environmental impacts, has been added. IMPACT can help to address questions such as: what potential bottlenecks exist in the form of capital, manpower, and materials in implementing a given strategy? What are the implications of these strategies on macroeconomic indicators?

Given its scope and aggregate geographical resolution (seven world regions), this model system cannot provide disaggregated information on impacts (in terms of economic sector, geographic detail, regional built environment, etc.) needed for economic assessment in the case studies. But the system contains model components that have structures and analytical capabilities appropriate for specific economic impact assessments, and have therefore been adopted as part of other model systems.

The strategic environmental assessment system (SEAS) model

SEAS was initially developed as an economy—environment model to provide a systematic assessment of emissions and abatement costs associated with economic growth and various pollution abatement policies (Lakshmanan and Krishnamurthi 1973). After 1973—74, as energy policy issues came to the fore, the scope of SEAS was broadened to include specification of energy supply, demand, and investment components so that it evolved into an integrated economy—environment—energy model (House 1977, Lakshmanan and Ratick 1977, 1980, Ratick and Lakshmanan 1983). The component modules of SEAS are interrelated within and between the three substantive areas by functional relationships and data matrices to form a large, medium-term (15—20 years) model (Figure 6.3).

The core model of SEAS is a 200-sector dynamic I—O forecasting model called INFORUM (interindustry forecasting model of the University of Maryland; Almon *et al.* 1974), which is linked to the Wharton macroeconomic model. INFORUM generates annual forecasts of sectoral activity in the context of some macroeconomic assumptions and final demand. Given the environmental focus of SEAS, the 200 sectors were disaggregated into many more product and technological subsectors (expressed in physical terms) in the INSIDE module, in order to delineate different pollutant emissions. The ABATE module computes the capital and operating costs of pollution abatement in any one year, for feedback into the capital and current accounts of that year in INFORUM, to obtain the relevant economic impacts for the next year.

The energy subsystem incorporates the reference energy system in the energy system network simulator (ESNS), three end-use energy demand models, and an energy investment model. The investment requirements corresponding to the energy supply technologies in the ESNS feed back to the energy demand modules and INFORUM.

The environmental modules estimate emission levels by type of pollutant and by type of technology from all production and consumption processes. REGION converts in a "top-down" fashion national economic and pollution forecasts into a variety of geographical areas — states,

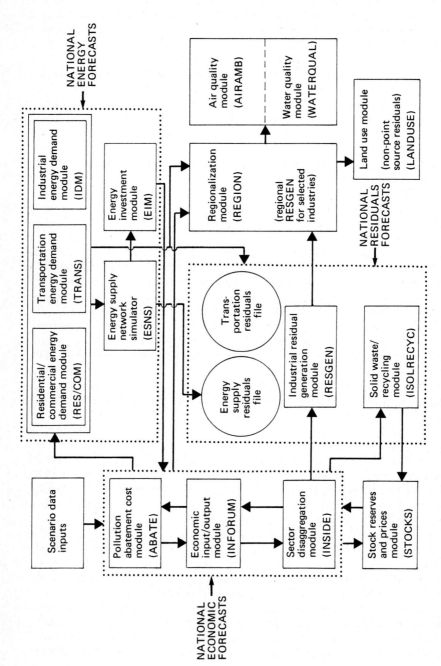

Figure 6.3. The SEAS model system (from Lakshmanan and Ratick 1980).

metropolitan areas, and spatial units relevant to air and water quality control.

SEAS provides an elaborate set of conditional forecasts of the effects of alternative energy strategies. The full capability of SEAS (such as it is, given the primitive and purely top-down nature of its regional submodel), is not utilized in the US Department of Energy where most of the SEAS effort in the US government is currently located. The institutional location of SEAS in the Environmental Assessment Division of the DOE has limited its application to environmental issues. The economic part of the model is constrained to accept output generated by the mid-term energy forecasting system (MEFS, a renamed version of PIES) and other economy—energy models, partly due to its current inability to handle factor substitution and multiregional modeling. In any case, its role in the US case study (see Chapter 5) was primarily as an environmental assessment tool.

The Swedish regional—national modeling system

The architecture of the impact model system used in the Swedish case study is in many ways appropriate to the analytical scope of economic assessment (Johansson and Snickars 1982). Each major component of the economic impact system (macroeconomic, multiregional, regional energy demand and supply) is recognized and represented by an existing model component (Figure 6.4). This sytem permits regional—national and, to some degree, international interactions, as well as traditional linkages between the energy sector and the national economy.

The macroeconomic model used in the Swedish case study is the Bergman model, a computable general equilibrium model for an open economy. As Bergman points out "the costs associated with the process of adjustment [to large-scale fuel switching] are left out of the analysis, and thus the impact analysis is confined to comparisons between different equilibrium conditions" (Bergman 1981, p270). In this respect, the second model proposed, MACROINVEST (Persson and Johansson 1982) is more helpful since it analyzes adjustment paths through vintage notions. Both models generate sectoral levels of employment, production, investment, energy uses, etc.

The multiregional modeling was carried out with MORSE (PROMISE is available as an alternative for this purpose), a multiregional, multisectoral model with eight regions and nine sectors (Lundqvist 1980). This hybrid model uses a bottom-up approach with regard to consumption and most production sectors, and a top-down approach for energy consumption, capital formation, and international trade. A variety of models drawn from analyses of housing and employment, building structures, and land-use planning helped to define the future spatial distribution of energy demand. These models were drawn from earlier metropolitan

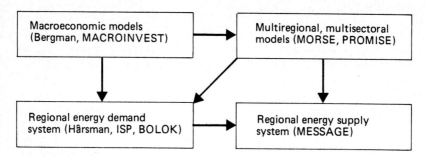

Figure 6.4. The Stockholm economic impact model system.

Stockholm planning studies. The energy supply system was detailed by the adaptation of the IIASA model MESSAGE to the Stockholm region.

A summing up

The problems of assessing the economic impacts of large-scale energy projects are analytically more complex than typical economy–energy impact problems. Given the multidimensionality of national–regional interdependences, the requisite model must integrate various analytical traditions. The scope of impact analysis methodology is to choose appropriate components and to link them together. The Swedish model system provides a good example for the case of energy development in a major metropolitan area. There are also analytical components appropriate for assessing the impacts of energy projects in resource frontiers.

While the above comments refer to model architecture, the attributes of particular model components still need to be matched with analytical requirements. Thus we observed that important adjustment paths in the case of major fuel switching in the Stockholm study are not handled by the Bergman model and perhaps MACROINVEST would have been better. This raises the general issue of key, unresolved, analytical issues in economic impact modeling, to which we now turn.

Future Directions for Economic Impact Modeling

Five analytical issues must be addressed if a model system is to be fully responsive to the requirements of information on economic impacts of large-scale energy projects: distributional issues; public expenditure and service quality; dynamic adjustment processes; regional, national, and international linkages; and the modeler–decision maker interface.

Distributional issues

A number of distributional issues arise when there is an increase in energy supply or fuel switching in a region. The income distributional issues arising from such large-scale changes have not been explored, yet one would expect that the development of an energy resource frontier would lead to an uneven distribution of benefits and costs — depending on whether one owned resource assets, or when older residents on fixed incomes get caught in boom town expansion, or there is curtailment of public services or labor dislocations. Indeed, it could be argued that much of the conflict between "old" and "new" groups in "boom towns" results from a failure to take these distributional outcomes into account and to incorporate them in politically responsive planning processes.

In the case of a large-scale fuel switching and development of new energy forms in a metropolitan market, there is a wide range of distributional outcomes. The Swedish model system currently generates welfare outcomes and environmental performance criteria at a broad subregional level. Yet the interactions between energy supply options and demand densities will generate energy price responses whose effects on different economic groups may be uneven. It is therefore important to model the income distributional effects of these energy developments at the local and regional levels. Such an analysis will become even more important in impact analysis if the economic growth rates of developed countries slow down considerably. Most multiregional models (including MORSE or the REGION module of SEAS) do not possess the capability, and it is here that recent microsimulation modeling in the US is relevant (Orcutt *et al.* 1976). These models, developed in the US Poverty Program at the Urban Institute, University of Wisconsin Poverty Institute and MATHEMATICA, utilize recently available data on household behavior, and provide information on labor supply, savings, consumption, migration, and other responses to external change and public policy by income class. In the US Department of Energy, such models as MATH and CHRDS illustrate these microsimulation models.[3] Another class of distributional effects is spatial and is incident on local government jurisdictions due to the changing distribution of households and enterprises resulting from large-scale energy system changes. The consequent interjurisdictional shifts in public revenues and expenditures are of interest to local decision makers and also need to be identified (see Chapter 7).

---

[3] Microanalytical transfer of households (MATH), and comprehensive human resource data system (CHRDS).

Public expenditure and service quality

A major consequence of a large-scale energy project is the burgeoning demand for local public services and expenditures, particularly in resource frontier areas. The boom town and other local economy models developed in response to this need are reviewed in Chapter 7. At present these models effectively represent a combination of accounting models and automated versions of simple notions such as economic base theory. But while they possess the virtues of simplicity and comprehensiveness, their outputs are not sensitive to many policy measures at the disposal of local governments.

There is thus considerable room for incorporation of mainstream economic theory into this area (e.g., the use of the median voter model in specifying rigorously local public expenditure; see Lakshmanan 1981, 1983). Further, it would be desirable to model public service quality measures since the latter may change in response to energy system changes.

Dynamic adjustment processes

The large-scale energy projects described in the case studies can be seen as mechanisms in the transition from an era of cheap fuel to one of expensive energy from different fuel mixes. An understanding of the nature and incidence of the costs incurred in this transition is both intellectually interesting and also vital to the implementation of the transition policies. It is useful to distinguish between three types of adjustment processes:

- *Short term* (three months to one year) in which the response of the economy to an energy shock results in changes in production rates, lay-offs or recalls, orders, and shipping, or in modifying production processes by changing wages and prices by hiring, training, etc.
- *Medium term* (2–5 years) in which new plants can be built, households can relocate, new technological processes be designed and installed, new sources of raw materials can be developed, new legislation passed, and new supportive public investments implemented.
- *Long term* (10–20 years) when plant, equipment, and some types of capital stock become obsolete, and some energy sources are exhausted.

These response times will clearly differ markedly with industrial sector, type of household, and public agency. The various economic, behavioral, and technological relations incorporated in regional and national economic models will vary for each dynamic adjustment process. Fixed model parameters in the short term become variables in longer adjustment periods (e.g., if gasoline prices climb steeply, in the short term consumers will take a car type as given and will reduce their driving distances; over a 3—4 year period, they will change their capital stock by buying more fuel-efficient cars). Since economic, social, technological, and urban development phenomena in the real world embody such dynamic adjustment processes, satisfactory economic models must incorporate them for the time periods over which they are believed to be appropriate; otherwise conditional or policy analysis predictions made from the model will be grossly inaccurate.

Econometric and I—O models obtained by fitting historical data implicitly assume that the estimated parameters are constant. Mathematical programming, based on engineering estimates of processes, can incorporate technological processes at future points in time, but they do not easily make the transition from the present to the future. Some economic models distinguish between short- and long-term price elasticities, while others let I—O coefficients vary with relative prices (Hudson and Jorgenson 1974). While these developments are relevant, they are only a partial treatment of structural change processes to which energy prices or large-scale energy developments are likely to lead in the form of changing technological and industrial mixes, and the location of population and production.

Some recent modeling efforts have begun to address this problem. The ideas of Berndt *et al.* (1979) in developing dynamic adjustment models of industrial demand have been applied at the regional level (Lakshmanan 1983, Anderson and Lakshmanan 1983) and could be easily incorporated into regional—national models. Another example is the specification of adjustment processes via vintage modeling techniques as in MACROINVEST (Persson and Johansson 1982). Thus there is a potential for better specification of economic adjustment processes than is currently the case at the national and multiregional levels.

At the intraregional level, knowledge of the dynamics (interaction of variables and speed of adjustment) in models of employment, housing, and land use (whether in boom towns or the Stockholm region) is primitive. Generally, the interactions of variables are myopic (with current decisions entirely dependent on the outcomes of current parameter values) and adjustments are close to instantaneous. At the local level, dynamic processes of stock adjustment have not yet been analytically explored. Housing stock turns over slowly; productive and human capital much faster, leading to stock mismatches and disequilibria, with potential impacts on the quality of the urban environment. Analytical improvements in this area are a research frontier in urban and metropolitan modeling.

Most of the models dealing with the economy, energy processes, or the urban environment are derived from a neoclassical framework that does not pay much attention to technological innovation, yet dynamic processes such as innovation, innovation diffusion, and capital investment are obviously part of the adjustments to energy-related developments. Behavior-oriented models of households and firms that depict information generation, flows, communications, and processing are needed, and could lay the foundation for the understanding necessary to identify dynamic adjustment processes in the various components of a large-scale energy system.

Regional, national, and international linkages

The need for the regional–national interactive linkages is a staple of contemporary multiregional modeling literature (Bolton 1982, Lakshmanan 1982). The demand for such information in the case studies has been demonstrated in earlier chapters.

Figure 6.5 shows the nature of these two-way linkages in multiregional models; it shows two-way information flows between regions and the nation in a hybrid approach. National economic variables can be exogenous or endogenous. Among the latter some are spatially uniform while others are spatially variable. Spatially uniform endogenous variables (e.g., investment in some production sectors) can be specified in a top-down format, while the spatially variable group (e.g., investment in housing or the retail sector) is determined at the regional level in relation to regional demand and supply variables and selected national variables (e.g., interest rates) and summed up to the nation. The key point is that economic impact models should build in such two-way regional–national linkages. The multiregional, multisectoral model MORSE used in the Swedish case study provides an example of such desired regional–national linkages.

A second major component of model linkages relates to the international dimension. Since the world is one large energy-producing and energy-consuming entity, the policies pursued in one nation, such as conservation, fuel switching, or large-scale supply enhancement, have broad ramifications. Thus, major developments in conservation and domestic energy production will affect not only the prosperity of oil exporters such as Mexico or Venezuela, but also (through their effects on world oil prices) the economies of affluent (e.g., Sweden) and poor (e.g., India) nations. Thus large-scale import reductions in a large consumer country such as the US have a "public good" character that requires consideration by others. The lower energy prices will reduce the stress on the financial system and help in the faster adjustment of oil-importing economies. While the Bergman model captures some of these relationships between the Swedish economy and the rest of the world, this is as yet a poorly explored field. At this stage of oil market development, the importance of the effects of national and international politicoeconomic linkages on energy prices and supply, and various investment policies on large-scale energy developments is too obvious to belabor. Future modeling efforts must take explicit account of national–international linkages.

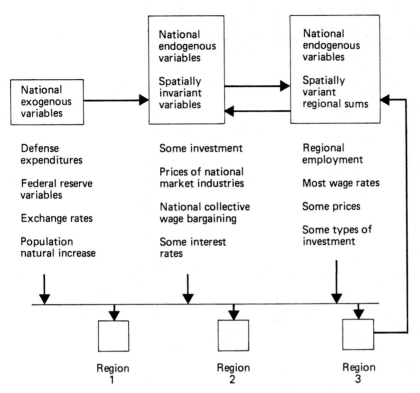

Figure 6.5. The hybrid approach: an illustration.

Modeler—decision maker interface

In spite of the widely touted contribution that economic modeling can make to energy decision making, the interface between the producers and users of models has been a bothersome barrier to its success. While this topic is discussed elsewhere in this volume, it may be useful to note here that differences in knowledge, functional roles, and time scales of operation between modelers and decision makers account for this barrier.

Policy issues in large-scale energy developments tend to be complex, ill-structured, and amorphous. Model systems are rather monolithic in the sense that the overall objective function determines optimality, while the real world has pluralistic decision structures, is interactive, and full of conflicts. These models thus tend to be useful in centralized decision contexts (as in typical operations research contexts). More often, in the public policy arena, economic modeling is inadequate in that it does not yet provide a method for strategic analysis that allows, in a context of adversarial procedures and bargaining, an orderly approach to balancing model results and judgment.

It is in this context that one can understand the strong demand for interactive multilevel modeling (with operational algorithms; see Lakshmanan and Roy 1984). While a few such modeling procedures have been sketched in carefully delimited contexts, their potential in the complex, ill-defined arena of energy decision making is still limited. The most likely and feasible avenue is currently the development of regional–national economic models as described in this chapter, as a means of enhancing the mutual understanding of the issues and problems among modelers and the multilevel participants in decision making. Developments in decision analysis, to sharpen this process of mutual understanding and learning, are sorely needed.

References

Ahn, B., *et al.* (1977) *Driving Variables and Scenario Definitions for the Coal in Transition 1980–2000 Study*, Energy Modeling Forum 2.3, Palo Alto, CA (mimeo).

Almon, C. *et al.* (1974) *1985: Interindustry Forecasts of the American Economy* (Lexington, MA: D.C. Heath).

Anderson, W. and Lakshmanan, T.R. (1983) *A Model of Regional Dynamic Adjustment in U.S. Manufacturing*. Working Paper (Boston: Department of Geography, Boston University).

Bergman, L. (1981) The impact of nuclear power discontinuation in Sweden. *Regional Science and Urban Economics* 11:269–86.

Berndt, E.R., Fuss, M.A., and Waverman, L. (1979) *Dynamic Adjustment Models of Industrial Demand: Empirical Analysis for U.S. Manufacturing 1947–1974* (Palo Alto, CA: Electric Power Research Institute).

Berndt, E.R. and Wood, D.O. (1975) Technology, prices and the derived demand for energy. *Review of Economics and Statistics* 57(3):259–68.

Bolton, R. (1982) The development of multiregional economic modeling in North America, in B. Issaev, *et al.* (Eds) *Multiregional Economic Modeling: Practice and Prospect* (Amsterdam: North-Holland) pp 157–70.

Cazalet, E.G. (1977) *Generalized Equilibrium Modeling: The Methodology of the SRI–Gulf Model* (Palo Alto, CA: Decision Focus Co.) (mimeo).

Cazalet, E.G. (1978) *The DFI Energy–Economy Modeling System*. Final Report prepared for the US Dept of Energy (Palo Alto, CA: Decision Focus, Inc.).

Dantzig, G.B. and Parikh, S.C. (1976) On a PILOT linear programming model for assessing physical impact of the economy of a changing energy future, in F.S. Roberts (Ed) *Energy: Mathematics and Models*. Proc. SIMS Conference on Energy, Salt Lake City, July. pp 1–23.

Fields, B.C. and Grabenstein, C. (1980) Capital energy substitution in U.S. manufacturing. *The Review of Economics and Statistics* 62:207–12.

Fuss, M.A. (1977) The demand for energy in Canadian manufacturing. *Journal of Econometrics* 5:86–116.

Griffin, J.M. and Gregory, P.A. (1976) An intercountry translog model of energy substitution responses. *American Economic Review* 66:845–57.

Häfele, W. (1981) *Energy in a Finite World*, 2 vols (Cambridge, MA: Ballinger).

Hårsman, B. (1981) *Housing Demand and Housing Market Models for Regional and Local Planning*. Document D13:1981 (Stockholm: Swedish Council for Building Research).

Helliwell, J.F. (1979) Canadian energy policy. *Annual Review of Energy* 4:125–229.

Helliwell, J.F. et al. (1976) *An Integrated Model for Energy Policy Analysis*. Resource Paper No. 7 (Vancouver: Department of Economics, University of British Columbia).

Hoffman, K.C. (1972) *A Unified Planning Framework for Energy System Planning*. PhD Thesis, Polytechnic Institute of Brooklyn, New York.

Hogan, W.W. (1975) Energy models for Project Independence. *Computer and Operations Research* 2:251–271.

Hogan, W.W. and Parikh, S. (1977) *Comparison of Models of Energy and the Economy*. Stanford Energy Modeling Forum, Working Paper, Energy Modeling Forum, 19.

House, P. (1977) *Trading Off Environment, Economics and Energy* (Lexington, MA: D.C. Heath).

Hudson, E.A. and Jorgenson, D.W. (1974) U.S. energy policy and economic growth. *Bell Journal of Economics and Management Science* Fall:461–514.

Institute of Energy Economics (1973) *The Long Term Energy Demand Model for Japan* (Tokyo: IEE) (mimeo).

Johansson, B. and Snickars, F. (1982) *Large-Scale Introductin of Energy Supply Systems*. Working Paper WP-82-121 (Laxenburg, Austria: International Institute for Applied Systems Analysis).

Khazzom, J.D. (1975) An application of the concepts of free and captive demands to the estimating and simulating energy demand in Canada, in *IIASA Proceedings of the Workshop on Energy Demand* May 1975 (Laxenburg, Austria: International Institute for Applied Systems Analysis), pp 181–232.

Klein, L.R. and Finan, W.F. (1976) *The Structure of the Wharton Annual Energy Model*. Paper presented at the Energy Modeling Forum, Washington, DC, October 1971.

Kononov, Yu. (1976) *Modeling of the Influence of Energy Development of Different Branches of the National Economy*. Research Report RR-76-11 (Laxenburg, Austria: International Institute for Applied Systems Analysis).

Kononov, Yu. and Por, A. (1979) *The Economic Impact Model*. Research Report RR-79-8 (Laxenburg, Austria: International Institute for Applied Systems Analysis).

Kydes, A.S. et al. (1979) *The Brookhaven TESOM*. BNL 21223 (Brookhaven National Laboratory).

Lakshmanan, T.R. (1981) *A Multiregional Model of the U.S. Economy, Environment and Energy Demand*. Paper presented at the Southern Economic Association.

Lakshmanan, T.R. (1982) Integrated multiregional economic modeling for the USA, in B. Issaev et al. (Eds) *Multiregional Economic Modeling: Practice and Prospect* (Amsterdam: North-Holland) pp 171–88.

Lakshmanan, T.R. (1983) A multiregional model of the economy, environment, and energy demand in the U.S. *Economic Geography* 59(3):296–320.

Lakshmanan, T.R. and Krishnamurthi, S. (1973) *The SEAS Test Model: Design and Implementation* (Washington, DC: Environmental Protection Agency).

Lakshmanan, T.R. and Ratick, S. (1977) *The Economic and Environmental Effects of Energy Development Scenarios: A Strategic Assessment*. Paper presented at the Soviet–American Seminar on Urban Development, Northwestern University, Evanston, IL, May 1977.

Lakshmanan, T.R. and Ratick, S. (1980) Integrated models for economic—energy—environmental impact analysis, in T.R. Lakshmanan and P. Nijkamp (Eds) *Economic—Environmental—Energy Interactions: Modeling and Policy Analysis* (Boston, MA: Martinus Nijhoff) pp 7—39.

Lakshmanan, T.R. and Probir, R. (1984), in J. Spronk, P. Nijkamp, and M. Despontin (Eds) *National Regional Linkages in Multiregional Models: Alternative Perspectives in Macroeconomic Planning with Conflicting Goals* (Amsterdam: Springer).

Lakshmanan, T.R. and Roy, P. (1984) Regional—national linkages in multiregional models, in M. Despontin, P. Nijkamp, and J. Spronk (Eds) *Macro-Economic Planning with Conflicting Goals* (Berlin: Springer Verlag).

Lakshmanan, T.R., Anderson, W., and Jourabchi, M. (1980) *A Multiregional Model of Factor Substitution*. Paper presented at the World Regional Science Congress, Cambridge, MA.

Lakshmanan, T.R., Anderson, W., and Jourabchi, M. (1984) Regional patterns of factor and fuel substitution in U.S. manufacturing. *Regional Science and Urban Economics* 3. Sweden.

Lundqvist, L. (1981) *A Dynamic Multiregional Input—Output Model for Analyzing Regional Development, Employment and Energy Use*. Paper presented at the European Regional Science Congress, Munich, 1981.

Orcutt, G. *et al.* (1976) *Policy Exploration through Micro Analytical Similarities* (Washington, DC: Urban Institute).

Persson, H. and Johansson, B. (1982) *A Dynamic Multisectoral Model with Endogenous Formation of Capacities and Equilibrium Prices: An Application to the Swedish Economy*. Professional Paper PP-82-9 (Laxenburg, Austria: International Institute for Applied Systems Analysis).

Pindyck, R.C. (1979) Interfuel substitution and industrial demand for energy: An international comparison. *Review of Economics and Statistics* 61:169—79.

PLANCO (1979) *Survey of Research into Economic—Energy Interactions*, prepared for US Department of Energy, April 1979.

Ratick, S. and Lakshmanan, T.R. (1983) An overview of the strategic environmental assessment system, in P. Nijkamp and T.R. Lakshmanan (Eds) *Systems and Models for Energy and Environmental Analysis* (London: Gower Press).

Schrattenholzer, L. (1981) *The Energy Supply Model MESSAGE*. Research Report RR-81-31 (Laxenburg, Austria: International Institute for Applied Systems Analysis).

Ziemba, W.T. and Schwartz, S.L. (Eds) (1980) *Energy Policy Modeling* (Boston, MA: Martinus Nijhoff).

Large-Scale Energy Projects: Assessment of Regional Consequences
T.R. Lakshmanan and B. Johansson (Editors)
Elsevier Science Publishers B.V. (North-Holland)
© IIASA, 1985

CHAPTER 7

Energy-Related Boom Towns: Problems, Causes, Policies, and Modeling

Chang-i Hua

Introduction

When a large-scale energy project is undertaken, its net benefits in terms of increased energy supply are diffused throughout a wide area, and its effects are only lightly felt by an individual at any particular time. In contrast, the local community in which the project is implemented bears the brunt of the construction; the community residents suddenly become distinct beneficiaries or victims. This kind of impact follows any large-scale civil or military construction, and it has been most dramatically demonstrated in the last 15 years in the energy-related developments in the western parts of the US and Canada. The impacted communities in these regions are known as boom towns, a term ripe with historical association. The effects of such construction schemes are most clearly discernible in regions with low population densities, remote from urban centers. For this reason, the boom town phenomenon and its accompanying problems summarized in this chapter have been mainly a North American experience.[1]

A boom town might appear to be a dream come true for a stagnant community striving for growth, if spared the negative effects reported in the literature. Indeed, the local unemployed and underemployed enjoy

---

[1] In Western Europe, some Scottish and Norwegian coastal towns have undergone similar but attenuated experiences during the North Sea oil exploration stage. From the limited information available, such as in Chapter 2 of this book, one senses that certain characteristics of the North American boom town also appear in Siberia. However, the most drastic effects of large-scale energy developments are perhaps to be found in the Persian Gulf area, where the boom town phenomenon has affected all of the Arab states and the problems cause societal transformation and cultural change.

new job opportunities, while many others may strike it rich from the windfalls brought by rapid development. But the experiences shared by these communities have been the basis for so many horror stories that the term "boom town effects" has only negative connotations. Many reports on boom town development portray mainly the regrettable consequences of large-scale energy projects. Rock Spring and Gillette in Wyoming, for example, are classic examples of these communities as victims. However, not all residents of such communities would accept such an interpretation; some researchers suggest that the negative aspects have been overemphasized, and have appealed for more balanced, objective research in this area.

This chapter reviews existing boom town studies in order to highlight their common problems and suggests some approaches to mitigate them. The assumption is that some information from the literature may still benefit planning for future energy projects in specific situations. This chapter therefore deliberately focuses on the negative aspects, even though these are somewhat exaggerated in certain studies.

Boom Town Problems

A definitional digression

It may be useful to begin with a clarification of the term boom town. In the US most states on both sides of the Rocky Mountains have witnessed a rapid growth of towns and counties due to various types of energy extraction activites. Areas most famous for boom towns are the Four Corners, the Powder River basin, and central Utah. In Canada, there are many resource towns in British Columbia and Alberta, but there is no comprehensive list because of the difficulty in defining what a boom town is.[2]

There is a continuum of community growth rates. For our purpose, we may conceptually define an "ideal type" boom town as an existing community that experiences a period of extraordinary growth and expects a period of rapid decline as the project is phased out. The boom town differs from the more familiar new town type of development in two ways. In the boom town a bust phase is expected, even though it may not materialize, and there is a clearly identifiable organization — the energy corporation and its construction company — that is responsible for the whole process. On the other hand, a boom town differs from a resource

---

[2] The US Department of Energy sponsored one survey in 1979 that listed 325 fast-growing communities affected by energy development. The most well known boom towns that have drawn many studies include Rock Spring, Wyoming (coal mining and power production), Gillette, Wyoming (coal mining, oil, gas), Craig, Colorado, and Colstrip, Montana (coal mining and power production). In Canada, Fort McMurray, Alberta (synthetic crude oil) typifies the boom town.

extraction company town in that the former has a local community and local government to provide goods and services, whereas in the latter these are internalized by the company. These simple distinctions lead to a set of boom town characteristics that deserve special analysis.

In this chapter a boom town is an abstraction of this ideal type. Needless to say, there are always exceptions; for example, a sequence of projects that impact the community may be spread relatively smoothly over time, rather than causing just one big boom and one bust. The corporation may dominate the local government to such a degree that the situation does not much differ from the company town case. There may not be just one local government involved but layers of tax jurisdictions, which make the meaning of "town" and the identity of a community unclear. Construction may be aborted even before it starts, yet the community will have gone through the shock and experienced the boom town syndrome all the same.

Shortage of goods and services and inflation

When a boom starts, the local economy lags behind. The goods and services originally provided in the community suddenly run short and their prices soar, while many others demanded by the new immigrants are not available at any price. The degree of market disequilibrium, the extent of price increases, and the length of the adjustment period all depend on the location of the town and the type of goods and services demanded. The farther away from population centers the town is, the more severe is this market dislocation problem. Here the population potential index of the town (the sum of the populations of all other places discounted by effective distance) may, in its inverse, serve as a gauge of the potential severity of the problem. This index reflects the spatial friction of market adjustment due to transportation costs. The lag in adjustment reflects the fact that the capital required to produce the goods or services takes time to put in effect. Even those goods and services that are not capital intensive command much higher prices in a boom town, reflecting the higher wages and levels of expected capital return; that is, the opportunity costs of inputs at the time. Fundamentally, resources in a boom town fall short of demand; and this, in turn, leads to inflation.

A salient example of the lagged market response is the shortage of housing, which has become the foremost boom town problem in most cases. It takes time to build houses even if land, materials, and skilled labor are available. But residential land has to be developed from virgin land, together with roads and utilities. In fact, the housing shortage is such a restrictive factor that the capacity of local builders alone may determine the development pace of an energy project. For the project construction company the solution is not in the market; it must provide accommodation for its workers in the form of mobile home parks or man-camps. This kind of instant settlement, which is often the source of social problems, has also become part of the boom town image.

Public services and municipal financing

Parallel to the housing shortage is a more severe inadequacy of various public services that complement housing needs: water, sanitation, medical care, civil safety (all urgent needs of the first order), and later, recreation facilities, schools, etc. There is much documentation of the overburdening of the public sector in boom towns and of the slow response of local government to the demand for municipal services, partly due to the necessary lag of capital adjustment in infrastructure similar to that in private capital stock. It takes time to expand or build new roads, plants, utilities, hospitals, and schools. Another factor is the nature of public goods, which, unlike market goods, cannot be adequately financed through user charges, and collective decisions on supply have to be reached through political procedures. Unless there is a strong rational planning process that is able to anticipate the need for municipal services, the local government's response is always a reactive one, i.e., a delayed action in response to demand.

The delay also has a fiscal cause. A large proportion of local revenues, particularly for small towns, comes from property taxes. While it is true that property values, or the tax base, jumps by leaps and bounds in a boom town, there is again a time lag before the increased market value can be translated into revenue through land and building assessment and tax collection. The property of the energy project itself cannot be assessed and taxed until it is fully completed, often many years later. But fundamentally, the growth of the tax base not only lags, but in many towns it never catches up with the growth of service needs.

Such a rapid growth calls for urban planning, but in actuality the local government is always understaffed for the task of planning and programming the huge increase in capital investment. Facing a crisis and under pressure to get things done, planners and decision makers in the town, or their consultants, have to grope for immediate solutions rather than programming things carefully according to a long-term plan. Decisions on capital spending have to be rushed to meet deadlines, usually with inadequate consideration of locational coordination among facilities. There is rarely a land-use plan to guide development, in contrast to new town development practice. The price paid for this unplanned growth, which essentially sacrifices logical spatial relationships for time expediency, is the perpetuated inefficiency of land use in later years.

Environmental deterioration

The environmental impact of energy projects is a major issue in itself, which is best addressed in relation to a specific project. Many types of environmental effects are concentrated in the local community and its surrounding area, particularly air and water pollution. It should be noted that it is the relative change of environmental quality, not the absolute level, that is relevant to local residents. After the project is in place, the air quality may still be higher than the national standard, but the residents who are used to clean air, particularly those who settled there partly because of it, are affected. In many cases it is the potential risk rather than the actual environmental change that is borne by the local community. There is no need, for example, to elaborate on the threat of a nuclear power plant to nearby communities.

In most cases it is not the operation of the energy project itself but the construction work that turns a once tranquil community into an unbearable environment. Several years of heavy noise, smell, and traffic congestion are long enough to cause an exodus of residents who do not have to stay. After the construction phase is over, the transformed town may become an unsightly place forever. Aesthetic decline is difficult to quantify, but it is one of the frequently cited causes of regret.

Social disruption and deterioration of life quality

The social aspects of boom towns have gained more attention than the other problem areas outlined above. Numerous reports (e.g., Kohrs 1974, Gilmore and Duff 1975) vividly describe the social disruption and the stress of the boom town.[3] The sudden influx of large numbers of male construction workers, only a small portion of whom bring families with them, quickly changes the demographic profile and consequently the atmosphere of the community. These workers must adjust themselves to the new environment, bearing with such realities as severe weather, adverse working conditions, and poor accommodation, as well as the lack of normal recreation facilities after long working hours. The spouses, who live in crowded mobile homes, suffer no less in a strange, isolated place without adequate services and social life. As the loneliness of the workers and their spouses grows, alcoholism and drug abuse often spreads. Violence and crime increases, as do the incidences of mental illness and suicide attempts.

Such behavioral tendencies, which sociologists call alienation, are not only confined to the transient men and women in town but affect the whole community. In addition, the town is injected with a new materialism brought by the economic boom. The school dropout rate jumps, juvenile delinquency emerges, and the divorce rate increases. In short, the old social fabric deteriorates. During this destabilization process, schisms and conflicts between the newcomers and the original residents develop and grow.

This type of social disruption is manifest in two kinds of turnovers. Those original residents who do not benefit from the new economic prosperity and who regret their lost lifestyle, eventually leave town when they have the chance, while those workers who were initially attracted to the

---

[3] The literature is reviewed and evaluated in Wilkinson *et al.* (1982) and Freudenburg (1976).

town by high wages, quit their jobs after they either become disen-
chanted or have fulfilled their original plan of working a definite period of
time. The high rate of either type of out-migration only compounds the
problem by tending to reinforce the transition. The latter type of workers' transition has been emphasized in the literature as being intrinsic to
the vicious cycle of a boom town (Gilmore and Duff 1975).

It should be noted here that most reports on the boom town
phenomenon have not been based on rigorous scientific research methodology. Furthermore, sociological and psychological studies are particularly subject to controversies due to their theoretical and interpretive
nature. On the subject of changes in the quality of life and the alienation
of boom town residents there have been conflicting conclusions (see the
works cited in footnote 3).

The Roots of the Problems

The problems described above have their logical roots; a demographic diagram can aid in our understanding of them. Figure 7.1
presents typical population growth in a boom town over time. The shape
of the overall population change (curve PP) characterizes boom town
development: a rapid population increase in a few years is succeeded by
an equally rapid decline, and is then followed by stable growth. This
overall population actually comprises three distinct groups: construction
workers (curve CW), new residents (curve NR) who come to settle in the
community as a consequence of the economic expansion, and the original
residents (curve OR), whose number declines over time due to out-
migration. Both curves CW and NR are the net result of two much more
volatile gross in- and outflows of people. However, the severity of boom
town problems may be measured by the proportion of the original
residents who would otherwise have stayed but actually have left the town
(curve OR*).[4]

The turbulent swing of the total population curve conceals underlying changes in sex and age distributions, which are the source of many
social problems. On the other hand, much of the boom town's economic
difficulties in both the private and public sectors can be attributed to the
bulge in the total population curve. The inadequate supply of goods and
services is partly due to the supplier's expectation of the forthcoming
bust, and high prices reflect the excessive capital costs.

---

[4] This can be obtained by dividing the area between OR and OR*, (the population had
there been no energy project, which should not be difficult to project from past trends)
by the total area under OR*. The proper time may be selected as that between t_1, when
the population starts to deviate from the expected trend OR*, and t_2, when stabilized
population growth begins. (The latter point may be where a course parallel to OR*
resumes, but a certain refinement is needed here, as the demographic structure has
changed such that the exact parallel course is attainable.)

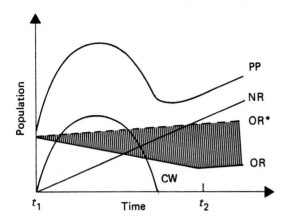

Figure 7.1. Typical population growth in a boom town over time.

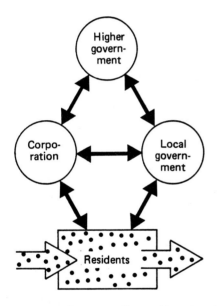

Figure 7.2. An interaction pattern in a boom town community.

Should the community be composed of homogeneous households with identical interests, then the intrinsically high cost of goods and services could simply be compensated for by higher wages, and passed on to the nation. Optimum investment levels could then be determined, as has indeed been proposed in an economic theory formulated specifically for the boom town with its excessive capital stock in the later period (Cummings and Schulze 1978). But a boom town should not be treated as a firm, as it is in theory; it is in fact composed of diverse interest groups with different objectives, and with varying levels of political power or channels of influence. The decision processes and interaction patterns among these groups are indeed complex, and this is yet another source of many problems.

The construction workers need adequate services immediately and are least concerned with the long-term fiscal consequences to the town. They have no direct voice in local decision processes, but are represented through the company. It is difficult to generalize the relationship between the company and the local government. More often than not, the higher level of government (state or province) that sponsors the energy project in the first place, and whose duty it supposedly is to protect local community interests, has a crucial role in affecting the local political process through both legislative and intergovernmental financial powers. The interests of the higher government do not necessarily coincide with those of the local community and the company. The corporation does not hesitate to apply pressure on local government through its influence on higher levels of government. What complicates the problem further is the fact that what local government represents is not always clear, as the community itself is in a state of flux. In particular, as indicated in Figure 7.2, as the number and structure of residents changes, new interest groups develop.

There is yet another fundamental problem in boom town development that cannot be graphically demonstrated: built-in uncertainty in both the short and the long terms. Because the development hinges upon one energy project, about which decisions are made in the remote headquarters of the corporation, the boom town is inherently vulnerable to world events (including oil price movements) that may suddenly lead to a halt in construction during the boom stage or a shutdown of production in a later period. But even after a town has successfully gone through the boom and bust stages and stable growth may be under way, its long-term fate is still uncertain because most energy projects ultimately terminate upon the depletion of the resource. Unless the boom town can, over time, expand its economic base from the single industry (or just a single plant) to a diversified, mature economic structure, there is always a threat that it will become a ghost town. These short- and long-term uncertainties are very real in the risk calculations by bankers, which in turn hinder private capital formation and add to the cost of community development.

Development Policy Recommendations

Despite the severe problems discussed above, the crisis faced by the boom town can generate unusual opportunities.[5] The situation truly tries

---

[5] It has been pointed out that the word "crisis" in Chinese also means "dangerous opportunity". This may be an overinterpretation of the two original Chinese monosyllables, but nevertheless seems quite an appropriate description of the boom town situation.

the wisdom and leadership of the decision makers and planners, but it is difficult to recommend specific actions. The existing rich body of literature on urban planning techniques and theory is relevant to boom town development but, again, specific applications cannot be found. On the other hand, certain general policy guidelines may be proposed, in the light of the unique problems and resources available.

The central actor in boom town development is of course the energy corporation, which has both financial and personnel resources, and, more importantly, has the relevant information and makes the basic decisions. In the past, the corporation and its construction company have tended to minimize their involvement in community affairs beyond what is necessary, but there is now a growing awareness that the social environment of a boom town has a direct bearing on the workers' productivity. Furthermore, the power of denial, delay, and regulation of construction vested in higher government in order to protect the local community is becoming an increasingly significant cost factor. The corporation must realize that the social costs external to construction should be absorbed by the project. Not only is this more equitable, but it is also more effective and efficient. Once this notion is accepted, the planning and management of boom town development will be fundamentally different.

There is at least one advantage in planning boom town development. Although the future of a boom town as a whole is uncertain, the specific development scenario in terms of population size, facility needs and demands, and fiscal resources over time is, paradoxically, more predictable than in the case of normal community development because all the quantitative aspects of development can be traced, with reasonable reliability, to one single source: the construction company or energy corporation payroll. In the final analysis, the corporation is a decision maker. (In contrast, it is difficult for an ordinary community to determine and forecast its sources of growth or decline or reasons for change in its basic activities.)

This predictability implies that community growth can be controlled. If the corporation regards the community welfare as internal to its operation, then there is a foundation on which to formulate policies for a successful development. The following policies may be effective.[6]

(1) *Control the maximum growth rate.* Past experience indicates that the strain caused by the shortage of goods and services begins to be felt when a community's population growth rate exceeds 5% per annum. Many boom town phenomena become evident when this rate is sustained at a 10% level for several years, and social disruption becomes more severe and even chaotic when the rate exceeds 15%. Although the situation also depends on the location of the town, several indicators (the duration of the rapid growth period, the imminence of the bust period

---

[6] Some parts of these policies are proposed in Susskind and O'Hare (1977).

ahead, and the planning effort) can serve as general benchmarks for planning. The central determinants of the growth rate are, of course, the size of the construction workforce and its distribution over time, both of which are subject to planning decisions in the corporation and its construction company.

The scale of an energy project, which in many cases is part of an overall plan, could be a variable. Alternatives do exist in many cases between a very large-scale, centralized project and several scaled-down projects spread over different communities. Given any particular project, different schedules can achieve different workforce distributions over time. All of these decisions should be made with reference to the social costs implied in the various population growth rates. If possible, the population of the community should not be allowed to double within five years (at approximately 15% per annum).

(2) *Full compensation to the "victims"*. Many native residents of the boom town, particularly the landlords, the unemployed and under-employed, achieve substantial economic gains from the development that may more than offset their losses from social and environmental change. But most residents do suffer, and there is no effective mechanism to transfer the windfalls from the former group to the latter. The corporation and government should take the responsibility to compensate the losers; this is not only social justice but may also facilitate the development of the project. Unaddressed grievances serve to form a political force that resists development and incurs costs. On the other hand, proper compensation (especially if not through lump-sum payments) may reduce the out-migration of original residents and therefore contribute to social stability, which significantly affects labor productivity. Identification of the "victims" and means of compensation are two topics that still need research. The corporation should also adequately contribute to municipal finances and to community facilities.

(3) *Maximizing the use of local labor*. Corporations tend to hire their workers from outside the community due to their skill requirements, time, or union pressure. However, given past experience of high labor turnover and low productivity in boom towns, corporations should seriously commit themselves to maximum training and use of local labor — employing both native residents and new migrants who have settled in the community on their own initiative. The training costs will not be trivial, and the newly acquired skills may not be reliable, but this policy should pay off in the long term, since resident workers have very different behavior patterns and need least help. This would be a stabilizing force not only to the corporation, but also to the community. The employment of residents can be thought of as an integral part of the compensation scheme. Furthermore, the training of local labor paves the way for long-term economic development, as discussed below.

(4) *Long-term economic development*. The corporation and higher government, in conjunction with local government, should map out a long-term economic development program and actively implement it from the outset, with the goal of expanding the local economic base from the single, or dominant, industry. The fate of the community ultimately depends on the success of diversification of local industries.

The boom town has unique assets for economic development. It has a tremendous surplus of both labor and capital stock during the bust period that many industries could take advantage of, so that planning and timing are crucial. Since it usually takes several years to establish a new industry in a community, planning and promotion should start at the very beginning of the boom period. To begin with, there should be a thorough location analysis of the town in its regional context, which will lead to the identification of appropriate industries. If the energy corporation is a conglomerate, there is a better than even chance of identifying its own industries that could and should be brought in during the bust period. Higher government should also use tax incentives, site permits, and licensing, etc., to aid local economic development.

(5) *Resolving local disputes by negotiation and mediation*. Even if the corporation has the best intentions and adopts all the above policies, disputes among various parties with conflicting interests will inevitably arise. Whether the disputes are addressed by legal means or through open confrontation, the cost is extremely high. Issues surrounding nuclear power plant construction are a case in point. Except in extreme cases, rarely are the disputing parties left no room for reconciliation (the "Pareto frontier") particularly when compensation, not necessarily in financial form, is possible. Negotiation and bargaining should thus be regarded as the major means for resolving conflicts in boom towns instead of steps secondary to legal approaches. The art and science in this area of negotiation and mediation are more advanced than is commonly recognized, and their application to environmental issues has become apparent (Susskind *et al.* 1978). The higher government has a specific role in promoting this approach. Formal mediation and arbitration procedures should be adopted, rules of information generation and sharing should be set, and legal backup of implementation should be planned for.

(6) *Issue of conditional permits with contingency plans*. To guard against possible adverse consequences, the traditional government method is regulation, or setting standards for development, such as subdivision bylaws. When development impacts are uncertain but possibly severe, which is often the case, such prior regulation is either too lax or unnecessarily restrictive. Alternatively, permits or licenses should be granted on condition of alleviating *de facto* harm. The developer is responsible for preparing and implementing contingency plans, or providing financial compensation to offset the real impacts. Application of this *ex post* approach instead of prior strict specification is fair, efficient, and

applicable to many boom towns, if the legal terms are well formulated and impact measurements are agreed upon. This can expedite project site approval and may subsequently affect the whole course of development. A prerequisite for this approach is a reliable monitoring system, which is needed for other aspects of boom town development in any case.

Modeling Boom Town Development

The implementation of such policies requires measurement, simulation, and monitoring of the events and processes. Independent of this source of need, the dramatic emergence of boom towns across North America in the past 15 years, together with the uncertain course of development in these towns, has pointed to the need for modeling. Consequently, various types of models have been adopted or proposed to simulate or forecast the impact of energy projects on certain aspects of development. The quick response to this need, as measured by the number of published papers and documents on boom town models, is impressive. As early as 1977 a review of the methods and models applied to forecasting the local impacts of energy projects covered more than 50 publications, while admitting its incomplete coverage at the time (Sanderson and O'Hare 1977). Since then, more models have been designed specifically for boom town applications. It is beyond the scope of this chapter to review and assess these models individually, but certain general observations can be offered on some of their common features and problems.

(1) As mentioned above, the best known boom town phenomena are its social problems, but these have not been the targets of the existing models. They are indeed difficult to model; in fact, some social problems are the subject of conceptual or measurement controversy in the first place (e.g., "alienation"), and others are still beyond our knowledge to explain and predict adequately (e.g., crime). Even in the more familiar economic area, suppliers' behavior in a specific context, such as a boom town, where the town's location is important, is very difficult to specify.

Thus, most models concentrate only on certain aspects of development. Typically, a model starts by forecasting jobs and population, using the results to forecast the housing market demand and public facility and service needs, and then to assess the municipal fiscal impact in terms of costs and revenues. This is a standard urban and regional planning modeling procedure that has been refined in the last two decades. The readily available modeling procedure explains why there has been a rapid increase in the number of boom town models: it does meet a specific need, for local fiscal uncertainty is one of the basic issues.

(2) The urban job—population—housing—fiscal model that is most often adopted is a static equilibrium one. It suppresses the lagged adjustment process, which is one source of boom town problems. Forecasting is done by applying the parameters estimated from past data to the changed exogenous variables in a future time. Most relationships in the model are linear and the parameters are simply average ratios. But even in those models where parameters represent marginal ratios (the log-linear models), the fundamental assumptions are the same: there is no structural change in the modeled system. Yet it is precisely this structural change that characterizes a boom town. Although violation of this assumption is commonly acknowledged in boom town models, the damage to model performance has not been assessed. In fact, few such models have been empirically evaluated.

The economic module in most boom town models illustrates this problem of structural change. No matter whether the module applies economic base, input—output (I–O), or econometric approaches, it is operated on some ratios or regression coefficients estimated from local pre-boom period data or borrowed from national or regional data, assuming they have remained constant after the boom. This can hardly be true in a boom town where shortages of goods, services, and labor induces imports and in-migration. Hence, the job or income multiplier is likely to change over time and should, therefore, not be treated as constant, as is usually the case. Most questionable is the application of the I–O linear production function by many models (which rely upon certain techniques to "regionalize" the national I–O technological coefficients for local use). Not only should the linear relationship be expected not to hold at such a disaggregate level, but the basic assumption of the I–O model — that there is no supply bottleneck — is certainly invalid in the boom town case.

To remedy the weakness of treating variables as parameters in a structurally changing environment, the modeler should frequently update the coefficients used. This again requires a monitoring system, but nothing of this sort has yet been established. Alternatively, a model should have more coefficients that can be changed into endogenous variables. This means a break away from adopting existing urban models for boom town applications and calls for advances in the state of the art of urban/regional modeling.

(3) Parallel to the economic module, the demographic module in most boom town models reflects the difficulty of adopting a standard urban/regional model for the local community. Among the three components of demographic change (births, deaths, and migration) migration is the most difficult to forecast, but its importance is inversely related to the community size and it becomes a crucial factor in the boom town case. In addition, the two gross figures of in- and out-migration account for most boom town problems, rather than the statistical artifact of net migration. Unfortunately, most boom town models follow the standard practice of forecasting only net migration to be consistent with job

changes, probably taking into account the local labor supply as predicted by cohort survival methods. This is equivalent to applying a model befitting a closed population system rather than a very open boom town system.

The gross in- and out-migrations are perhaps both the causes and effects of high labor turnover, given any employment level in a boom town. This should therefore be determined jointly, probably in conjunction with the labor force participation rate. Other variables, such as housing, amenities, and the location of the town, may be important explanatory variables in addition to real wages. This interaction between migration and jobs should distinguish such a boom town model from a standard urban/regional model.

Finally, we conclude this chapter with some brief comments on two models that have been specifically developed for the boom town. The Cumulative Impacts Task Force (CITF) model designed by Mountain West Research for northwestern Colorado (see Chapter 4.2) can be regarded as the result of pragmatic planning modeling techniques over the last two decades. The other is the BOOM-1 model and its extensions designed at Los Alamos Scientific Laboratory, which breaks away from the traditional modeling approach (and is therefore not subject to the two comments made above). The two models represent radically different approaches that contrast in every respect. (Another major approach is the econometric model, which, because of its extensive historical data requirements, has seldom been proposed for a boom town application.)

The CITF model is an extension of an earlier one developed to forecast regional growth in Arizona, which was in turn based on a core notion of regional economics that jobs and population in a region mutually determine each other, with basic activities in the regional economy and natural demographic growth as exogenous variables. In practice, the average ratios computed from recent data are used as parameters for forecasting. Applying these to a boom town, the model thus has the weaknesses noted above; it treats the boom town region in a business-as-usual manner when the region is probably undergoing structural change. Perhaps for this reason, the modeler disavows that the model is a predictive one and only allows it to be used as a simulation tool for examining the implications of whatever input assumptions the user would like to make. However, its use as an examination tool is meaningful only to the extent that what the model tells will indeed be realized. Thus any sensitivity analysis cannot be really free from the burden of empirical performance of prediction. Furthermore, the gross in- and out-migration, job switching, and labor force participation are either suppressed or treated as model parameters. Consequently, many boom town phenomena cannot be simulated.

The CITF model has many virtues nonetheless. It is one of the rare large-scale models that has been seriously designed for full, sustained implementation by the users themselves. The structure of the model and the logic of its working procedures are open and transparent, understood perhaps by a college student with minimal experience of computer simulation and regional economics. The model has a database as an explicit working component, accessible to public examination and subject to flexible change and updating. Its unique way of classifying activities, and its requirement of using worker profiles as input, combine to simulate certain important features of the boom town economy. The distinction and interaction between income and jobs in the model is a contribution to clarifying the relationship between the two type multipliers. Still, the basic strength of the CITF model lies in its "user friendliness", which is seldom achieved in computer simulation modeling. It is perhaps a necessary feature for application to a boom town or a region where the model must serve as a public forum for diverse interest groups. One learns political as well as modeling reality from CITF.

BOOM-1 is based on the systems dynamics methodology, but does not follow the structure of Forrester's urban dynamics. The model builders started anew to apply the nonlinear delayed feedback system to modeling certain boom town phenomena. As previously mentioned, many phenomena arise from the time lag in adjustment and certain self-reinforcing causal relations. Thus, systems dynamics appears to be the right tool for simulating them. It seems for this reason that BOOM-1 became a generic model from which no less than a dozen extensions or modifications have been made by several researchers to study various aspects of the boom town. The most noticeable extension is the BOOM-H model, representing a joint effort between the Los Alamos Laboratory and the University of Alberta.

One focus of BOOM-1 is the vicious cycle of labor turnover and low productivity, whereas in BOOM-H the focus is shifted to the housing sector. What seems to distinguish this dynamic model and the past urban dynamics family is that more attention has been paid to formulating a model structure that has relatively clear, understandable causal relations. Moreover, efforts have been made to parametrize the equations in a more or less empirical way. It is reported that the application of BOOM-H to Fort McMurray has been able to "backtrack" empirically the changes in the housing market during the early 1970s. Perhaps the most remarkable feature of BOOM-H is its explicit incorporation of price as the junction between a supply and a demand loop. This price variable was conspicuously absent in urban dynamics or other previous systems dynamics models.[7]

---

[7] Price does appear in one earlier dynamic model of land (Mass 1974), but its role in the model is not clear — the "demand" side loop is driven by speculation rather than by price. Forrester justifies the suppression of price by referring to the long time framework of the models: the market clearing mechanism can be neglected from a process concerning the result of 100 years' interaction. This justification does not apply to the boom town case, however, where the price behavior is all-important.

The difficulties of applying systems dynamics to boom towns have not been adequately reported. One can understand the problems of estimating parameters in a nonlinear system that cannot be fully calibrated by data. How to optimize the mix of coefficients obtained from "expert opinion" and empirically estimated parameters is an interesting question. Price determination should be the key to a successful market behavior model, and there seems to be room for improvement in the current model.[8]

There are some disadvantages of adopting a systems dynamic model. It has a holistic behavior that cannot easily be related to individual model components. The modeler sometimes has difficulty in tracing a counter-intuitive result to its causes, let alone in explaining it to the public. It is not a flexible model subject to modification at any time; newly obtained data cannot be easily utilized. Its operation and maintenance have to be done by people with special skills, so the public ultimately has to trust the experts to run the model and interpret the results. But controversies may exist even among experts over the implications of running the same model, and that would confuse the public — a situation caused by urban dynamics and world dynamics models.

Could the advantages and strengths of both the CITF model and the systems dynamics model be combined into a new style of modeling? It is presently difficult to conceive of a way of integration or reconciliation. A reflection on the shortcomings of both approaches and the obvious need to overcome them leads one to believe that the boom town, in spite of its small size, is the place from which to challenge urban and regional modeling.

References

Cummings, R.G. and Schulze, W.D. (1978) Optimum investment strategy for boom towns: A theoretical analysis. *American Economic Review* 68:374–85.

Freudenburg, W.R. (1976) *The Social Impact of Energy Boom Development on Rural Communities: A Review of the Literature and Some Predictions.* Presented at the annual meeting of the American Sociological Association, August, 1976.

Freudenburg, W.R. (1981) Women and men in an energy boom town: Adjustment, alienation and adaptation. *Rural Sociology* 46:220–24.

Gilmore, J.S. and Duff, M.K. (1975) *Boom Town Growth Management: A Case Study of Rock Spring, Green River, Wyoming* (Boulder, CO: Westview Press).

---

[8] In BOOM-H, housing price is a function of vacancy alone. This needs theoretical analysis. A low housing vacancy rate does not cause high prices if the community is becoming more stagnant in population growth. It seems to be the change of vacancy duration, which is vacancy rate divided by purchase (absorbing) rate, that affects the price movement. Vacancy duration can be interpreted as the ratio of supply to demand, or it can be used to explain the seller/landlord's behavior according to the monopolistic competition theory in microeconomics (Hua 1977).

Hua, C. (1977) *The Equilibrium of Housing Vacancy and Waiting Time.* Working
    Paper (Pittsburgh, PA: Carnegie-Mellon University, School of Urban and
    Public Affairs).

Kohrs, E.V. (1974) *Social Consequences of Boom Town Growth in Wyoming.*
    Presented at the annual meeting of the Southwestern and Rocky Mountain
    Section, American Association for the Advancement of Science, April.

Mass, N.J. (1974) Urban dynamic model of land pricing and urban land allocation,
    in N.J. Mass (Ed) *Reading in Urban Dynamics: Volume I* (Cambridge, MA:
    Wright—Allen Press).

Sanderson, D. and O'Hare, M. (1977) *Predicting the Local Impact of Energy
    Development: A Critical Guide to Forecasting Methods and Models* (Cam-
    bridge, MA: Laboratory of Architecture and Planning, MIT).

Susskind, L. and O'Hare, M. (1977) *Managing the Social and Economic Impacts of
    Energy Development.* Summary Report: Phase 1 of MIT Energy Impact Pro-
    ject (Cambridge, MA: Laboratory of Architecture and Planning, MIT).

Susskind, L.E., Richardson, J.R., and Hildebrand, K.H. (1978) *Resolving Environ-
    mental Disputes: Approaches to Intervention, Negotiation, and Conflict
    Resolution* (Cambridge, MA: Laboratory of Architecture and Planning, MIT).

Wilkinson, K.P., *et al.* (1982) Local social disruption and western energy develop-
    ment: A critical review. *Pacific Sociological Review* 25:275—96.

Further Reading

The items listed here have been selected for their representative-
ness and availability. A large and rich body of boom town studies has
been presented in various conferences or reported on in the form of
working papers, but has not been formally published. The reader may
contact the following institutions for full information on their studies on
boom towns: Argonne National Laboratory, Los Alamos Scientific Laboratory, Denver Research Institute, Laboratory of Architecture and Planning
of Massachusetts Institute of Technology, Department of Social Work and
Center for Urban Regional Analysis of University of Wyoming, Department
of Sociology/Anthropology of North Dakota State University.

Albrecht, S.L. (1978) Socio-cultural factors and enregy resource development in
    rural areas in the west. *Journal of Environment Management* 7:73—90.

Auger, C.S., *et al.* (1978) *Energy Resource Development, Socio-economic Impacts,
    and the Current Status of Impact Assessment: An Eleven State Review*
    (Boulder, CO: Tsoco Foundation).

Baldwin, T.E., Dixon-Davis, D., Strenejhem, E.J., and Woloko, T.D. (1976) *A
    Socioeconomic Assessment of Energy Development in a Small Rural Com-
    munity,* Vols. 1 and 2 (Argonne, IL: Argonne National Laboratory).

Bender, L.D., Temple, G.S., and Parcels, L.C. (1980) *An Introduction to the COAL-
    TOWN Impact Assessment Model* (Washington, DC: US Environmental Pro-
    tection Agency).

Bradbury, J.H. (1980) Instant resource towns policy in British Columbia:
    1965—1972. *Plan Canada* 20(1):19—38.

Brookshire, D.S. and D'Arge, R.C. (1980) Adjustment issues of impacted commu-
    nities or, are boom towns bad? *Natural Resources Journal* 20:523—46.

Champion, D. and Ford, A. (1980) Boom town effects. *Environment* 22(5):25–31.

Cortese, D.F. and Jones, B. (1977) The sociological analysis of boom towns. *Western Sociological Review* 8:76–90.

Denver Research Institute (1979) *Socioeconomic Impacts of Western Energy Development* (Washington, DC: Council for Environmental Quality).

Ford, A. (1976) *Summary Description of the BOOM-1 Model*, LA-6424-MS (Los Alamos, NM: Los Alamos Scientific Laboratory).

Gilmore, J.S. (1976) Boom towns may hinder energy resource development. *Science* 191:535–40.

Krutilla, J.V., Fisher, A.C., and Rice, R.E. (1978) *Economic and Fiscal Impact of Coal Development: North Great Plains* (Baltimore, MD: Johns Hopkins University Press).

Leistritz, F.L. and Murdock, S.H. (1981) *Socioeconomic Impact of Resource Development: Method of Assessment* (Boulder, CO: Westview Press).

Leistritz, F.L., et al. (1982) Local fiscal impact of energy resource development: Application of an assessment model in policy-making. *North Central Journal of Agricultural Economics* 4:47–57.

Lucas, R.A. (1971) *Minetown, Milltown, Railtown: Life in a Canadian Community of Single Industry* (Toronto: University of Toronto Press).

Murdock, S.H. and Leistritz, F.L. (1979) *Energy Development in the Western United States: Impact on Rural Areas* (New York: Praeger).

Murdock, S.H., et al. (1979, 1976) *Texas Assessment Modeling System: User's Manual* (College Station, TX: Texas Agricultural Experimental Station, Texas A&M University, 1979); *North Dakota Regional Environmental Assessment Program, the REAP Economic Demographic Model 1: User's Manual* (Bismarck, ND: State Capital, 1976).

Rink, R. and Ford, A. (1975) *A Simulation Model for Boom Town Housing*, LA-7324-MS (Los Alamos, NM: Los Alamos Scientific Laboratory).

Rose, R. (1980) Policies to improve the economic impact of energy resource development. *Growth and Change* 11:41–7.

Stelter, G.A. and Arthise, A.F.J. (Eds) (1978) Canadian resource towns. *Plan Canada* 18(1).

Stenehjem, E.J. (1978) *Summary Description of SEAM* (Argonne, IL: Argonne National Laboratory).

US Department of Energy, Denver, Colorado Region VIII (1979), *Regional Profile of Energy Impacted Communities: Region VIII* (DOE/TIC-10001).

Large-Scale Energy Projects: Assessment of Regional Consequences
T.R. Lakshmanan and B. Johansson (Editors)
Elsevier Science Publishers B.V. (North-Holland)
© IIASA, 1985

CHAPTER 8

Assessing the Environmenal Consequences of Large-Scale Energy Projects

---

Samuel J. Ratick, with S. Creed and G. Rylander

Introduction

In the US the National Environmental Policy Act was signed into law on 1 January 1970 establishing a national policy that was to "... encourage productive and enjoyable harmony between man and his environment; to promote efforts which will prevent or eliminate damage to the environment and biosphere and stimulate the health and welfare of man; to enrich the understanding of the ecological systems and natural resources important to the Nation ...". The Act required that all plans and programs related to the federal government be preceded by a full and adequate analysis of all environmental effects of those actions. During this period similar laws or required environmental assessment processes were promulgated in other countries as well, representing a culmination of a worldwide concern over the environmental consequences of anthropogenic activities. In the 1960s and 1970s neither reliable scientific information on environmental processes nor adequate analysis and assessment tools appeared to be available, but these are now being developed and used in environmental assessment activities.

A number of scientific, technical, and policy questions impinge on the successful performance of an environmental assessment for a large-scale energy project. Can important factors be determined? Can the effects of an action be measured accurately over an appropriate time scale and for an appropriate spatial area? Can existing methods characterize and replicate the interaction of environmental components and predict how they will respond to the activities that comprise the projects? Are there recognizable individuals or groups in positions of decision authority whose preferences for the project can in some way be understood? If the project has conflicting goals, can consensus or compromise be reached? Can the interactions of the decision makers be characterized as a part of the assessment process? How can the scientific and technical information generated by an environmental assessment best be used in this decision process? It is difficult to determine the attributes of a useful environmental assessment; not only may its purposes be obscure but also the accurate determination of the consequences of an action requires the understanding of complex webs of dynamically interacting and changing processes operating in many different spheres (physical, ecological, economic). In the absence of knowledge about these processes, studies may attempt to be as complete as possible, measuring all that it is possible to measure. But completeness alone may not be sufficient, as is noted by Holling (1978): "however intensively and extensively data are collected, however much we know of how the system functions, the domain of our knowledge of specific ecological and social systems is small when compared to that of our ignorance." He suggests that an environmental assessment should be an organic process characterized by an acceptance of the limitations of existing techniques, a recognition of the certainty of uncertainty, and a willingness to allow for some flexibility in project and process design.

This chapter organizes and reviews some of the issues in the use of systems methods for the environmental assessment of large-scale energy projects. In order to address this topic systematically it has been necessary to arbitrarily "linearize" the order of explanation. First, the attributes of environmental assessments are discussed in relation to large-scale energy projects. Second, the policy and decision framework in the USSR, Canada, the US, and Sweden are reviewed. Third, some existing assessment methods are described, together with a brief review of a comprehensive, integrated model system SEAS (strategic environmental assessment system). Any order would be as relevant and as incorrect for such a dynamic, interrelated subject.

Technical Description

Environmental assessment is described as measuring and evaluating the environmental impacts of an activity. In order to measure the magnitude of an impact at any point in time a projection of the unaffected state of the environment at that time, as well as a measure of its affected state, needs to be made (see Figure 8.1). Many of the assessments discussed in the Canadian case study (Chapter 3) were designed to produce a baseline of current environmental conditions before the resource extraction process was begun. As with other consequences of energy projects, these are multidimensional and, as such, can be measured along a number of dimensions.

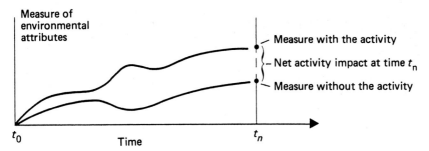

Figure 8.1. Measuring environmental impacts (from Jain *et al.* 1977).

Categories of environmental consequences

Environmental impacts can be classified according to physical consequences such as air and water pollution or solid waste generation. These categories can be further subdivided to include the component parts (e.g., particulate emissions, or specific elements that comprise these particulates), and then to the level at which an impact can be measured.

Consequences can be direct, indirect, or induced. They may also be measured along both temporal and spatial scales. Environmental effects may be temporary or persist for a long time after the project has ceased. Likewise, spatial effects can be localized to the project site or be noted on a global scale. In this chapter the spatial scale is divided into three categories:

- *micro* (restricted to the site of the activity that produced it), e.g., production of a non-hazardous and nontoxic solid waste that is effectively disposed of at the project site;
- *meso* (only within physically or naturally defined regions, such as air or watersheds), e.g., the production of oxygen-demanding water pollution that degrades within the watershed;
- *macro* (beyond the boundaries that define the meso category), e.g., SO_2 emissions transported to another region and deposited as acid rain, or the global atmospheric distribution of CO_2 (see Chapter 4).

These categories can also be further subdivided to include the degree to which there is interaction between consequences and media, as with hydrocarbons and nitrogen oxides to form photochemical oxidants, or solid wastes leaching groundwater contaminants.

In addition to the taxonomic problems of categorizing environmental consequences is the problem of determining and classifying the degree to which a particular environmental consequence is considered by society to be harmful or undesirable. The determination of acceptable levels of risk by society is, of course, both a difficult scientific task and complex social decision process. Figure 8.2 demonstrates some of the

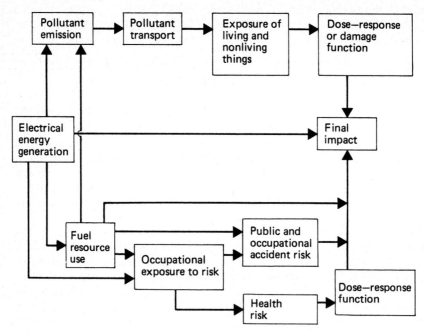

Figure 8.2. Impact pathways for electricity generation (from Foell *et al.* 1981).

steps that are necessary to determine the quantitative impacts of electricity generation. Quantifying each step of the impact assessment process, emissions of pollutants and diffusion of these emissions, measuring the level of exposure to the pollutant, and determining the response of living organisms to this pollutant level, or the degree to which property will be damaged, is a process that is, for most pollutants, only partially understood. Society must, with such incomplete information, determine whether or not and to what degree this type of consequence is in keeping with its objectives. Thus, different consequences will effect different sections of society and in different ways, and will be evaluated by each in relation to its goals and objectives.

In the US, for example, primary and secondary air quality standards are designed to protect air quality so as to promote the health and welfare of its population. Primary standards reflect the scientific analysis of effects of ambient air quality on human health, and secondary standards the effects on other animal species and vegetation, as well as aesthetic characteristics such as visibility and the destruction of environmentally protected areas. These standards differ not only in their allowable concentrations but also in the frequency of permissible violations of the standard concentrations and the lengths of time that standards can be exceeded. The Endangered Species Act prohibits any activity that will adversely affect the habitats of endangered species. Thus the protection of public health, croplands, property, parklands, and wildlife represents both the scientific determination of harmful consequences and the concerns of diverse interest groups about social welfare goals.

Examples of environmental consequences from energy activities

The processing, transmission, and use of fossil fuels accounts for the majority of air pollutants. However, natural gas, coal, and oil extraction also produce these pollutants during mining and drilling activities. At the micro level, in subsurface coal mining coal and rock dust particulates can pose both short- and long-term health effects. The major source of air pollution in surface mining, and in drilling for oil and natural gas is the combustion processes in the extraction machinery, which emit primarily carbon monoxide, nitrogen oxides, and hydrocarbons.

Combustion products from the transmission of fuels will have the same short-term effects, but diffused over a wider area. Some other compounds emitted from processing plants are sulfur oxides, sulfurous and sulfuric acids, nitrates, and various nitrogen oxides; they are usually distributed on the micro and meso levels. On a global level the effects of air pollution from energy projects on climate are more difficult to determine.

Energy projects also have impacts on the land through the generation of solid wastes, which may affect wildlife and vegetation. The most dramatic effects of surface mining are due to disturbances of the topsoil, vegetation, and wildlife. Over the long term, such disturbances may irrevocably alter the types of plants and wildlife that can inhabit these areas, even after the mines are closed down. Thus the severity of long-term impacts depends on the success of land reclamation programs.

Synfuel processing, oil and gas refining, and basic coal processing also affect the land on the micro level through the generation of large quantities of solid wastes. The wastes become meso level problems if they are transported for burial, or if groundwater contamination is likely. Operations like tar sand and oil shale recovery create large amounts of spent material and wastes from cleansing and refining of fossil fuels; these tend to be high in sulfur, and occasionally in heavy metals which can leach into the soil and groundwater over the medium to very long term. Environmental effects on land tend to occur at all temporal levels but are generally concentrated at the micro scale. Meso level effects may result from ecosystem changes due to land disturbances which are very long term and are difficult to predict.

One of the most serious long-term environmental consequences of energy projects is the adverse effect on water quality. Eventually, most pollutants will find their way into a water body, either through leaching and runoff or by being rained out of the atmosphere. In the short term, runoff from mine sites and wastewater from processing plants increase levels of sediment, metals, salt, sulfur, heat, and petroleum byproducts in water systems. These pollutants react with dissolved oxygen to increase biological oxygen demand (BOD) loadings and deplete the stream of oxygen. Over the medium to long term, this affects the ability of the water to sustain plant and animal life. When many affected water bodies form larger ones within a watershed, the consequences escalate to the meso level. The change in water quality may affect human health in the long term, especially when non-degrading pollutants (toxic metals such as lead, cadmium, mercury, and beryllium) are present.

The cumulative effects of water pollution from energy projects are important but difficult to measure on the macro level. The effects on air, land, and water, and their resultant consequences derive directly from energy project activities, but indirect consequences associated with construction and maintenance are also important. Local and regional populations may increase, creating environmental stresses that need to be dealt with. Measures of this magnitude of induced growth are made with the techniques such as those used in the Colorado and Swedish case studies, which focused on the infrastructure needs of energy and economic development in the project areas. The US synfuels study and the Canadian case study, in comparison, focused on the direct environmental consequences of energy extraction and processing activities.

Policy and Decision Frameworks for Environmental Assessment

A great deal of public policy debate and action over environmental concerns took place during the late 1960s and early 1970s. That there has been such a strong policy response to ensure that the environmental effects of proposed activities be properly assessed is not surprising. Since pollution rarely respects jurisdictional boundaries and cannot be expected to remain one generation's problem, the debate over the degree and extent of socially acceptable environmental risk is necessarily undertaken within a public policy arena. Clean air, potable water, and usable land are in many ways public goods that are necessary inputs into more economic activities and whose quality needs to be ensured for this and future generations. As described above, environmental consequences are often ubiquitous, and affect society on many different levels and over differing time frames, making it difficult to establish who is being harmed and what is causing the harm. The persons who are to make decisions concerning the fate of large-scale energy projects are easier to determine than those who will be affected by their unwanted consequences. The required environmental assessment activities described in this section can be viewed as the ways in which societies ensure that environmental externalities are internalized as can best be done, in the design of projects and in the determination of the distribution of a project's costs and benefits. Each of the four countries reviewed approached the problem of environmental assessment in different ways, modifying both the type of methods and models that were employed and, perhaps more importantly, how these techniques and the information they imply were used in the assessment process.

Each country's environmental philosophy forms the basis of the requirements for the assessment of activities. These requirements will often determine the scope of the assessment, the information needs, and methods that are to be used. In this section the institutional and legal settings within which environmental assessments of energy projects are required in the US, Canada, Sweden, and the USSR will be reviewed.

The United States

In the US an assessment of environmental impacts is required for any federally initiated and funded project under the National Environmental Policy Act (NEPA). This law states that any action must be preceded by an environmental assessment (EA), which analyzes all direct and indirect, short- and long-term, desirable and undesirable effects. The President's Council on Environmental Quality (CEQ) was created by the Act as an oversight and review agency responsible for enforcement of the law. The CEQ was empowered to issue guidelines to help sponsoring agencies carry out assessments as efficiently as possible so as to ensure that adequate and accurate information would be available to decision makers. The EA is contained in an environmental impact statement (EIS), which provides evidence of the completion of the EA and provides a unified and comparable flow of information to all concerned. Some states in the US have subsequently adopted their own versions of NEPA.

The strategy behind NEPA is to force consideration of potential environmental effects of a proposed action at the earliest possible planning stage, rather than to decide the fate of any particular project solely on the basis of its environmental advantages or disadvantages. Other than the requirements that an EIS be prepared, NEPA does not contain any provisions that would prevent environmentally unsound projects from being undertaken. This capability is found in other US environmental laws, notably the Clean Air Act and Clean Water Act, which require the federal government to set standards for ambient air and water quality (e.g., allowable pollutant concentrations). States have the planning and enforcement responsibility to meet federal standards, and the federal government maintains a review and oversight function, primarily through the Environmental Protection Agency (EPA). With regard to air quality, states submit a State Implementation Plan (SIP) to the EPA which contains their plans to meet and maintain these standards. The legislation also enables states to grant air and water quality permits for energy project activities that may have adverse air and water quality impacts. The information generated by the EA in the EIS is often used during this procedure (see Figure 8.3).

Other US environmental laws, such as the Resource Conservation and Recovery Act (which regulates the disposal of hazardous and non-hazardous solid wastes) and the Endangered Species Act, can affect the

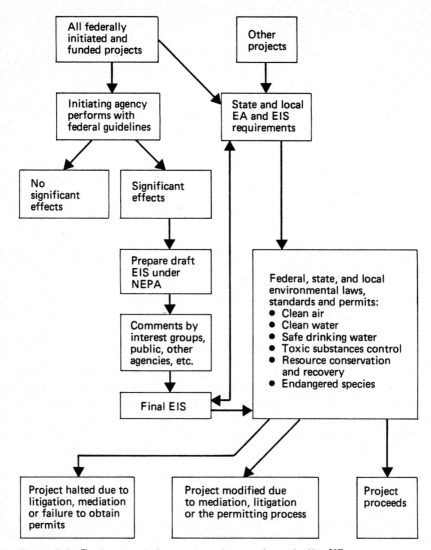

Figure 8.3. Environmental assessment procedures in the US.

design of an energy project or determine whether or not it will be initiated.

In a pluralistic society such as the US, environmental decision authority is generally widespread and diffuse. Projects whose environmental consequences are unacceptable are often subject to interest group action in the form of litigation or mediation that can sometimes prevent a project from being undertaken or require severe design modifications. State governments may also stop a project or cause it to be modified by refusing to grant the necessary permits. Even when states are willing to issue such permits, the federal government, in its oversight capacity, may slow or block approval. Since it is often difficult in the US to determine which persons or groups will be the most influential in the environmental review of an energy project, the EA requirements of the NEPA are very comprehensive and require extensive information gathering.

Canada

As opposed to the legal requirements for environmental assessment in the US, Canada has established an environmental assessment and review process (EARP), in which all federal agencies are invited to participate (see Figure 8.4). The provinces have adapted similar policies. This process applies to all projects initiated or funded by federal agencies and to those that use federal land. It is based upon a self-assessment approach for which the Department of Environment issues guidelines to help each agency screen the projects for which it is responsible.

This screening process yields one of three initial assessments: (*a*) there are no or no significant anticipated environmental effects — the EARP is then stopped and the agency is directed to take feasible measures to alleviate any adverse effects; (*b*) the effects of the project are indeterminate based on the initial screening; and (*c*) significant adverse effects are anticipated and the agency is to submit the project to the Department of Environment for a formal review. If the agency arrives at conclusion (*b*), it then continues the process by producing an initial environmental evaluation (IEE), a higher-order assessment for which the Department of Environment issues a set of project-specific guidelines requiring a more analytical assessment of the potential hazards.

> The IEE provides a description of the project; of the existing environment and resource use; of potential environmental effects and impacts; of measures proposed to mitigate or prevent certain anticipated environmental effects; and a judgement concerning the impact of those effects that remain after all known measures for prevention and counter-action have been specified. In this description, the alternative ways of accomplishing the project are examined and the preferred alternatives identified (Duffy and Tait 1979).

In undertaking the IEE, agencies are encouraged to seek information and advice from many sources, including five regional screening and coordinating committees set up for this purpose. Based on IEE findings the agency determines whether or not significant adverse effects will result. If they will not, the EARP is stopped, as in case (*a*): if they will, then, as for case (*c*), the agency submits the project for a formal review.

An environmental assessment panel (EAP, or an environmental

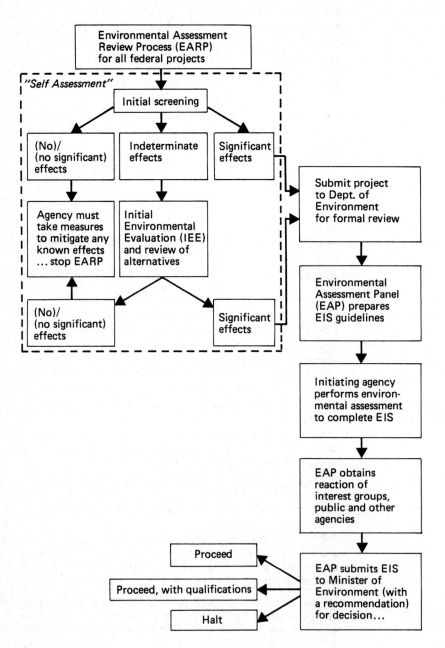

Figure 8.4. Environmental assessment procedures in Canada.

review board[1]) is formed to review the project and begins by issuing guidelines for preparation of an environmental impact statement (EIS). Unlike an EIS in the US, the Canadian one is project-specific. When the EIS is completed, the EAP obtains public reaction to the project through a series of meetings. The panel then submits the EIS, and all related evidence, to the Minister of the Environment with a recommendation to halt the project, proceed, or proceed with qualifications. The minister, in consultation with the initiating department, makes the decision. If there is disagreement, the matter goes to the cabinet.

For Canada, in comparison with the US, the persons responsible for making decisions on the environmental viability of a project are better defined. The Canadian environmental review process can therefore be specific and targeted to provide information for both public and ministerial review.

Sweden

There is no one specific law (such as NEPA in the US) or mandated process (such as the Canadian EARP) in Sweden that requires an environmental assessment, but this function is an integral part of the national physical planning process and, as such, is a part of a number of laws and processes that relate to the determination of the environmental consequences of proposed energy projects (see Figure 8.5). Three statutes that embody Sweden's requirement for environmental assessment are the Building Act (1974), the Environmental Protection Act (1969) and related ordinances, and the Nature Conservancy Act (1964). The National Environmental Protection Board (NEPB) is the central administrative authority for the environmental sector that has functions similar to those of both the EPA and the CEQ in the US and the Minister of the Environment in Canada. However, NEPB shares responsibility for legislative enforcement with county administrators.

The Building Act generally concerns regulation of the location of factories, machinery and installations, etc., and specifically states that the location of industrial activities that relate to energy management must be approved by the government, and issued a permit by the NEPB. Permits for land use granted under the Building Act are legally binding and pre-empt other land-use legislation. Municipalities have a right of veto on any permits issued by the government.

The Environmental Protection Act and its accompanying ordinances are operationally similar to the Building Act, except that they are direct environmental laws operating on a permit basis, whose purpose is to minimize environmental disruption from specific types of plants,

---

[1] An ERB is composed entirely of experts from the private sector, while the more common EAP comprises government experts. The Minister of the Environment may opt to use a review board for preparation of EIS guidelines if he feels that the nature of the proposed project warrants it.

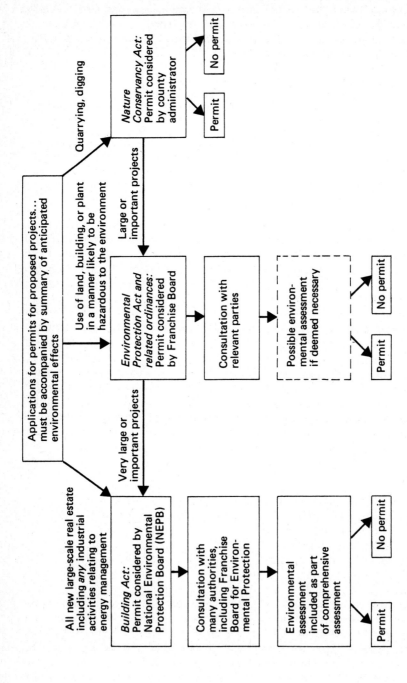

Figure 8.5. Environmental assessment procedures in Sweden.

buildings and land uses listed in the ordinances. Permits are awarded by the Franchise Board for Environmental Protection, except in unusual cases when permitting authority may be deferred to the NEPB for an exemption. In order to coordinate the overlapping aims of the Building Act and the Environmental Protection Act:

> A new rule in the Building Act provides that the question of establishment is first to be considered by the government. The government shall hereby make a comprehensive assessment relating considerations of environmental protection and planning to, e.g., considerations of labor market policy, regional policy and industrial policy. In order that the government's decisions be as broadly based as possible, opinions are normally requested from authorities, union bodies, industrial organizations, etc. Authorities which are normally consulted include the National Franchise Board for Environment Protection (OECD 1977).

The Nature Conservancy Act contains a set of area classifications, one of which is "natural environment", for which a permit from the county administrator is required before any disruptive work is begun. For larger-scale projects, the county administrator must consult with the NEPB.

In the US, Canada, and Sweden litigation through the courts for parties who perceive they are being adversely affected is always a possibility and therefore, as in the US case, any project may be halted or modified by judicial ruling. In the US adversarial procedures are an expected part of the review process for a large-scale energy project, whereas in Sweden cooperation and consensus are seen as being more important. In addition, Sweden, in comparison to the US and Canada, does not treat environmental assssment as separate from comprehensive socio-economic assessments; "comprehensive assessment" is implied in its law and applied to all relevant (as defined by the laws) activities, not just those initiated or sponsored by the federal government.

The USSR

The USSR has exacting technical legislation relating to environmental protection, most of which is based on emission and effluent limits and the maximum "carrying capacity" of a specific ecosystem, etc. The aims of an environmental assessment are to "give maximum satisfaction to the demands of society, restore, and improve the environment and to satisfy both of these goals at minimum cost" (Munn 1979). Environmental assessment, then, is part of the overall planning process in the USSR and is accomplished within a systems planning framework (see Figure 8.6). A State Committee on Hydrometeorology and the Environment (Gidromet) was created in 1978: "Gidromet and the US Environmental Protection Agency may be viewed as comparable regulatory agencies which function outside the production processes of their respective systems" (Ziegler 1982). Thus environmental protection is institutionalized and systematically pursued in the USSR. The enforcement agencies are the Councils of Ministers of the individual republics who ensure that local production facilities and environmental goals are incorporated in these plans. Information concerning the potential environmental effects of a proposed project is supplied to the ministers by research institutes and universities.

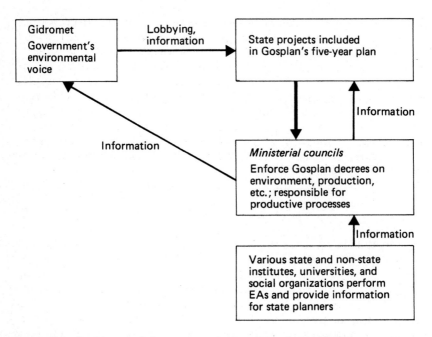

Figure 8.6. Environmental assessment procedures in the USSR.

Like Sweden, the USSR incorporates environmental goals into its comprehensive national goals. Gosplan is the Soviet state planning agency — all of the country's social, economic, and environmental goals are incorporated into its five-year plans whose directives are legally binding. A great deal of information is channeled to decision makers from many non-state social organizations and interest groups.

Summary

The US and Canada do not have strong centralized planning functions, but rather rely on the market, individual interests, and some government regulation to determine the course for environmental protection. Their procedures are therefore geared to produce comprehensive information about the potential environmental consequences of energy projects. Sweden and the USSR, however, do engage in physical planning processes and their laws have been designed to ensure that environmental objectives are considered along with other planning goals. These differences in approach to the environmental assessment process, in some ways, determine the types of methods that are used to perform these assessments.

Methods and Models used for Environmental Assessment

The amount of information on environmental consequences required to aid decisions on large-scale energy projects can be substantial and quite varied, involving a number of different fields and areas of expertise. There are a number of techniques to assist in the generation, organization, and analysis of this information, which, like the environmental consequences they address, can be classified in many ways. In this section, these techniques are organized into four categories according to their intended purposes; organizational methods, descriptive (predictive) methods, decision support (prescriptive) methods, and integration. These categories and some of the techniques they embody are listed in Table 8.1 and are discussed below.

Table 8.1. Model or system purpose.

Data organization
      Map overlays
      Matrices
      Indices
      Value paths

Description (prediction)
      Quantitative and qualitative simulation
      Input–output analysis
      Regression
      Spatial time series
      Systems dynamics

Decision support (prescription)
      Cost–benefit analysis
      Mathematical programming
      • linear/integer/nonlinear
      • multiobjective
      • dynamic
      Multicriteria decision methods
      • concordance analysis
      • multidimensional scaling
      Game theory methods
      Decision analysis

Integration
      Linking of models and methods for systematic
      and comprehensive analysis of consequences

An overview of methods

Organization methods have as their primary function the organization and display of environmental information. Map overlays (applied in the DOE study of synfuels) involve the superimposition of graphs and maps of environmental characteristics. Matrices display the impacts of different project activities on various aspects of the environment. Indices are similar to matrix methods in that they provide a composite value for the matrix by weighting and combining the degree of impact. Finally, value paths provide a two-dimensional display of alternative solutions to a multiobjective analysis.

Descriptive (predictive) methods provide an abstract, analytical, and mathematical description of the system being modeled. They enable conditional, "what would happen if" type analyses to be performed. Table 8.2 provides a summary of some environmental consequences and corresponding methods of analysis.

Table 8.2. Summary of descriptive methods (adapted from EPA 1979).

Model/decision area	General type	Important characteristics
Air quality		
Air pollution standard evaluation, monitoring	Probability distribution of pollutant concentration	Uses data to obtain a probability distribution of pollutant concentrations, which can be used to find out how often a proposed standard will be violated.
Air pollution standard evaluation, monitoring control	Probability distribution of maximum concentrations	This distribution can be used to find out how often a proposed standard for maximum concentrations will be violated.
Prediction of pollutant concentrations, identification of significant factors causing pollution, and economic analyses of air pollution	Regression model	Based on data we can evaluate what factors cause pollution. We can also predict concentration levels based on specified values of the significant factors.
Prediction and forecasting of pollutant concentrations, identification of trends	Time series analysis models	Using historical data we can forecast individual values of future pollutant concentrations. We can detect trends in pollution levels.

Table 8.2. *Continued*

Model/decision area	General type	Important characteristics
Air quality (cont.)		
Prediction of pollutant concentrations at different points in an area	Diffusion models	Using some data on wind velocity, wind direction, and other meteorological parameters, concentrations at various points in space can be predicted.
Water quality		
Pollution impact on water bodies	Analytic simulation statistics	Shows impacts on physical parameters of water bodies due to waste inputs (usual parameters are dissolved oxygen, nutrients, salinity, and temperature).
Ecological modeling	Simulation	Models address broad strategy of organisms and specific tactics.
Urbanized storm runoff modeling	Simulation statistics	Shows quality aspects of urban runoff and allows both land-use and structural controls.
Pollution impacts on groundwater	Simulation	Temporal and spatial dispersion of pollutants.
Watershed and catchment area models	Simulation	Shows the response in terms of runoff to a rainfall intensity and pattern.
Synthetic rainfall and stream flow generation	Statistics	Generates long-term synthetic rainfall and stream flow data traces which have similar statistical properties to short-term observations.
Groundwater modeling	Simulation	Movement and availability of groundwater.
Solid waste		
Generation prediction	Forecasting	Uses historical data to forecast amount of waste generated.
Generation prediction	Input—output	Permits examination of impact of changes in one sector on waste streams in other sectors.

Decision support (prescriptive) methods are used to provide a normative evaluation of alternative plans and activities. They are also applied to prescribe actions according to given decision criteria (social objectives). Figure 8.7 describes how multiobjective decision methods can be combined with various decision-making contexts (see Cohon 1978). A review of decision support methods is provided in Nijkamp (1980) and Rietveld (1980). An outline is given in Table 8.3.

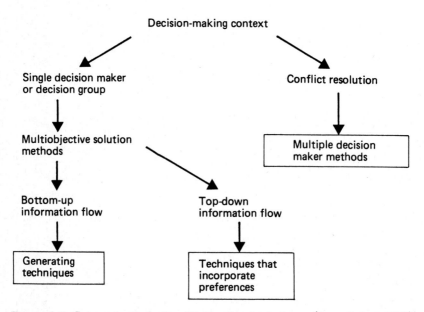

Figure 8.7. Categorization of multiobjective techniques (from Cohon 1978).

Integration

Several attempts have been made to integrate analysis procedures in different sectors, such as energy, economy, and the environment, to provide comprehensive assessments of the consequences of activities (see Lakshmanan and Nijkamp 1980, 1983). One such system, the strategic environmental assessment system (SEAS), has been used in various US government agencies such as the EPA and the DOE since the early 1970s to provide forecasts of the potential economic, energy, and environmental consequences of various economic growth assumptions. SEAS is a descriptive modeling system for conditional analysis to evaluate national policies and activities systematically (see Ratick and Lakshmanan 1983). It is an integrated series of computer models and

Table 8.3. Summary of decision support methods (adapted from EPA 1979).

Model/decision area	General type	Important characteristics
Air quality		
Optimization of resources planning strategies, making decisions	Linear, nonlinear, or multi-objective programming, multi-criteria decision methods	Gives us a strategy for optimum allocation of limited resources such as fuels, monitoring equipment, etc., to minimize the control costs of an air pollution program.
Water quality		
Investment scheduling and sequencing	Dynamic optimization	Project scheduling under budget constraints.
Pipeline and aqueduct network design	Optimization/simulation	Sizing and configuration analysis.
Gauging station location	Optimization/simulation statistics	Gauging location to maximize information.
Technology design	Optimization (dynamic or geometric programming)	Optimal sizing and choice of subsystems for treatment.
Models of treatment technology	Optimization/simulation	Helps to design, size, and cost treatment facility.
Models of the economic and social impacts of water pollution control	Input–output analysis, simulation systems, analysis games, statistics	Attempts to define economic and demographic changes and to aid in implementation.
Economic and social impacts of water resource development	Simulation, systems dynamics, statistics	Models for predicting economic, demographic, recreational effects of projects.
Regional waste management	Optimization	Investment models for: regional least-cost treatment, equitable cost distribution, treatment plant location, low-flow augmentation, instream aeration, bottom deposits, storm water.
Solid waste		
Site selection	Integer programming	Selects sites for facilities from among specified alternatives; considers costs of transportation, construction, and operation.

databases depicting economy—energy—environment interactions (see
Chapter 6). In this chapter we focus on the environmental model components in SEAS.

The system provides medium-term forecasts (15—20 years) of
activity levels and magnitudes of environmental consequences in
response to exogenous growth assumptions such as economic, population,
and energy demand projections. The significant level of detail in each
module allows these overall levels and magnitudes to be disaggregated to
provide information on the sectoral composition and spatial distribution
of effects.

SEAS can be partitioned into three functional areas; economic,
energy, and the environment (see Figure 6.3), each of which comprises a
number of modules designed for specific purposes. These modules are
interrelated within and between partitions by functional relationships
and data matrices. Central to the economic partition is a dynamic
input—output forecasting model, INFORUM[2] (Almon *et al.* 1974), which
produces annual forecasts of activity levels of 200 economic sectors over
the forecast horizon in response to macroeconomic projections of final
demand over the same timespan.

For many energy and environmental assessments the 200-sector
detail is not sufficient, so that many important economic sectors are
disaggregated into subsectors, by product or technological process, using
algorithms of the module INSIDE. The type of information provided by
this module includes the amount of physical product produced by process
and by industry. The physical amounts correspond to the levels of
economic activity forecast by INFORUM for each year.

SEAS was developed to help EPA decision makers to anticipate
environmental problems that could result from differing economic and
technological assumptions. Although the outputs of the economic and
energy partitions are useful and informative, the primary purpose of cal-
culating this information in such a consistent manner is to provide accurate and comprehensive forecasts of pollution generation, ambient
environmental quality, and environmental costs and benefits.

The environment partition relates the level of activity calculated by
the economic and energy partitions to concomitant levels of residuals
(pollution) generated. The investment, operation, and maintenance costs
for user input levels as regards degree of abatement, are also calculated
and "fed back" to the economic partition. The amount and composition of
pollutants generated by specific economic or energy-related activities
forecast by SEAS, are dependent upon the technologies employed for that
activity. Calculation of the total amount of pollutants generated nationally has only limited usefulness. It is therefore necessary not only to
relate activity levels to specific technological processes, but to locate

---

[2] Interindustry forecasting model of the University of Maryland (INFORUM), developed
and maintained by Professor Almon and his associates.

these processes spatially within the US. The linking of economic and demographic activities to detailed technological processes is accomplished in part within the INSIDE module.

REGION converts national-level forecasts into forecasts of activity in federal regions, states, standard metropolitan statistical areas, air quality control regions, aggregated hydrologic subareas, and river basins.

The generation of residuals (environmental pollutants) is estimated within the RESGEN module. Under user-specified (or programmed default) assumptions about the level and type of abatement activity, RESGEN calculates net residuals and secondary residuals (e.g. captured air pollutants that have become solid or liquid waste). The output of this sector is quite detailed, and provides information by category of pollutant (e.g., particulates), components (e.g., particulate lead), or by economic or energy sectors (e.g., chemicals or electricity generation). This output is provided for each forecast year and can be obtained under changing assumptions of scheduling and degree of abatement. This could be done on a national or regional basis.

SEAS is operationalized using exogenous input scenario assumptions and user input changes. In the extreme every data element, parameter, and algorithm can be changed for any given run. However, the system has been designed to accept certain trends of changes quite easily. The system is used primarily to perform conditional analyses of the impacts of alternative environmental or energy strategies by comparing the results of different scenario runs in terms of levels of effects, their sectoral composition, and their spatial distribution each year over the forecast horizon.

SEAS has been used to assess the economic and environmental implications of the US National Energy Plan, to provide an annual assessment of the environmental consequences of energy technologies, to assess solar energy growth scenarios, among other uses.

Conclusions

As can be seen from this brief survey of environmental assessment models and methods there are many ways in which an analysis can proceed. Each country's requirements for environmental assessments in some way determines which methods are used and, perhaps more importantly, how these methods are employed. For the US and Canada descriptive assessment methods are prevalent, providing information to interest groups who will use it in adversarial public policy debates, and in litigation to promote, modify, or prevent energy project undertakings. For the USSR and Sweden there is a reliance on decision support methods, such as large-scale LP models to balance environmental concerns with other physical planning objectives and to attempt to achieve consensus. The success of both of these approaches depends upon the effectiveness of the techniques employed.

In reviewing the availability of methods to perform adequate environmental assessments and to incorporate this information into a rational decision context, it seems that the decision support methods for using information have outpaced our ability to understand and describe environmental systems. Ongoing scientific research analyzing complex environmental interactions will improve our ability to make better decisions in these areas. There is also work in new directions for decision support methods that aim to improve our ability to make decisions with limited or incomplete data or to allow for some "irrationality" in decision making. The applicability of these techniques will in some ways depend upon the willingness of those with decision authority to utilize their results.

The attributes that a good analysis methodology should have varies with the reaons for and type of environmental assessment that is to be done. Accuracy, replicability, flexibility, economy, and understandability have been used as a guide by Coleman (1977), who concluded that there is no clearly superior method. Nijkamp (1980) details the prerequisites for a satisfactory environment—economy analysis: (1) a satisfactory degree of disaggregation and variation; (2) interactions within and between subsystems should receive sufficient attention; (3) an empirical analysis should, in principle, be possible; and (4) the analysis should provide sufficient and relevant information for policy makers. Holling (1978) also lists the attributes for which techniques for evaluation and prescription within this field should allow: generation of alternative objectives; effective policy design to achieve these objectives; and communication and interaction between those who design, choose, and implement policies, among others.

It has been pointed out that the models, the model builders, and the analysts are evaluated in the decision process that they are to serve. Not only will the model or system be evaluated based upon the criteria summarized above, but also the analysts will be evaluated as to how well they understand decision makers' problems and how well they interact. As the number of successful applications of these models and methods grow and as the familiarity with the vocabulary and technology used by technical analysts become understandable to the persons in decision authority, their usefulness will increase. Perhaps a new type of analyst could be promoted, one who is not only well trained in the technical nuances of systems analysis, but who is also trained to recognize the subtle interactions that characterize the policy process.

References

Almon, C., Buckley, M.R., Horowitz, L.M., and Reimbold, T.C. (1974) *1985 Interindustry Forecasts of the American Economy* (Lexington, MA: D.C. Heath).

Cohon, J.L. (1978) *Multiobjective Programming and Planning* (New York: Academic Press).

Coleman, D.J. (1977) Environmental impact assessment methodologies: A critical review, in M. Plewes and J.B.R. Whitney (Eds) *Environmental Assessment in Canada: Processes and Approaches* (Toronto: Institute for Environmental Studies, University of Toronto).

Duffy, P.J. and Tait, W.S. (1979) Canada's policy on environmental assessment for federal activities, in R.E. Munn (Ed) *Environmental Impact Assessment: Principles and Procedures, SCOPE 5*, 2nd edn (Toronto: Wiley).

EPA (1979) *A Guide to Models in Government Planning and Operations*. Report Contract No. 68-01-0788 (Washington, DC: Environmental Protection Agency).

Foell, W.K. *et al.* (1981) *The Wisconsin–IIASA Set of Energy/Environment (WISE) Models for Regional Planning and Management: An Overview*. Research Report RR-81-17 (Laxenburg, Austria: International Institute for Applied Systems Analysis).

Holling, C.S. (Ed) (1978) *Adaptive Environmental Assessment and Management*, IIASA International Series on Applied Systems Analysis, vol. 3 (Chichester, UK: Wiley).

Jain, R.K., Urban, L.V., and Stacey, G.S. (1977) *Environmental Impact Analysis: A New Dimension in Decision Making* (New York: Van Nostrand Reinhold).

Lakshmanan, T.R. and Nijkamp, P. (Eds) (1980) *Economic–Environmental– Energy Interactions: Modeling and Policy Analysis* (Boston, MA: Martinus Nijhoff).

Lakshmanan, T.R. and Nijkamp, P. (Eds) (1983) *Systems and Models for Energy and Environmental Analysis* (London: Gower Press).

Munn, R.E. (Ed) (1979) *Environmental Impact Assessment: Principles and Procedures, SCOPE 5*, 2nd edn (Toronto: Wiley).

Nijkamp, P. (1980) *Environmental Policy Analysis: Operational Methods and Models* (New York: Wiley).

OECD (1977) *Environmental Policy in Sweden* (Paris: OECD).

Rietveld, P. (1980) *Multiple Objective Decision Methods and Regional Planning* (Amsterdam: North-Holland).

Ratick, S.J. and Lakshmanan, T.R. (1983) An overview of the strategic environmental assessment system, in P. Nijkamp and T.R. Lakshmanan (Eds) *Systems and Models for Energy and Environmental Analysis* (London: Gower Press).

Ziegler, C.E. (1982) Centrally planned economics and environmental information: A rejoinder. *Soviet Studies* XXXIV(2):296–9.

Large-Scale Energy Projects: Assessment of Regional Consequences
T.R. Lakshmanan and B. Johansson (Editors)
Elsevier Science Publishers B.V. (North-Holland)
© IIASA, 1985

CHAPTER 9

Regional Information Systems and Impact Analyses for Large-Scale Energy Developments

Peter Nijkamp

Introduction

Public policies and proposals require careful and critical judgment, which may take several forms:

- an assessment of all relevant consequences (*ex ante*);
- an evaluation of all relevant choice alternatives (*ex ante*);
- a validation of the impacts of the choices made (*ex post*).

Ideally, all these steps would be the main components of an appropriate and useful policy analysis. Suitable information systems and reliable impact analyses are necessary ingredients for such judgments of public policies.

There is a specific reason why current large-scale energy policies deserve special treatment in this respect. The sharp rise in oil prices in the 1970s, the slow growth ("slowth") of most economies in recent years, and the drive for energy self-sufficiency (or at least for a diversity in energy supplies) have stimulated many nations to exploit their own energy sources to the full (see Wilbanks 1983), leading to the implementation of many large-scale energy supply systems: nuclear power, coal mining, integrated heating systems for urban areas, solar and wind energy programs, and so forth.

In this chapter a large-scale energy system is regarded as a set of long-term, connected, and integrated energy supply activities that serve the energy needs of a relatively large number of people. To a great extent such a system may be considered as a particular kind of public infrastructure marked by the following features (see Biehl *et al.* 1982):

(*a*)   *General*
*   a high degree of publicness
*   a high degree of immobility
*   a high degree of indivisibility
*   a high degree of nonsubstitutability
*   a high degree of monovalence.

(*b*)   *Specific*
*   strong socioeconomic and environmental repercussions
*   drastic (potential) shifts in demand
*   rapid technological developments
*   long pay-back period
*   strong geographical dimensions.

Large-scale developments tend to have strongly differentiated regional impacts depending on the geographical distribution of the energy sources concerned and on the specific policy being pursued (see Lakshmanan and Nijkamp 1983). The speed of the introduction of such supply systems has, however, not left ample time for a deliberate consideration of all options and of their consequences. For instance, small-scale supply systems such as district heating may have adverse effects compared with the current tendency to opt for large-scale energy solutions. Therefore it is extremely relevant, and even urgent, that regional evaluation studies of large-scale energy developments are undertaken. This chapter contributes to this issue by presenting some methodological reflections on information systems and impact studies that are necessary for a mature regional policy analysis of large-scale energy systems.

The Needs and Content of Information Systems

Information systems for policy analysis

Since the development of modern computer software, information systems have become an important tool in policy analysis. *Information* has to be distinguished from *data* (see Burch *et al.* 1979, Nijkamp and Rietveld 1984): data are numerical attributes of phenomena, whereas information means *structured* data (by means of monitoring, modeling, forecasting, etc.) that serve the aims of policy analysis, i.e., prior assessment, prior evaluation, and posterior validation. Consequently, information systems are a necessary ingredient for decision analysis. The *ex ante* and *ex post* aspects of information systems can be synthesized to indicate whether or not a particular decision can be justified (see Table

Table 9.1. Combinatorial analysis of rational and favorable decisions.

Prior analysis ╲ Posterior analysis	Choice has been made		Choice has not been made	
	Choice is *ex post* desirable	Choice is *ex post* undesirable	Choice would *ex post* have been desirable	Choice would *ex post* have been undesirable
Choice is *ex ante* desirable	+	Δ	−	□
Choice is *ex ante* undesirable	□	−	Δ	+

+ rational and (*ex post*) favorable decision.
− irrational and (*ex post*) unfavorable decision.
Δ rational and (*ex post*) unfavorable decision.
□ irrational and (*ex post*) favorable decision.

9.1). This table bears some resemblance to type I and type II errors in statistics, and may be useful in judging policy decisions, based on *ex ante* rationality criteria and *ex post* social benefit criteria.

Particularly for planning problems, information systems (for instance, in the form of monitoring and learning systems) may be helpful in adjusting policy choices to new circumstances by means of feedback mechanisms. The case studies described in this volume would no doubt have been richer if closer analysis of rational choice aspects had been undertaken.

Elements of information systems

The rise of computers, microelectronic equipment, and tele-communications have led to a rapid growth of information systems. In general, data in an information system can be measured on two scales: qualitative (nominal and ordinal) or quantitative (interval and ratio). In the past, most socioeconomic variables have been defined on a quantitative scale, but recently much effort has been put into the development of qualitative (or soft) data methods (see Nijkamp and Rietveld 1983, Wrigley 1980). Such analytical methods are *inter alia* based on rank correlation methods, scaling methods, logit and probit analysis, contingency table analysis, and latent variable methods. In any case, data measured on a lower measurement scale should not be left out of consideration. Each numerical attribute that leads to an increase, decrease, or confirmation of existing certainty regarding a phenomenon is a relevant element of an information system.

Information systems can be used for description, impact analysis, or policy evaluation. In the case of regional large-scale energy developments, they may be based on a general systems approach so as to provide a coherent and complete picture of a complex system. In particular, monitoring systems may serve as important tools in (energy) policy analysis. Such systems should take into account the existence of multiple interdependent regions, the energy planning orientation, and the (potential) usefulness of modeling. Hence, such an information system should meet the following criteria:

timely availability	policy relevance
up-to-date representation	multidimensionality of variables
easy accessibility	interregional and intertemporal comparability
consistency	flexibility
completeness	versatility

Clearly, the elements of an information system for regional energy impact analysis are especially determined by the *specific* elements of a large-scale energy system listed above. A good example of a mature energy data system has been given by Fels (1981) who, on the basis of feasibility criteria (such as data availability, modest costs, short implementation times, and easy retrievability) has attempted to design an integrated state energy supply—demand picture. The goals of his system are to monitor energy supply and demand on a timely, noncrisis basis; to allow monthly/annual reporting of the state's energy profile; to provide immediate answers to basic public policy questions; and to support energy emergency, management, and planning activities.

Information for energy analysis

The general remarks made above on information systems for policy analysis also hold for the analysis of the effects of large-scale energy developments. Energy demand patterns caused *inter alia* by changes in lifestyles (such as transportation behavior) are strongly influenced by energy supply and by energy policies. Furthermore, both demand and supply have strong repercussions on the geographical distribution of household and entrepreneurial activities. Thus, there are strong interdependences between the energy situation and the socioeconomic position of a region (see Figure 9.1). An adequate information system for the regional dimensions of energy policies should thus take into account demand—supply linkages, land-use patterns, transportation systems, and socioeconomic development (cf. Sassin 1982).

The energy question is indeed a complex one; therefore, the design and implementation of relevant and manageable energy policy models is a prerequisite for assessing the regional and urban dimensions of energy developments. Obviously, this requires large amounts of data, but unfortunately sufficiently long time series are poorly developed so that behavioral analyses are very rare. Only recently have more systematic

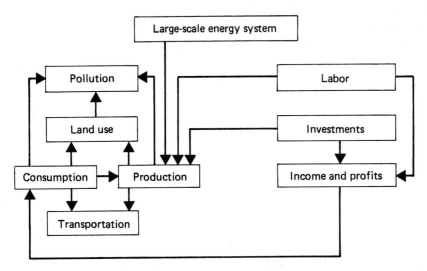

Figure 9.1. An interdependent energy systems framework.

attempts been made to create information systems on energy issues that will serve the needs of an appropriate energy policy analysis. The majority of such information systems, however, usually address energy issues at a national level and only seldom at a regional level (see Nijkamp 1983). Thus especially the *geographical* dimensions of large-scale energy projects deserve particular attention (see also Laconte *et al.* 1982).

A particularly intriguing problem arises if a new resource frontier area (such as Colorado) is being developed. In such cases, there are few prior data, though often in a short time policy decisions with tremendous impacts have to be taken. Many adverse effects may then occur, as is also shown by various *ex post* policy analyses. What can be done in such cases?

The best available strategy for designing information systems on phenomena for which no direct data exist is based on two approaches: *information from previous experience elsewhere* and *scenario analysis*. Information from prior experience of rapid development of new resource areas elsewhere (e.g., boom towns; see Chapter 7) may provide comparable insights into the complex mechanism of chains of changes imposed on a new area being developed from a so-called zero situation that is exposed to sudden external perturbations. Such insights can be used systematically to develop a *core information system* for any new resource frontier area, whatever the specific details may be. Further details of other aspects may then be added by making more elaborate assumptions regarding the time trajectory of the development of the area. This can most efficiently be based on a scenario analysis, which aims to portray an uncertain future on the basis of a description of feasible ways of changing the present situation.

On the basis of previous experiences and scenarios, further insights may be gained into future development paths, and particularly into potential bottlenecks. Further elaboration of an energy information system should then focus specifically on uncertainties and bottlenecks in the evolution of the area.

Impact Analysis in Regional Planning

A systems view of impact analysis

Impact analysis serves as an important analytical tool in an information system by assessing all relevant expected and foreseeable consequences of changes in key variables (e.g., external circumstances, policy controls, etc.) of a system. Overviews of regional impact analyses can be found in Glickman (1980), Nijkamp (1981), and Pleeter (1980). In the context of this chapter, regional impact analysis will be taken to be a way of assessing the regional consequences of policy decisions related directly or indirectly to large-scale energy systems.

The structure of such an impact system is essentially a stimulus—response system that takes into account impacts of key variables (external factors and internal policies/decisions). Impacts are registered as changes in effect variables. The stimulus—response analysis must include interactions between effect variables, as well as between key variables and effect variables.

Important aspects of a stimulus—response approach

Three important aspects of the stimulus—response approach should be mentioned: discrete versus continuous analysis, single versus compound impact analysis, and regional versus supraregional analysis.

The first aspect concerns whether or not the number of alternative states of a large-scale energy system is finite. A *discrete* energy impact analysis refers to a situation in which the number of alternative choices is limited (e.g., locations for hydropower plants). If different effects are to be distinguished, the outcomes of such a discrete impact analysis can be included in an impact matrix.

A *continuous* energy impact analysis is based on a situation in which no significant indivisibilities exist (e.g., the number of megawatts produced by a power plant). Such impact analyses usually require the use of continuous (econometric or statistical) models (see below). Continuous problems often arise in the operating stage of a system.

The second aspect focuses on single and compound impact assessments. A *single* impact assessment attempts to trace a specific effect (e.g., financial) of a single policy measure (e.g., a certain percentage change in energy taxes), whereas a *compound* impact assessment aims at gauging the combined effects of changes in multiple key variables for multiple-effect variables. Clearly this situation, typical of the case studies, requires the use of interdependent regional models in order to disentangle the specific direct and indirect regional effects of different policy measures (see Folmer and Nijkamp 1983, Moore and Rhodes 1974).

Finally, the *spatial* dimensions of energy impact analysis have to be mentioned. A large-scale energy project can interfere with the development of a region in various ways: top-down and bottom-up patterns, and combinations thereof (see Issaev *et al.* 1982).

Having discussed an integrated *ex ante* assessment of impacts, we will now turn to an *ex ante* evaluation of alternatives and an *ex post* validation of actual results.

Policy Analysis for Large-Scale Energy Systems

Conflicting effects

In general, large-scale energy systems serve to provide an efficient energy supply, but they also lead to various (often conflicting) effects that have to be evaluated carefully. Although the nature of these effects may vary over time and space, the following should be considered in practical evaluations:

(*a*) the extent to which security of energy supply is guaranteed;
(*b*) the costs of producing energy (including the consequences for energy demand);
(*c*) the environmental repercussions (including diffusion, accumulation, synergistic effects, and risks);
(*d*) the socioeconomic impacts on various economic sectors (especially employment and investment); and
(*e*) the spatial effects (especially equity and mobility effects such as migration, transportation, and residential choices).

These should be evaluated with regard to their temporal and spatial dimensions, taking into account their interdependences. The interdependences create the most difficult problems in integrated studies for policy analysis since they require the design and assessment of an operational systems model (see below).

It is clear that such effects will differ with the energy supply alternative chosen, since each exerts a different impact on the multidimensional welfare profile of a region (see Nijkamp 1978, 1979, 1980). Profiles encompassing these effects can be constructed for individual regions of a spatial system. A meaningful policy analysis should then attempt to evaluate the (incommensurable) consequences of each option, based on elements from conflict theory.

Multidimensional *ex ante* policy analysis

Given the conflicting nature of large-scale energy systems with respect to other policy areas, careful *ex ante* evaluation is necessary. Given the incommensurable and sometimes even intangible nature of the successive effects implied by the various choice options, conventional evaluation methods like cost–benefit or cost–effectiveness analysis (for discrete-choice problems) or programming techniques (for continuous-choice problems) are unsatisfactory. Therefore, attention will now be called to compromise principles from multicriteria analysis (for discrete-choice problems) or multiobjective programming analysis (for continuous-choice problems). Both assume that policy analysis should aim to ensure a rationalization of choice problems related to conflicting options (see Rietveld 1982, Spronk 1981, Voogd 1982).

The compromise approach is illustrated here with a hypothetical example in which a decision regarding various energy systems is to be based on two conflicting criteria: energy conservation, c, and economic growth, g. Clearly, a choice in favor of rapid economic growth will normally lead to reduced energy conservation, and vice versa. The extent to which these two options are mutually conflicting can be identified by means of a formal model that describes all structural relationships between variables (see Figure 9.1).

The conflict between c and g can be described formally by means of the notion of a Pareto (or efficiency) frontier, indicating all feasible and efficient solutions of one variable for any given value of the other, and vice versa. These Pareto solutions indicate that c cannot be increased in value without decreasing g, and vice versa. All such Pareto points can, in principle, be identified through parametric variation of the trade-offs between c and g. The particular level that represents an optimal compromise solution for the choice between c and g can theoretically be determined by assuming a "master" objective function $\omega(c,g)$, in which the weights attached to c and g reflect the trade-offs inherent in this conflict analysis. Clearly, an optimal solution might then be achieved by means of the well known marginality rule:

$$\frac{\delta\omega}{\delta c}\bigg/\frac{\delta\omega}{\delta g} = -\frac{dg}{dc} \ . \tag{9.1}$$

However, since the weights in $\omega(c,g)$ are usually unknown, the latter condition does not give an operational solution. Within the framework of multicriteria analysis and multiobjective programming, a wide variety of methods and techniques has been developed, which aim to identify compromises between divergent objectives. In recent years, interactive methods have become especially popular (see Rietveld 1980, Spronk 1981).

Interactive policy analysis is based on a systematic exchange of information between a decision maker D and an analyst A. Such methods are especially useful in process planning, in which decisions are not taken just once but require consideration at several stages during a certain time period. The steps normally undertaken are:

- A proposes an initial (trial) solution to D.
- D indicates whether or not he is satisfied.
- A uses the information from D as a constraint in the next stage of the analysis and suggests an adjusted solution to D.

By repeating this procedure, an ultimate compromise solution can be obtained. The specific methods applied to identify a compromise solution may be based on ideal-point or min—max strategies.

The use of multicriteria analyses and/or multiobjective programming methods may be an important contribution to large-scale energy planning with conflicting objectives. Many applications have already demonstrated the validity and operationality of this approach in policy analyses with conflicting objectives.

Multidimensional *ex post* policy analysis

Ex post evaluation is important as a learning process for both the analyst and the policy maker. Analysts can learn about the (in)validity of their assumptions in model techniques used (stability of parameters, exogenous data, etc.), while policy makers can gain more insights into the reasons for the success or failure of their decisions (e.g., behavior patterns of the general public).

The judgment of the results of a prior impact analysis with respect to the actual outcomes once a plan has been finalized, is too often neglected. Especially in a new area such as large-scale energy planning, with its many uncertainties and counter-intuitive effects, an *ex post* judgment is extremely important. Particular attention may then be given to a systematic typology of failures in scientific analyses and policy decisions (e.g., due to model mis-specifications, a wrong discount rate, an incomplete set of policy alternatives, etc.).

The *ex post* judgment of the success of a policy measure is not straightforward due to the wide variety of goals involved. Some may be achieved, others over- or underachieved. Depending on the *ex post* weights attached to the successive goals, a policy maker will judge a certain policy measure as more or less successful. This problem is again multidimensional in nature and the same principles of multidimensional policy analysis apply here.

**Toward a Framework for Large-Scale Energy
Impact Assessment**

We now attempt to synthesize in a systems framework the various
notions inherent in a comprehensive assessment system for large-scale
energy developments (cf. Gibson and Binkley 1982). In general, energy
development comprises various stages (Schliephake 1977):

- energy research and development
- exploitation of energy resources
- transportation of raw resources
- conversion and processing of energy resources
- transportation of usable energy resources
- end-uses of energy.

Usually, each of these stages includes some substages, such as building
and construction activities, and operating activities.

In assessing large-scale energy projects, all relevant choice options
or alternatives for regional development have to be identified, in relation
to the main purposes of the energy project at hand. Consequently, in
order to design and judge the successive energy supply alternatives, all
relevant policy goals have to be specified. National and regional aspects
of energy policy have to be taken into account.

Then the expected impacts of each alternative regional energy
development have to be assessed (e.g., by using some of the impact
methods or models described above, in order to account also for interdependences in the system). Here specific attention has to be given to
the temporal and interregional dimensions of the various effects. Then
an appropriate evaluation method has to be applied. In general,
minimum threshold values (e.g., due to indivisibilities) and bottlenecks
related to the energy system or the broader socioeconomic system also
have to be identified. Finally, an *ex post* evaluation has to be undertaken
(see Figure 9.2).

Recommendations

This chapter concludes with a set of recommendations for research
and policy analysis emerging from the above discussion.

- Before decisions on large-scale energy developments can be made, a
  regional energy impact analysis should be carried out to provide a
  systematic and comprehensive assessment of all relevant potential
  impacts.

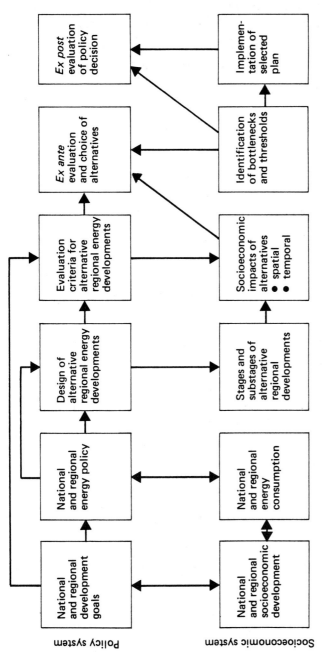

Figure 9.2. A comprehensive assessment system for large-scale energy development.

- Given the frequent lack of precise data, information systems on regional energy plans should take explicitly into account uncertainties (by appropriate measurement techniques, probabilistic methods, fuzzy set analysis, trichotomous decision analysis, "soft" data techniques, etc.); in any case, a sufficient documentation is necessary, in which the missing data should also be mentioned.

- Energy impact analysis should have an explicit policy orientation; a multidimensional policy evaluation based on conflict analysis and compromise principles may be a very helpful tool in identifying trade-offs or conflicts between competing policy goals, interest groups, policy agencies, institutional and decision levels, and so forth. Both *ex ante* and *ex post* policy *and* research evaluations are necessary.

- The issue of regional self-sufficiency with regard to energy supply deserves further attention, since the higher efficiency (in terms of a lower vulnerability at a regional level) has to be judged against interregional inequalities due to shifts in regional energy prices.

- The spatial dimensions of large-scale energy developments should be analyzed very carefully, since urbanization and locational patterns and their related mobility and transportation flows may severely — and sometimes in diverse directions — be affected by regional and national energy policies.

- The construction of integrated, dynamic energy, economy, environment, and land-use models may be an operational way of arriving at systematic and comprehensive assessment and evaluation models that are suitable for practical large-scale energy policy analysis at a regional or urban level.

References

Biehl, D., *et al.* (1982) *The Contribution of Infrastructure to Regional Development* (Brussels: Regional Policy Division, EEC).

Burch, J.J., Strater, F.R., and Grudnitski, G. (1979) *Information Systems: Theory and Practice* (New York: Wiley).

Fels, M.F. (1981) Proposed: A fundamental energy data system for states, in R.A. Fazzolare and C.B. Smith (Eds) *Beyond the Energy Crisis* (Oxford: Pergamon), pp 215–22.

Folmer, H. and Nijkamp, P. (1983) Linear structural equation models with spatiotemporal auto- and crosscorrelation, in M.M. Fischer and G. Bahrenberg (Eds) *Models in Geography* (Bremen: Bremer Beiträge zur Geographie) Heft 5.

Gibson, J.E. and Binkley, J.R. (1982) Systems and models in urban design: A tutorial overview, in P. Laconte *et al.* (Eds) *Human and Energy Factors in Urban Planning: A Systems Approach* (The Hague: Martinus Nijhoff) pp 7–34.

Glickman, N.J. (Ed) (1980) *The Urban Impacts of Federal Policies* (Baltimore, MD: Johns Hopkins University Press).

Issaev, B., Nijkamp, P., Rietveld, P., and Snickars, F. (Eds) (1982) *Multiregional Economic Modeling: Practice and Prospect* (Amsterdam: North-Holland).

Laconte, P., Gibson, J., and Rapoport, A. (Eds) (1982) *Human and Energy Factors in Urban Planning: A Systems Approach* (The Hague: Martinus Nijhoff).

Lakshmanan, T.R. and Nijkamp, P. (Eds) (1983) *Systems and Models for Energy and Environmental Analysis* (London: Gower Press).

Moore, B. and Rhodes, J. (1974) The effects of regional economic policy in the United Kingdom, in M. Sant (Ed) *Regional Policy and Planning for Europe* (London: Saxon House) pp 87–110.

Nijkamp, P. (1978) *Theory and Application of Environmental Economics* (Amsterdam: North-Holland).

Nijkamp, P. (1979) *Multidimensional Spatial Data and Decision Analysis* (New York: Wiley).

Njkamp, P. (1980) *Environmental Policy Analysis* (New York: Wiley).

Nijkamp, P. (1981) *Urban Analysis in a Spatial Context*. Research Memorandum 1981-5, Department of Economics, Free University, Amsterdam.

Nijkamp, P. (1983) Regional dimensions of energy scarcity. *Environment and Planning C: Government and Policy* 1(2):179–92.

Nijkamp, P. and Rietveld, P. (1983) Soft econometrics as a tool in regional discrepancy analysis. *Papers of the Regional Science Association* 49:3–21.

Nijkamp, P. and Rietveld, P. (1984) *Information Systems for Integrated Regional Planning* (Amsterdam: North-Holland).

Pleeter, S. (1980) *Economic Impact Analysis* (Boston, MA: Martinus Nijhoff).

Rietveld, P. (1980) *Multiple Objective Decision-Making for Regional Developments* (Amsterdam: North-Holland).

Rietveld, P. (1982) *Multiple Objective Decision-Making and Regional Planning* (Amsterdam: North-Holland).

Sassin, W. (1982) Urbanization and the global energy problem, in P. Laconte *et al.* (Eds) *Human and Energy Factors in Urban Planning* (Boston, MA: Martinus Nijhoff), pp 207–34.

Schliephake, K. (1977) *Oil and Regional Development* (New York: Praeger).

Spronk, J. (1981) *Interactive Multiple Goal Programming for Capital Budgeting and Financial Planning* (Boston, MA: Martinus Nijhoff).

Voogd, J.H. (1982) *Multiple Criteria Analysis in Public Planning* (London: Pion).

Wilbanks, T.J. (1983) Energy self-sufficiency as an issue in regional and national development, in T.R. Lakshmanan and P. Nijkamp (Eds) *Systems and Models for Energy and Environmental Analysis* (London: Gower Press) pp 28–49.

Wrigley, N. (1980) Categorical data, repeated measurement research designs, and industrial surveys. *Regional Studies* 14:445–71.

PART III

Decision Frameworks for
Energy Assessments

The case studies and analyses presented in Parts II and III reveal how the actual application of basically similar methods and models differ as the decision framework varies. This framework is not only a reflection of the national institutional settings, but also depends on the constellation of sponsors, clients, and interest groups that determines the coordination and game-like structure of objectives and constraints that surround an assessment study. Moreover, the framework varies as the spatial extension of the problem changes to include local, regional, national, or international decision problems. The decision situation may also temporarily be embedded in a consensus- or conflict-oriented framework, and this may partly change in character during the course of the assessment process.

In Part III those alternative decision structures are illustrated. Chapter 10 examines policy analysis in theory and practice on the basis of experiences from North America and, in particular, from the US. It focuses on the links between the design of the assessment study, the translation of research results to policy conclusions, and the final integration of such conclusions into the policy formulation process. The presentation also investigates the different case studies of Part I within the framework outlined in the chapter.

Chapter 11 provides summary conclusions about energy decisions and models, and outlines some prospects. An attempt is made to answer the question: What have we learned from the comparative study?

Large-Scale Energy Projects: Assessment of Regional Consequences
T.R. Lakshmanan and B. Johansson (Editors)
Elsevier Science Publishers B.V. (North-Holland)

CHAPTER 10

Policy Analysis in Theory and Practice

T.J. Wilbanks and R. Lee

Introduction

We who do policy analysis believe that science can help make policy better, to the larger benefit of society. Attracted by any chance to link our technical skills with our impulse to be useful, we have spent a major part of our professional lives trying to make this happen. But deep within our hearts, we know that a lot of our effort goes for naught. Even worse, some of it gets misused by the policy-making process in the pursuit of policies that we believe misguided.

Because *doing* policy analysis has its own satisfactions and rewards, regardless what happens to the results, we often carry on as if we are being useful, reducing the pressure from our policy idealism by paying more attention to scientific idealism or institutional imperatives. In the meantime, however, the connection between science and policy making remains tenuous, and many of our hopes for social relevance go unrealized.

Many of us are frustrated by this gap between aspiration and reality in what we do — together with our conviction that the gap is usually contrary to the public interest. In IIASA's terms, we sense the existence of a "universal" problem here and, by pooling our experience, we hope to find some avenues that offer us real prospects of solving it.

As a rather tentative step in such a direction, this chapter starts by very briefly reviewing policy analysis as an ideal and indicating how this idea is manifested in the five case studies. It then considers the "real world" of policy analysis — how the process usually works in practice — and how this process differs from the ideal, using the case studies as examples. Finally, it suggests some directions for closing the gap between theory and practice in policy analysis.

Policy Analysis in Theory

As a kind of activity distinct enough to carry its own label, policy analysis emerged at about the same time as systems theory, systems analysis, operations research, cybernetics, and other quasi-disciplinary efforts to apply formal analytical methods to large, complex problems. Experiences during World War II with planning and management had suggested to a great many people that science need not be reductionist in order to work: that "bigness" was an inescapable part of the modern world and that applying the perspectives and tools of science to this bigness could become one of the great intellectual enterprises of the twentieth century.

In one way or another, this postwar movement affected nearly all fields of science and engineering. In the US it appeared within political science as a fascination with the "policy sciences" (Lerner and Lasswell 1951) and with the perspectives of systems analysis (Easton 1953). As these themes intermingled in the work of political scientists such as Dye and Sharkansky, one of the terms that came to be applied to the nascent specialty was policy analysis. Since then, of course, just as with systems analysis and its other cousins, "policy analysis" has become an ever-larger umbrella for professional activity, to the point that it no longer means anything very disciplinary or very narrowly defined.

For the purposes of this chapter, we will define policy analysis simply as *the systematic investigation of characteristics and implications of policies*. "Systematic investigation" implies a concern with formal analytical structures, measurement, and the use of quantitative techniques where appropriate. "Characteristics" are qualities or attributes, known or hypothetical. "Implications" refer to a focus on relationships between means and ends: an evaluation of "if this — then that" relationships in the disorderly world of real human systems. "Policies" are courses of action or guiding principles that involve wide ramifications, relatively long time perspectives, and call for considerable information and thought (Bauer 1968), in contrast, say, with administrative decisions.

In this sense, policy analysis is a type of applied systems analysis, intended specifically to contribute to policy making. Although mathematical models are an important part of its tool bag, policy analysis is broader than modeling alone, and it tends to differ from modeling in its preoccupation with results rather than with manipulations.

What policy analysis is and how it works

What makes policy analysis special is not how it proceeds scientifically, but how it connects with a policy-making process. According to a rational view of policy making, this process works more or less as depicted in Figure 10.1. Analysis can contribute to most of the stages of

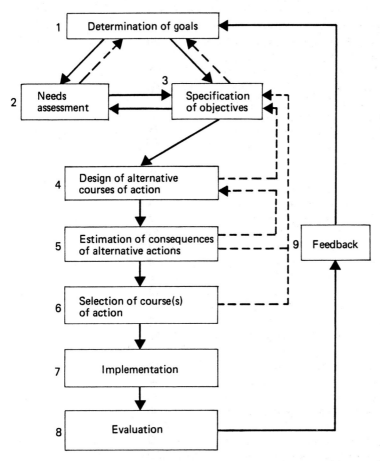

Figure 10.1. Stages in the policy-making process (Mayer and Greenwood 1980, p 9).

the process. For example, it is usually a part of a needs assessment (step 2); it can help in identifying alternative courses of action (step 4); and it can provide a way to evaluate policies after the fact (step 8). But the heart of policy analysis is its relationship to policy decisions (step 6).

In this respect, a policy analyst is generally interested in either (*a*) choosing a course of action (analysis *for* policy), or (*b*) evaluating a course of action already taken (analysis *of* policy).[1] The policy analysis literature on the latter subject differs from the program evaluation literature in that it is generally more concerned with why actions were taken than what they have accomplished; its central purpose has been to

---

[1] This distinction is drawn from Jenkins (1978).

help understand policy making rather than to inform it (a purpose that
lies outside the policy-making process as such).

We are therefore being reasonably faithful to the concept of policy
analysis as an applied art and science, as well as to the subject of this
book, in focusing on policy analysis as a component of step 5 of the process: estimating the consequences of alternative actions in order to help
policy makers select the best alternatives.

In contributing to step 5, nearly everyone agrees that the purpose of
policy analysis is to provide heuristic insights, not to determine choices
per se, even if it uses techniques whose purpose is to "optimize" (Meadows
et al. 1982, pp 279–80, Hogan 1978, House and Williams 1981).[2] It is one of
many bases for policy decisions. But if the policy-making process is
rational and the policy analysis is well targeted and well done, in principle the outcomes from the analysis should include such benefits as a
reduction in the number of options being considered seriously, improved
information about the pros and cons of those that remain, and a fuller
application of the various ways that each option connects with other
matters.

The case studies in this book reflect this broad view of what policy
analysis is and how it works.[3] They share the ideal. All represent
attempts to estimate impacts of energy developments comprehensively —
in the future, if not as a basis for current decisions. All seek to use available quantitative methods, at least in connection with a limited range of
questions, and to take some steps beyond them. All emphasize the
nature of policy analysis as a continuing, multiphased activity; and they
all confront some of the theoretical issues in analyzing impacts on a
regional scale. Moreover, all are concerned in one way or another with
interactions between policy analysis and its users.

On the other hand, they all differ from the ideal in that the link
between policy analysis and policy making is fuzzy at best (see below),
and they illustrate the diversity of forms that policy analysis can take.
One of the differences is in their contexts. The US case was concerned
with the feasibility of a fairly specific national policy, not so much in
order to contribute to a decision about what the policy should be as to
explore its implications after the direction had been set. The case of
Swedish policy on nuclear energy was similar in its objective, but the policy analysis appears to have been structured more formally into the
national and regional policy-making apparatus. In Canada, the analysis
was likewise concerned with implications after the fact, but the focus
seemed to be on implications for an impacted region (as a gesture toward

---

[2] An exception is Nagel, who talks in terms of methodologies for optimizing choices (e.g.,
Nagel and Neef 1979).

[3] For convenience, we will refer to the five case studies (Chapters 2–5) as follows: the US
synfuels acceleration program, *US*; tar sands development in Alberta, *Canada*; impact
evaluations in Sweden, *Sweden*; CITF experience in northwestern Colorado, *Colorado*;
and natural gas development in Siberia, *USSR*.

conflict resolution) rather than implications for national policy. In Colorado, the entire context was one of regional and local planning, where the role of the expert was not to analyze policies but to provide tools for local parties to use as they see fit. In the USSR case, specific analytical and policy questions about the project were overshadowed on the one hand by international issues, and on the other by the broad philosophical context of regional planning.

The five cases also seem to differ in the reasons for the policy analysis activity. In Canada and perhaps in the US, a major part of the motivation was a need to satisfy regulatory requirements; without these legal constraints, less might have been done. In the USSR, the policy analysis was an expression of a rather elaborate and standardized process for centrally planning and implementing large projects. In Sweden, more than any of the other cases, the analysis seems to have arisen as a response to the expectation of society at large — closer to the ideal. In Colorado, it appeared because of the interest of some of the parties in policy discussions in reducing conflicts over decisions, not because of broad social expectations or regulatory requirements.

Finally, the case studies can be compared in their balance of concern with applying existing tools of analysis versus developing new and better ones. In all cases, the analytical tools used for the actual policy analysis were already available, although the tools selected for the different cases varied considerably. The Canada study (AOSERP) was limited to compiling baseline data, with the only modeling effort being the use of a Gaussian distribution to model SO_2 dispersion. The US study used a pollutant emissions—econometric model, together with a site rating method, to evaluate counties appropriate for synfuels development. The Sweden (REGI) study harnessed a battery of existing input—output, econometric, Markov chain, LP, and entropy-maximizing models. The USSR project planning effort was based partly on a system of large quantitative models, with a considerable emphasis on optimization (see Issaev *et al.* 1982, Albegov *et al.* 1982). The Colorado study utilized a computer software package consisting of a basic economic activity module, county population projections, and spatial allocation. In Canada (AOSERP) and Sweden (REGI), however, the policy analysis activity led to a research effort to improve capabilities for the future; recent work by Issaev, Snickars, and others at IIASA might be considered a parallel for the USSR. In the US and Colorado, no such effect is reported.

Theoretical issues in policy analysis

As the case studies make clear, no one pretends that analysis, even in theory, is perfect. To policy analysts, in fact, it is more interesting because it is not; there are still mountains to climb, not just fields to plough. In getting closer to the goal, the main challenge is that, in theory, policy analysis takes a systems view of political life and its relation to society. This poses several difficulties, none of which has been very satisfactorily resolved so far:

(1) *The complexity of causation:* When the objective of policy analysis is to estimate the effects of a specified policy, it is frustrating to recognize that the consequences are at least as likely to depend on *other* actions and influences as upon the policy itself. It has been argued, for example, that policies are more often facilitative than causative (Dye and Gray 1980, pp 13–14); certainly, they have more impact when they flow with the prevailing currents than against them. In particular, it seems clear that the effects of a policy are shaped by how it is implemented, not just by its substance. The consequences depend on organizational effectiveness, societal commitment, voluntary compliance. In this sense, it is sometimes useful to distinguish between policy *analysis* as an ideal and policy *implementation* as an ideal. The former is concerned with policy *before* it is determined; it is essentially scientific, taking the means of an action as given, more or less, and focusing on implications of the ends. The latter is concerned with policy *after* it is determined; it is essentially pragmatic, taking the ends of an action as given, more or less, and focusing on means to reach those ends. In the actual conduct of policy making, these two purposes are often intertwined; and they are linked in theory as well, because both call for good information about likely policy achievements and effects. But the two aims are fundamentally different; an analysis that is optimal for one may not be optimal for the other.

Another complication is that a policy itself usually changes as feedback is received, which means that its content through time has an interactive relationship with its effects. This puts the analyst in the position of estimating the values associated with a single arrow in a very complex systems model (see Figure 10.2), when that arrow has a very limited meaning if considered apart from all the others. Part of the significance of this complexity is that, in theory, policy analysis deals with an immense number of variables and relationships, integrating a variety of different units and levels of analysis (Gregg 1976). This means formidable requirements for measurement and also for theory, and it makes specification error an ever-present danger (see below).

(2) *The relationship of analysis to decisions:* Although some analysts are able to separate their work from its use, most of us share the concerns of theorists about how policy analysis is plugged into policy decision making. The connection is relatively simple when one assumes that policy is the result of rational decisions by individual entities, but it is considerably less simple when one recognizes that policy making is often incremental rather than rational (e.g., Dye and Gray 1980) and that it usually reflects complex organizational behavior rather than individual or small-group behavior (Ackoff and Emery 1972, Dye and Gray 1980, Gregg 1976).

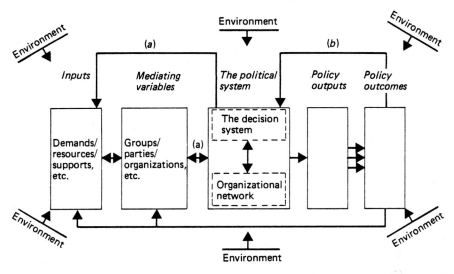

Figure 10.2. A systems model of the policy process (from Jenkins 1978, p22). Policy analysis is focused on the link between policy outputs and policy outcomes (triple arrow).

(3) *The objectivity of policy analysis:* In principle, one would like to think that scientific analysis is value-free, but we know it is not. Its purposes and mechanisms (even its language; see Olsson 1975) are conditioned by ideology. Its environment is shadowed by constraints on independence and openness. Its conduct is shaped by such influences as the analyst's instincts as a moral critic or his/her concerns about the consequences of the analysis for society. Within political science, at least, these have been treated as fundamental questions, not just practical ones (e.g., Rein 1976, Fischer 1980, Mayer and Greenwood 1980, pp 62–4).

Methodologies for policy analysis

Given the inherent complexity (and the potential ubiquity) of policy analysis, it is not surprising that its methodologies are so diverse. Itinerant analysts have arrived from all sorts of disciplinary starting points, bringing along their accustomed tools, nearly always finding ways to apply them, and leaving their experience as a part of the legacy of the profession.

In theory, the choice of a method depends on the context: the substance of the policy and its intended effects; the nature of the questions about it; the scale of the analysis; etc. Rose (1976), for instance, suggests that different views of the nature of changes in policy (i.e., linear, cyclical, or discontinuous) call for different methodologies. Mayer and

Greenwood (1980, pp 13—15) note that the methods of policy analysis often differ according to its purpose: to assess efficiency (cost—benefit or cost—effectiveness approaches); effectiveness (causal analysis); feasibility (political analysis); or ethical acceptability. Others distinguish between the desires to explore, describe, explain, and predict — or between short-, mid-, and long-range time horizons. This implies that, as an ideal, there is no such thing as a general methodology for policy analysis.

Almost by definition, most of the methodologies are quantitative; and most of them used in energy policy analysis are labeled models: simplified representations of reality that can be manipulated to investigate relationships. In many ways, models are the "technologies" of policy analysis, moving through the same stages of research and development (R&D) as a machine (basic research, applied research, development, demonstration, and commercialization) and, like a machine, representing a significant R&D investment (see Ziemba and Schwartz 1980, Greenberger *et al.* 1976, Lakshmanan and Nijkamp 1980, Albegov *et al.* 1982, Häfele and Kirchmayer 1981, Meadows *et al.* 1982). A variety of quantitative techniques are described in Greenberger (1977), Poister (1978), Bunn and Thomas (1978), and Scioli and Cook (1975). Larger modeling systems often combine many of these methods, as the Sweden and USSR case studies show (see Lee *et al.* 1982, Lee and Thomas 1983).

In its development, policy analysis has also been strongly influenced by efforts to develop the art of "qualitative analysis" associated with such concepts as scenario construction and formal approaches for seeking a consensus among respondents (expert or otherwise). Because of the complexity of policy issues and the limitations of available tools, some have argued the need for even less quantitative (but still systematic) approaches to policy analysis. In the field of energy, perhaps the best known example of this in the US is the approach to impact assessment developed at the University of Oklahoma, which stresses an interactive relationship with a diverse population of experts and affected parties, revolving around qualitative statements of issues rather than quantitative estimates (White *et al.* 1979).

Policy Analysis in Practice

From the quiet, formal gardens of science, we move now to the crowded, noisy streets of the world of policy making, full of excitement and opportunity, but also full of danger and disappointment. Here, to paraphrase Carol Weiss, one sees an image of policy analysis entering an arena that is already crowded — where analysis is certainly not irrelevant, but neither is it often a prime mover (Weiss 1977, p 1). In fact, it is sometimes so buffeted by others in the arena that it comes out battered beyond recognition.

The central challenges

In applying policy analysis as a practical art, an analyst runs into several general difficulties. Simply stated, it seems to be necessary to get "tangled up in a system that is dominated by social processes that operate independent of content" (Wilbanks 1982a); to reconcile the ideals of policy analysis with some very real limitations on what can be done; and to tiptoe through a minefield of pitfalls in order to set the right course. Too often, the result is that the relationship between analyst and policy maker is an unhealthy one, far removed from the lofty principles of this kind of enterprise.

Relating Science to Politics

There are profound differences between the scientific method and the political process, and these contrasts have turned the practitioners of the two ways of life into different cultures. At worst, they comprise

> two groups — comparable in intelligence, ... not grossly different in social origin, earning about the same incomes, who [have] almost ceased to communicate at all, who in intellectual, moral and psychological climate [have] so little in common that ... one might have crossed an ocean (Snow 1959, pp 2–3)

Such a dichotomy is clearly an exaggeration, but analysts and policy makers do tend to speak different languages, to respond to different reward systems, to define "important" and "satisfying" in different ways. Like highlanders and flatlanders or desert tribes and oasis dwellers, "they have a curious distorted image of each other" (Snow 1959, p 4). Policy analysis operates precariously at the intersection between these two cultures, where the problems of cross-cultural communication are formidable indeed (Wilbanks 1982b, pp 100–2; see also Majone and Quade 1980, pp 105–7, 116–37).

But even when these problems are solved, policy analysis must be injected into a policy-making process that is far too amorphous to fit the ideal. The determinants of policy are complex, hazy, and mysterious. Who decides? How are decisions arrived at? When? Harold Orlans speaks of

> countless proximate decisions ... reached in many offices, each with a different brew of fermenting knowledge — and, of course, much else besides knowledge — until ... an hour comes and goes in which, we later say, the matter was consummated. (quoted in Weiss 1977, p 11).

In this process, compromises are negotiated and coalitions form and disappear. To the analyst, it may appear that the truth gets enmeshed in a Byzantine world where strategies are often devious and motives often ignoble. At any rate, the role of analysis in all of this "game-playing" is exceedingly hard to determine. Often, it appears disappointingly slight.

One of the major reasons is that many important policies are themselves amorphous. Their concerns are general, their purposes multidimensional, their possible mechanisms diverse, their rationales obscure. They tend to mix interests in society with interests in organizational empire-building. Sometimes, it seems that policy analysis is merely a prop for a kind of great charade, used to advance special causes rather than to find out which options are truly better. Certainly, in translating a policy into a form susceptible to analysis — a set of specific actions and responses — it is virtually impossible to capture all the subtleties that are a part of the bigger picture, and this can relegate policy analysis to the role of a minor player in the drama.

A second problem is that the point of contact for policy analysis is often a unit in a bureaucracy, which is not necessarily the same thing as an important component of policy making. In many respects, it is unfortunate that this connection with decisions is so often so poor. Many "bureaucrats" are highly competent; they are well informed about critical issues, their judgment is sound, and their putative role is to provide staff support for policy making. But in case after case, we see these good people bogged down with administrative details and disconnected from important policy decisions. Maybe partly because of the many demands on the time of top officials, mid-level officials often seem to be one step behind policy making rather than helping to prepare the groundwork for it (Wilbanks 1982a). Furthermore, their jurisdictions are usually so limited that they can only make limited use of the results of comprehensive analysis, even if they are able to commission it.

This means that, if an analyst truly wants to influence public policy, he or she frequently finds it necessary to communicate with a broader audience: top officials, the people to whom they listen, the media, etc. But this suggests a paradox: the people most likely to be able to put the results of policy analysis to use are seldom the ones who support it financially. Such a channel to the top may even jeopardize future access to the financial support — both because to a user the support seems unnecessary (the advice flows in steadily without any direct investment in it) and because to the sponsor in the bureaucracy the outside channel serves further to reduce his or her role in the process.

More often, though, when policy analysis does have an impact on public policy, it does so indirectly. Rather than communicating directly with a policy maker, the analyst is successful in influencing the thinking of people the policy maker listens to. In a sense, the analysis serves an "enlightenment" function, helping to shape broad frameworks of thought in society, rather than serving an "engineering" function, helping to "fix" policy in specific ways (Weiss 1977, p 17).

In the end, the demand for policy analysis depends on how well the fruits of past efforts match up to society's expectations from them, and in the US in the 1980s we have a problem. Apart from the general tightening of public sector budgets, there appears to be "a broad-based disenchantment with this kind of work throughout society" (Kash 1982, p 6).

One reason, clearly, is that we have often seemed to claim more for our analysis (in both truth and objectivity) than we could deliver. Perhaps this has been partly because policy makers have asked unrealistic things from us. Perhaps users have often overlooked our careful statements of assumptions and qualifications, and we have felt misunderstood. Regardless of the validity of our excuses, the public's as well as the policy makers' evaluations of our analyses are based on the accuracy of their predictions; and here things leave much to be desired.

Another reason is that users have generally expected these applications of science to *reduce* uncertainty, but policy analysis in the 1970s (including impact assessment, technology assessment, etc.) has more often served to *increase* uncertainty by identifying problems or raising new issues (Kash 1982, see· also House and Williams 1980, p 20). As Joe Coates says, "any good technology assessment gives a bureaucrat bad news" (Coates, personal communication). This has tended to give it an aura of obstructionism, when the mood of the 1980s is more resolute, attracted to simple goals rather than troublesome complexities.

Living with Limitations

The second challenge is to produce valid and useful results under intense scrutiny, in spite of some serious limitations. To start with, there are limits to science. When an analyst is contemplating science and technology policy, in which many of the effects are to be expected decades into the future, the uncertainties swamp our capabilities for long-range forecasting. Perhaps, as Kenneth Boulding suggests, we need to build better bridges to the humanities to add to our capabilities for dealing with the trans-scientific questions that abound in policy analysis (Boulding 1979; see also Weinberg 1979).

But a bigger problem — probably the biggest of them all for policy analysis in practice — is that we never have the resources we need in order to do what we know how to do: the information, the time, the money, the audience. And our work inevitably suffers from the compromises that are necessary. For a person with a systems perspective, the most frequent (and most agonizing) trade-offs are between (*a*) comprehensiveness, with the kinds of integration and sensitivity that we seek as an ideal, and (*b*) timeliness. A true policy analysis is an extremely complex task, requiring countless methodological problems to be overcome (e.g., Buehring *et al.* 1978). Regrettably, however, policy decisions seldom wait for the analyst; our role is usually not that central (Wilbanks 1984). If we want to contribute, we often find ourselves under pressure to conduct our work in ways that many of our scientific colleagues consider unprofessional.

A second set of trade-offs also relates to the desire to be useful. In doing useful policy analysis, analysis alone is not sufficient. The task also calls for management (for example, to integrate the results of various contributors), communication with users, and other functions that draw upon an already limited reservoir of funds and people. This adds to the agonies associated with cutting corners, adopting *ad hoc* approaches, and making other compromises, because the competing demands for resources require more compromises to be made — and thus further increase our needs for management (e.g., quality assurance) and communication (e.g., to explain and defend unconventional methods). Allocating scarce resources is never easy, except in economic theory; in the conduct of policy analysis, it can leave an analyst in a virtually impossible position.

The other major resource limitations fall under the category of "state of the art": the data, tools, and theories at hand when the call comes for contributions to a policy decision. At this point, our technical resources are seriously constrained by five factors.

(1) Because policy analysis usually must produce in a hurry if it expects to contribute to policy decisions, we are stuck with the information and tools readily at hand. But "because analytical tools take a while to develop and test, they tend to reflect the questions and policy needs of the past, not the present" (Wilbanks 1982b, p 94).

(2) In our formal policy analysis, we rely heavily upon theories and techniques developed by the basic research community. But that community determines its priorities in different ways from the policy world, paying more attention to such things as disciplinary paradigms. As a result, we sometimes find an array of reosurces "quite capable of providing answers to many questions nobody is asking and incapable of responding to the needs of ... planning and policy" (Dacey 1971).

(3) At least partly because of differences in the questions asked by basic research scholars, we find ourselves especially limited in dealing with certain kinds of issues that are often critical in energy policy (Wilbanks 1982b): interaction effects across disciplinary boundaries, questions involving human and institutional behavior, the likelihood and effects of exceptional events, the uncertainties of program implementation, and the estimation of critical thresholds.

(4) Comprehensive policy analysis often calls for integrating the results of different kinds of activities; e.g., models that represent contrasting approaches. This "imposes enormous demands on the analyst's intuitive and rational faculties [because] there has been no good theoretical treatment of what meaning can actually emerge from [such] a system..." (Meadows 1981, p 24). It also places enormous demands on a management system (see Chapter 5).

(5) Year after year, policy analyses of various types are conducted, results are issued, decisions made, and the river of policy flows on. But as the effects of a policy begin to appear, we seldom return to the original estimates to see how good they were, partly because we analysts are too busy looking ahead at the next policy issue — but mainly because the

sources of support for analysis are likewise concerned with the future, not the past. The result is that we miss many chances to learn from our experience. In the meantime, even when we manage to improve our capabilities, the needs seem to expand even faster (Dror 1971).

Avoiding Pitfalls

Finally, even when we can find a way to connect effectively with the political process and to get the job done with our available resources, we face a landscape packed with traps; and we have all stumbled into them at one time or another, no doubt contributing to the skepticism with which our further efforts are received (Timenes 1982, p 106). Four problems crop up especially often in energy policy analysis, at least in the US: mistaking competence for usefulness, the lack of a systems perspective, questions about ethics, and hubris.

The first problem is one of "tunnel vision". Like other scientists, policy analysts like to do what we know how to do. We dislike having to perform in arenas in which we consider ourselves no more than well informed laymen. Especially when our love is quantitative methods, this sometimes creates "a tendency to turn to formalism, toward syllogisms, and not see beyond those syllogisms" (Schlesinger 1980). Sometimes, our affection for closed-form solutions leads us to reinterpret complex issues until they become more tractable problems,[4] even if the resulting analysis is distant from the core of the issues themselves (e.g., Majone and Quade 1980, pp 96–8). Our affection for mathematical elegance lets elegance become an end in itself (Majone 1980). Our preoccupation with manipulating our models distracts us from our search for insights (Timenes 1982, p 106). We select tools because they are familiar, without asking whether they are right (Majone and Quade 1980, pp 99–103). We fail to remember Tukey's axiom for social research:

> Far better an approximate answer to the right question, which is often vague, than an exact answer to the wrong questions, which can always be made precise. (quoted in Weiss 1977, p 23)

One difficulty for those of us who identify with the academic research community is that its reward systems keep pulling us in precisely this direction, away from the goals of policy analysis. It is not an easy choice. Another factor may be that, because the results of a policy analysis related to controversial issues are often scrutinized with a zeal that makes an academic journal look like a picnic, we feel far more secure

---

[4] An issue is "a fundamental enduring conflict among or between objectives, goals, customs, plans, activities or stakeholders, which is not likely to be resolved completely in favor of any polar position in that conflict.... A problem is a matter of the application of knowledge and choice in a definitive way. Problems can be solved, issues cannot" (Coates 1977).

sticking with topics and methods less likely to make us vulnerable to criticism.

The lack of a systems perspective is a related problem, but it stems less from a love of elegance as such than from mistakes in deciding which items to include in the analysis: specification errors. From a systems point of view, the scope of an analysis should be broad and eclectic. In practice, however, the scope is often narrow, not only because of time limitations, but for other reasons as well, such as the kinds of blindness that come with our disciplinary baggage or an agreement by the analyst to confine the study to the jurisdiction of its sponsor (Majone 1980). For example, Meadows (1981) has noted a lack of attention to "mechanisms of social control and adaptation" (p 25),[5] maybe partly because government sponsors of policy analysis fear accusations of social engineering.

Although these limitations on a systems perspective are seldom consciously dishonest or malign, they raise questions about the ethics of policy analysis in practice. Analysts can so easily get captured by the atmosphere of policy making (Timenes 1982, p 106), caught up in the drama, seduced by the apparent access to channels of influence.

> Gaining an understanding of the decisionmaker's problem may shade into learning to think exactly like the decisionmaker, into adopting uncritically the decisionmaker's point of view and sharing his or her biases and blind spots. (Majone and Quade 1980, p 111)

Clearly, in this way and others, the idealism of policy analysis as a "pure" scientific activity often gets mixed with the realism of career motivations (Weiss 1977, p 7) and the impulses of the analyst as a citizen, reflecting ideology and social consciousness.

Among analysts themselves, a particular concern is with censorship — not so much a situation where a sponsor says "you can't say that because it doesn't fit the policy line", but a situation where those people who fail to show loyalty to the sponsor have trouble keeping their support and access. This may cause some analysts to compromise their own integrity by censoring themselves; certainly, it tends to affect the scientific credibility of analysts dealing with controversial topics who keep their funding year after year.

These themes of integrity and scope become interwoven in almost every policy analysis. For whom is the analysis done — a sponsor or the broader community of users? To whom is it relevant? What is its sensitivity to such issues as political feasibility and institutional agendas? With which vested interests is it allied, in appearance if not in fact? For instance, because policy analysis costs money and usually requires a certain amount of sophistication to appreciate its purposes and approaches, it is likely to be associated with those parties in a policy debate that have the necessary money and sophistication; and it may be perceived by

---

[5] A common error of this type is a failure to distinguish between policy effects (e.g., risk) and social acceptance of those effects.

other parties as a strategic device rather than an open-minded search for truth.

An integrity issue arises in another connection as well. Policy analysis tends to pull us as scientists into risky territory. One of the challenges is that policy makers want a definite "bottom line"; and under pressure to deliver concrete recommendations, we sometimes ignore our presumed skepticism. Besides, policy makers want answers to *their* questions, not ours, even if they are questions we cannot answer as expert scientists. Because we are so often treated not just as individual specialists but as windows to the wisdom of all science, we feel pressed to give (or get) a good guess at an answer.

Finally, we are too often guilty of hubris: "claiming scope, applicability and certainty ... where modesty and temporizing would be more appropriate and insightful" (Timenes 1982, p 106). Like other scientists, we tend to fall in love with our own theories and methodologies. Like other scientists, we tend to develop love affairs with our own projects, losing a good bit of our objectivity toward them (Agnew and Pike 1978, p 201) — developing an additional kind of tunnel vision. And like other scientists, we sometimes perceive a need to "oversell" our capabilities and results in order to be heard — to compete with others shouting for the policy maker's ear or the funding agency's money. But a result can be that what we are seeing — and communicating — as a depiction of reality is in fact an artifact of our particular analytical approaches and views of the world (e.g., House and Williams 1981, pp 12–14), far less prescient and insightful than we ourselves think (Hoos 1972, cites a number of cases where analysts have overreached themselves in addressing policy problems).

Implications of a focus on regional consequences of large-scale projects

These challenges are especially acute when the art and science of policy analysis are focused on regional consequences of large-scale projects. As a result, it can be especially hard to do this particular kind of policy analysis well. Consider the implications for an analyst of a "large-scale project", compared with a smaller-scale activity:

(1) *Scope of analysis.* A large-scale project involves a bigger overall system to be analyzed, with more extensive connections, probably with complementary actions more significant in determining outcomes, and with unique features of the project more important (placing limits on inferences from other experience).

(2) *Horizon of analysis.* Because a larger project takes longer to implement, forecasts generally have to look farther into the future, which increases uncertainties in the analysis.

(3) *Project control*. Larger projects are usually bigger management challenges. The risk of something important going wrong is greater; the "worst" case can be expected to be substantively worse. Furthermore, bigness usually begets bigness; among the impacts of a large-scale project are a variety of institutional changes that imply secondary effects on economy, society, and the environment.

(4) *Project expense*. Larger projects are usually more expensive. They may have significant impacts on capital markets. They involve greater opportunity costs, which increases the importance of considering policy alternatives. And they mean bigger stakes for parties interested in a policy decision; they tend to be associated with certain pressures on analysts and to increase the scrutiny of their work.

(5) *Project requirements*. Larger projects make more intensive demands on the capabilities of their environments; e.g., to accept emissions or to provide labor. They are more likely to raise questions about capacity limitations.

(6) *Public attitudes*. Larger projects are more noticeable, in a sense more visibly symbolic, which means that they are likely to attract more parties who want to participate in major decisions — to help define the scope of analysis and evaluate its significance.

For these reasons, among many, our limitations as policy analysts are more problematic for large-scale projects or actions than for smaller ones. Similarly, a concern with "regional consequences" turns the associated policy analysis into a distinctive kind of activity, with its own set of complications:

(a) *Magnification of effects*. An effect, problem, or uncertainty associated with a particular project is almost certain to have a noticeable impact on at least a few localities, even if it seems relatively insignificant at a national scale. Impacts are therefore harder to ignore or dismiss at a regional scale.

(b) *Increased importance of variance*. At a national scale, average or "most likely" effects are usually the major concern; but at a regional scale the central question for analysis often has to do with the effects of extremes, departures from averages, the tails of probability distributions.

(c) *Importance of external linkages*. It is a simple principle that the smaller the area for which an analysis is performed, the more linkages are likely to cross the boundary of that area (e.g., the relationship between regional scale and regional multipliers). At a regional scale, therefore, an immense range of external linkages must be traced and estimated: ties between region and nation, interregional flows and transactions, spatial patterns and externalities.

(d) *Data limitations*. A region is often too small for needed data to be collected at that scale routinely, but too large to be able to afford to collect very much data nonroutinely. As a result, an analyst usually faces a trade-off between data quality and analytical detail; in order to get one, he or she must be prepared to sacrifice the other (Bolton 1979).

(e) *Theory limitations*. Theories are scarce about social processes at a "meso-scale," especially theories backed up by empirical evidence — and most especially by evidence about the processes under post-1973 conditions.

(f) *Salience of qualitative aspects of analysis*. As the scale of analysis approaches that of individual actors in society, the relationship between policy analysis (or at least *public* policy analysis) and its social context changes. It gets closer, more personal, in a sense more social and less scientific. For example, issue identification is more likely to include a bottom-up component, and users are more likely to expect a great many kinds of concerns to be integrated.

(g) *Communication limitations*. Compared with a national scale, at a regional scale the users of analysis are more likely to include parties without technical expertise. This affects the communication of results, methodologies, and sometimes even the justification of a major analytical effort.

Combining these two sets of challenges, one can see the difficulties for an analyst (Table 10.1). In a great many ways, the imperatives of a comprehensive policy analysis for a large project are hard to reconcile with very real constraints on rigorous work at a regional scale.

Table 10.1. Special challenges associated with a focus on regional consequences of large-scale projects.

Scale of resolution: regional	Scale of action: large
A given effect has a larger meaning in a smaller system	Impacts are larger and harder to control
Analytical detail is limited by scarce data	A bigger, more complex system requires more data to characterize it fully
Financial systems seldom operate at a regional scale	Financial and investment issues are more important
Theories of regional processes are scarce	Estimating effects requires more foresight, which calls for a better understanding of how processes work
Quantitative methods have only a limited ability to capture the major issues	Quantitative methods are needed to keep track of the abundance of data and interaction effects

The case studies as examples

The case studies in this book are a rich source of information about policy analysis in practice, and echo many of the points made above. Although it is always dangerous to generalize from so few cases, it appears that we can learn some lessons from them about several important questions.

Why Is Policy Analysis Done?

(1) Policy analysis sometimes only takes place because it must. In Chapter 3 Lonergan indicates that many assessments are commissioned not because policy makers want them or accept the notion that they are needed, but because regulations require them or political exigencies make them unavoidable. Although some of these pressures may be encouraging to the analyst, in the sense that they suggest society has a greater appreciation for impact information than many decision makers, the results of policy analysis would probably be used more effectively in the policy-making process if the underlying rationales for the analysis were more positive.

(2) Policy analysis sometimes takes place because society wants to improve its "climate of understanding" of a policy issue. Especially when a country or region is faced with some sort of a crisis, its citizens are likely to ask that certain questions be answered, and the answers must be supported by analysis in order to be credible. In an indirect way, at least, most of the case studies are responses of this sort to the concerns stimulated by the 1973 oil embargo.

(3) Rather than contributing to policy *formulation*, analysis often — by intention or by timing — ends up contributing instead to policy *implementation*: a continuing process of adding detail, seeking agreement, and making mid-course corrections for a policy direction already decided upon. In the US case in particular, the concern is not so much with whether the policy should be selected as with determining how it could be made to work. This role, which is played down in the theoretical literature (in fact, rejected by some of it), is a major part of the real world of the analyst. In a sense, a great deal of *policy-related* analysis is not policy analysis in the strictest sense; it is oriented toward purposes and ideals that are different from those of classic policy analysis.

(4) Policy analysis sometimes occurs because a body of laws, regulations, or precedents has made it a standard part of the policy-making process. Chapter 2 provides one example of this, based on a general philosophy of how policy should be developed. Another example, implicit in the US case, is the analyses of environmental impacts that have become virtually automatic for major federal government actions in that country since the passage of the National Environmental Policy Act — a kind of structural change in response to social concerns, with the nature and

scope of policy analysis defined rather formally and thus removed as a matter to be determined case by case.

How Do We Do Policy Analysis?

(*a*) A policy analysis effort is often expected to produce results very quickly, whether the analyst is ready or not. In the cases of both the US and Sweden, inputs to the policy-making process were requested (and provided) before a careful analysis could be completed. Although apparently not a factor in these cases, such provisional advisories always run the risk of producing policy positions that both the policy maker and the analyst later feel compelled to defend, regardless of further analytical results.

(*b*) Because we must respond so quickly, we generally find it necessary to rely on the tools already at hand, even if they were developed in connection with studies of other issues. In some cases, this can lead to an imbalance in our attention to the various questions raised, as we tackle those questions our tools can handle and treat the others in less detail, if at all.

(*c*) We must cope with substantial problems of operational definition. Often, in order to analyze policy, we must interpret it: redefine objectives in more concrete terms, make our own decisions about types of effects that should be examined, etc. In the process, we run the perhaps unavoidable danger of losing touch with some of the issues of greatest concern to policy makers — and of putting limits on a systems perspective.

(*d*) A large and complex policy analysis effort is a management challenge as well as a technical challenge. The description of the analytical support for the Commission on Consequences in Sweden offers a powerful example of the problems associated with integrating the work of many different contributors to a major effort. Similar experiences could probably have been recounted for the other cases as well; this is often the "Achilles heel" of policy analysis in practice.

(*e*) In contributing to the policy-making process, such classic aims of policy analysis as complexity and quantification may have limitations as well as potentials: limitations on time, resources, capabilities, and communication processes. In the US case (Chapter 5), Williams reports that at the outset, because of a time frame "eventually lengthened to one month" (!), certain analytical tools which had been developed so that impacts might be traced systematically could not be used; simpler methods were the only option. Later, when a more thorough job was possible, he notes user criticisms of the rather elaborate approach to rating areas as potential sites for synfuel plants and of an "unwarranted degree of precision" in reporting the results. At the same time, the extensive coverage of effects, clearly aiming at comprehensiveness, may have tended to invite readers to detect omissions: if they mention *this*, why not that? One suspects similar issues in the Colorado case and perhaps elsewhere.

What Difference Does a Regional Scale Make?

(1) When the concern is with implementing rather than formulating national policies, regional-scale analysis may be more important. The reason is that, whereas a key to national policy formulation may be impact *assessment*, the critical issue in policy implementation is often impact *acceptance*, and this is usually a highly localized matter. This became the core of the US case, at least in terms of compliance with environmental regulations, and there are hints of it in the Swedish and Colorado cases as well.

(2) Policy analyses at different scales can be difficult to relate to each other. In Chapter 5 Johansson and Snickars contribute a valuable discussion of the problems in relating analysis (and policies) at the national scale to activities at the regional and local scales: the difficulties in distinguishing regional effects from national, the frequent shortages of technical competence at more local levels, etc. Although the US and Colorado cases do not cite this as a problem, they support the point by showing the kinds of methodological contortions that are often required even to approach a link between different scales of concern.

How Is Policy Analysis Affected by its Environment?

(*a*) Ideology shapes analysis. The Swedish cases are strongly shaped by ideology, both in terms of the policy choice that stimulated the analysis and the ground rules established for it (e.g., stressing adaptability and flexibility over efficiency as criteria for evaluating options); and the USSR case shows how ideology can determine the role of analysis in a well specified, centralized planning process. In the other cases, ideology is less explicit in the discussion, although it certainly lies behind the strong push for domestic fossil fuel development in North America, the mechanisms for it, and the attitudes of many policy makers toward the roles of policy analysis in it. There is nothing wrong in this from the point of view of society, but it represents a departure from some of the standard visions of policy analysis as an ideal.

(*b*) Either the conduct of policy analysis or its uses may be limited by institutional constraints. The most powerful example of this is the decision of Canada's Berger Inquiry to ignore insights from the Helliwell model. Another example, perhaps, is the limitation of AOSERP investigations to the immediate region of the tar sands developments. From this evidence, it may be appropriate to suggest that reductionist policy making tends to generate reductionist analysis. When policy making is highly compartmentalized, topically or geographically, it can be hard to find a user (or a supporter) for broad, systematic policy analysis. Who in government or society, the systems analyst asks, is responsible for seeing the big picture? Regardless, it is clear that most policy analyses are subject to institutional constraints, especially if they are carried out by agencies with vested interests in the policy outcome. This does not imply dishonesty on the part of either the institution or the analyst. But operational decisions must be made about the way a policy will be interpreted, the scope of the search for effects, and the scenarios for the future to be considered. And these judgments often reflect institutional decisions; e.g., related to the institution's needs to coordinate that particular analysis with other activities.

(c) Policy analysis can appear to be a tool of political strategy rather than a search for truth. In the Colorado case (Chapter 4), Chalmers notes "an ever-present wariness by local officials" of a process with the "potential to reduce their autonomy", and he hints that there is some justification for this attitude: the CITF tools are likely in fact to "bound the negotiating space of local governments", and this is a principal reason for the participation of industry and state government. As a result, the entire effort has become a local political issue, and its future is uncertain.

(d) Where major national policy issues are concerned, a single policy analysis effort seldom stands alone. It is a part of a larger effort to assemble information and make judgments based on it. The US case is an especially valuable example of this. During the 1970s, the impacts of coal and oil shale development in the US were examined repeatedly by a wide range of parties. By 1979, when the Carter administration announced its plan to accelerate synfuels development, the literature was already immense, if "fugitive" (in the sense that much of it, consisting of reports rather than published articles or books, was inaccessible through standard reference systems). The issues were well understood; in fact, three influential books on national energy policy were published in 1979 (Landsberg *et al.*, Schurr *et al.*, Stobaugh and Yergin), sketching out an emerging consensus on synfuels development: essentially (a) that the US needed synfuels alternatives to be available for possible use in the 1990s, (b) that government action was required because the market alone was unlikely to take the necessary actions to develop and demonstrate these alternatives, but (c) too many uncertainties lay ahead, economic as well as environmental, to set ambitious production targets such as 2.5 million bpd within 10–15 years. The critical need was simply to get some plants built and operating, not necessarily to meet a specific future production level. The Energy Security Act of 1980, creating the Synthetic Fuels Corporation, was an outgrowth of this consensus (see Kash and Rycroft 1984); and the survival of the SFC in the 1980s indicates that the consensus is still alive. Appearing in this already well endowed kind of setting, the analysis described in the case study contributed mainly by reinforcing the growing consensus, by helping to show that different analytical approaches and perspectives led to the same general conclusion: that synfuels development could get started without unacceptable impacts (an example of another such study, done in quite a different way, is White *et al.* 1979). In other words, it was one component of a much broader stream of policy analysis — in fact, close to the mainstream, drawing information and momentum from the rest of the stream and, in turn, contributing its own.

What Are the Results of Our Analyses?

(1) The effectiveness of policy analysis is usually uncertain. Assuming that an analysis will suggest certain policies as more sensible than others, it is difficult to know whether these sensible policies will actually be implemented — or what such a decision depends upon. For instance, external conditions may change (as in the case of synfuels in the US) to the point that careful analysis becomes irrelevant. After several such experiences, it can be hard to maintain the morale of policy analysts who entered the arena because they were idealistic about helping to improve policy.

(2) Even if the product of a policy analysis is disappointing, the process can be educational. Chalmers suggests that many of the contributions of the Colorado case have been rather peripheral to the main purpose of the effort — e.g., improving local understanding of some of the basic concepts of regional economics. Other cases also come to mind, such as the Committee on Nuclear and Alternative Energy Systems (CONAES) of the US National Academy of Sciences, which conducted a comprehensive study of US energy policy during the 1970s. The resulting summary report, revised and edited so thoroughly that most of the substance was squeezed out, was panned by readers everywhere. But the CONAES process may have been the single most influential factor in convincing the US business community by the late 1970s that energy conservation is a good idea. Such "externalities" from policy analysis probably deserve more recognition and encouragement.

(3) A demand for policy analysis may lead to (more or less) fundamental research to improve the tools for policy analysis. Because our existing capabilities are so often inadequate, our response to a social need may be limited to starting a major effort to gather more data and develop better analytical capabilities — AOSERP and REGI are examples. This means that most of the contributions from careful analysis in these cases will be to decisions in the future, not now (which may raise questions in some parts of society about whether policy directions can be diverted once they are well established). As long as society is willing to be patient with us, however, such a situation is not without advantages, because it is one of the few ways to motivate the policy-making system to invest in work to improve our tools for policy analysis; in this sense, some of the efforts we label policy analysis end up benefiting science at least as much as they benefit policy.

How Can Policy Analysis Be Done Better?

(*a*) Interactions between analysts and policy makers are all-important if policy analysis is to have any utility for policy. This is a common theme in all five cases, most powerfully illustrated in the discussion of the Commission on Consequences (a marvelous name) in Sweden. Besides indicating the importance of these links, however, the case studies also suggest just how complex and hazy they usually are.

(*b*) If policy analysis is to be useful to a larger community of users, at least within a pluralistic policy-making system, it often works best if it is deliberately designed as a multiphased activity: provisional inputs to policy on the basis of a quick, usually *ad hoc* "first cut"; an after-the-fact version released for a broader audience; responses by this audience; further analysis and special studies to respond to comments, criticisms, and changes in the policy environment; and iterations of the same cycle. The US case study describes in some detail the role of analysis as a part of an ongoing interactive process of public policy dialogue: a catalyst for discussion and consensus formation, focused less on a specific policy result than on a general policy direction.

(*c*) Perhaps policy analysis can be made more effective if policy makers become more directly involved in it. The Colorado case is especially interesting as an attempt to put the tools of policy analysis directly into the hands of policy makers, so that they will be able to ask their own questions, get their own answers, and maybe — from first-hand experience — gain a better understanding of how the tools can help them in their planning. As we enter the age of a microelectronic revolution, this may give us a hint of a kind of future for which we should all be preparing, in which more policy analysis is done *by* policy makers, not just *for* them (see below).

Some Directions for Closing the Gap Between Theory and Practice

Clearly, then, the practice of policy analysis is often different from its theory, and one result is a strong sense among professional analysts that the gap needs to be closed. We believe that initiatives in four areas can help in this effort. These areas are: improving communications between policy makers and the policy analysis process; investing in preparations to meet future needs; creating portfolios of capabilities designed for meeting a variety of needs; and broadening the meaning of "analysis" in order to increase its relevance and credibility.[6]

---

[6] We omit one other possibility that is frequently mentioned in the literature: improving the quality and wisdom of the policy makers involved in the process (e.g., J.Q. Wilson in Lynn 1978, and Weiss 1977, pp 6–7; see also Wilbanks 1982a).

Improving communications

First, we need to confront the communication problem between
analysts and decision makers: developing ways to get the two communities in closer contact, cultivating specialized individuals and institutions
to bridge the gap, and together examining the way policy decisions are
made (Wilbanks 1982b, pp 106—8).

One approach is to provide more opportunities for the two groups to
spend a great deal of time together, so that they get to know each other
better as individuals and get a better understanding of each other's perspectives and needs (Sternlight 1978). "There seems ... to be no place
where the two cultures meet" (Snow 1959, p 17). Early experiments of
this sort have been "chastening, frustrating, but ultimately very reward-
ing" (Greenberger and Richels 1979, pp 483—4). A forum approach, organ-
izing working groups of analysts and users to explore key issues together,
has been one of the important innovations in recent years (e.g., the
Energy Modeling Forum at Stanford University). Among many things, policy makers learn just how important is the analyst's judgment in using
models and other formal techniques to develop estimates of policy
impacts; analysis is no cold, mechanical exercise. This, in turn, puts
pressure on the analyst to show that he or she has a deep substantive
knowledge of the issues, not just competence with analytical tools (Kash
1977).

These intensive periods of interaction have their limitations, however. One obvious reason is that both the analysts and the users need to
spend most of their time working in their own respective territories. As a
result, there is a critical need for people and groups to serve as bridges
between the communities of analysis and policy, passing analytical
findings, capabilities, and support needs in one direction and policy questions, perspectives, and priorities in the other. This calls for a special
kind of professional, "neither model builder nor model user, but in a middle position between the two, empathetic with [and knowledgeable in]
both" (Greenberger *et al.* 1976; see also Sundquist 1978, Papon 1979, Weiss
1977). It also calls for special kinds of institutions and support arrangements to protect the independence and credibility of the third-party professionals, especially when the issues are complex, multidisciplinary, and
controversial. Don K. Price (1954) characterized this middle-man role as
"an intervening layer for protection and lubrication" (pp 108—9). Given
improved communication channels, the two communities could work
together very effectively if the decision-making process is structured to
allow it (Wilbanks 1982b, p 108).

In addition to improving personal contacts between analysts and
users, we also need to address the current limitations on information
tools for policy makers. Too often to a user, the policy analysis activity is
a classic "black box": a question goes in, machinery grinds mysteriously,
and an answer comes out. The user is disconnected from the activity, not
a part of it. But we suspect that a policy maker is more likely to use

analysis — and to understand it, to value it, to trust it — if he or she has a more active involvement in it (e.g., Meadows 1981, p 270, Greenberger 1979); this idea lies behind the CITF effort in Colorado, for example, and several other experiments with interactive policy analysis as well (e.g., Donovan *et al.* 1975, Perez 1978).

Can we not start to use the new communication technologies to test this possibility and, if it works, implement it widely? In most of the developed countries — from offices to research laboratories — the trend is to move analytical tools closer to the user and make them more accessible, relying on such developments as desk-top computer terminals and "user-friendly" software. Some parts of the US government now predict that every manager will have a terminal and display unit on his or her office desk within five years. Linked to this trend, such techniques as simulation models and interactive computer graphics offer ways for policy makers to become quasi-analysts (see, for example, Bossel 1977, Loucks *et al.* 1982). If this were to happen, users of analysis could participate in real-time choices of parameters and see the impact on results (Vogely 1974), meeting some of their own needs for quick-response analysis themselves. In the meantime, professional analysts could spend more of their time concentrating on tool development, where their technical skills would be used more fully. In other words, it may be possible — by allying ourselves with emerging communication technologies and social trends — to accomplish two desirable things at the same time: (*a*) to bring policy and analysis closer together by bringing policy makers closer to us, rather than making all the adjustments ourselves; and (*b*) to reduce the pressure on us to play roles that underutilize our skills.

Investing in Anticipation

A further need, and a critical one in most countries, is to persuade both society and the policy-making system that good policy analysis must rest on a strong research base. We simply cannot do a very good job of answering questions about policy issues as they arise unless (*a*) the basic and applied research community provides us with building blocks of theory and methodology, (*b*) we can find support for model development and improvement as well as utilization, and (*c*) these activities are related to interactions that policy makers consider critical — or that they should, or that they eventually will.

In the US, it is an accepted principle that the national government has certain responsibilities for ensuring that the nation maintains an adequate "technology base": ongoing programs of basic research in the sciences that are fundamental for meeting such national needs as for energy, and a wide variety of other supporting research to ensure that problems can be solved and bottlenecks removed if they should appear in the future. For policy analysis, however, the difficulty is that this commitment has been focused almost entirely on the physical and life sciences and their extensions. For important questions that lie outside the domain of technological, ecological, and health research, an equivalent system of research support is not provided, even though the need is as great and the rationale is the same. As a consequence, too little basic and applied research is being done to help us reduce specification errors, deal with structural change, and meet other technical needs in policy analysis; and our performance suffers. By the standards of research support to the physical sciences, the cost of lessening these constraints can be small, and the long-term payoff per dollar invested is likely to be high.

Besides supporting relatively basic research, we need to invest in more practical model development. When policy issues are constantly changing and the state of the art is constantly advancing, merely supporting the use of available models and other analytical capabilities means that we are left with increasingly outdated tools. Every year, both the capabilities and the people who apply them fall farther behind the needs for their services. Perhaps the most effective way to address this problem is to take a hard look at our mechanisms for supporting policy analysis (e.g., Weiss 1977, pp 6–7, Wilbanks 1982a). For instance, many of the problems might be solved if we could find some ways to provide support at least slightly in excess of what is needed to meet urgent needs (if necessary, as a kind of surcharge) and to de-bureaucratize the process of supporting policy analysis, giving analysts more discretion in allocating resources and steering the overall effort. Two possibilities for this are a greater use of multi-year grants and contracts, adding stability to a policy analysis effort (allowing analysts to work on capability improvement in the lulls between crises), and greater use of general support grants to institutions, perhaps along the lines of the research institutes in the USSR and many European countries, holding them accountable over a period of time for their use of the support, but not specifying exactly what it is to be used for.

But none of these attractive options makes much sense for society unless they can be targeted to meet the future needs of policy analysis. In terms of both topics and technical capabilities, they must be anticipatory, related to emerging policy issues rather than just to the priorities of research disciplines. There is no *a priori* reason why basic research priorities cannot be established at least partly on the basis of policy and policy analysis needs. Some of the resulting work might be unconventional in disciplinary terms, but the new directions could turn out to advance the sciences as well as to advance the art of policy making.

Developing portfolios of capabilities

A constant challenge in policy analysis is the conflict between a need on the one hand to develop a comprehensive grasp of interaction effects, which implies large, complex models, and a need on the other hand to produce results quickly, which implies simple, lean approaches to analysis. Some of the gaps between policy analysis in theory and in practice may result from our tendency not to treat this latter need as professionally as the former — and our inability in so many cases to link the two different kinds of approaches.

One of the answers, it appears, is to see simplification as an important and interesting challenge for science (e.g., Wilbanks 1982b, pp 103–5; Issaev *et al.* 1982, pp 217ff). But such an effort should be linked directly with broader-scale work, not separated from it. Large, comprehensive models can be used as tools to help us decide which effects to emphasize in our simple ones; they can help us estimate and calibrate our quick-response capabilities; and they can be invaluable in developing a broader qualitative view of policy effects. In a sense, we need to work toward a nested family of models, with a set of simple, quick, well focused tools of analysis resting securely in the arms of more comprehensive modeling frameworks, the various levels drawing nourishment from each other symbiotically.

This is only one of several important respects in which our individual tools should be seen as modules within a larger framework. Another example pertains to scales of attention: regional-scale policy analysis as an interactive part of a system which also includes national and local policy analysis (see Chapter 1). For such a system, we need families of tools for each level, together with linkages so that we can assess interaction effects between levels. In the meantime, our portfolio is only as strong as its weakest part.

Broadening the meaning of analysis

Finally, we need to enlarge the frame of "policy analysis" to ensure that it does not exclude such important aspects of policy impact as processes (as contrasted with outcomes) and preferences. The fact that such factors may be hard — or even inappropriate — to quantify is no excuse for ignoring them in our attempts to deal with all sorts of relevant policy impacts in a systematic way. At this point, our most pressing deficiency is that we have trouble integrating the results of quantitative analysis, qualitative analysis, and expert judgment (Wilbanks 1982b).

The case studies in this book illustrate very clearly how important it is to combine formal analysis with consensual interactions between interested parties, and a growing literature on "integrated assessment" offers a wide range of experience with this. In addition, experiments are beginning to appear that attempt to integrate the preferences of decision makers and other interested parties into composite models (e.g., Buehring *et al.* 1978, Hafkamp and Nijkamp, in Lakshmanan and Nijkamp 1980, pp 162–8)

Conclusions

In conclusion, there is little disagreement about the state of policy analysis in practice as a professional activity. As analysts, we are convinced of the need for what we do; and we continue to see signs that society agrees with us, at least in principle. And we are convinced of the value of what we do; we believe we can demonstrate that policy analysis is often useful, perhaps not in making precise predictions, but certainly in developing qualitative insights about policy effects (e.g., Timenes 1982, House and Williams 1981, p 23).

Likewise, there is considerable agreement about the role our analysis plays in policymaking. Most of the time, our insights find their way into policy choices indirectly. As we release our results for public information and comment, they influence society's general "climate of understanding" about a policy issue, and this set of opinions flows in to decision makers from staff, acquaintances, and other parties in the political process (Weiss 1977). Consequently, our contributions are most important before decisions are made; afterward, they may be highly visible, but their influence is likely to be weaker (Timenes 1982, p 99). Finally, we generally agree that our analytical capabilities and usual modes of operation are often inadequate for the job to be done. In particular, we need to develop more effective, more direct ways to interact with policy makers themselves, and we need to find ways of filling some of the empty spaces in our tool bag.

In the meantime, we continue with policy analysis for the same reasons we started: we believe that science can help make policy better, to the larger benefit of society, and we find that the effort is intellectually interesting. The former motive helps to tide us over the times when the latter is not so true, and the latter helps to sustain us when we doubt whether the first is being realized.

References

Ackoff, R.L. and Emery, F.E. (1972) *On Purposeful Systems* (Chicago: Aldine-Atherton).

Agnew, N.M. and Pike, S.W. (1978) *The Science Game*, 2nd edn (Englewood Cliffs, NJ: Prentice-Hall).

Albegov, M., Andersson, Å.E., and Snickars, F. (1982) *Regional Development Modeling: Theory and Practice* (Amsterdam: North-Holland).

Bauer, R.A. (1968) The study of policy formulation: An introduction, in R.A. Bauer and K. Gergen (Eds) *The Study of Policy Formulation* (New York: Free Press).

Bolton, R. (1979) *Multiregional Models in Policy Analysis*. Paper presented at the Conference on Modeling and Multiregional Economic Systems, June 1979.

Bossel, H. (1977) *Concepts and Tools of Computer-assisted Policy Analysis* (Basel: Birkhäuser Verlag).

Buehring, W.A., Foell, W.K., and Keeney, R.L. (1978) Examining energy/environment policy using decision analysis. *Energy Systems and Policy* 2:341–67.

Boulding, K. (1979) In extremis. *Technology Review* August/September: 8–9.

Bunn, D.W. and Thomas, H. (Eds) (1978) *Formal Methods in Policy Formulation* (Basel: Birkhäuser Verlag).

Coates, J. (1977) *What is the Public Policy Issue?* Paper presented at the Symposium on Judgment and Choice in Public Policy, American Association for the Advancement of Science, February 1977.

Dacey, M. (1971) Some comments on population density models, tractable and otherwise. *Papers of the Regional Science Association* 27:129–30.

Donovan, J.J., *et al.* (1975) *Application of a Generalized Management Information System to Energy Policy and Decision Making* (Energy Laboratory, Massachusetts Institute of Technology).

Dror, Y. (1971) *Ventures in Policy Sciences* (New York: Elsevier).

Dye, T.R. and Gray, V. (Eds) (1980) *The Determinants of Public Policy* (Lexington: Heath-Lexington).

Easton, D. (1953) *The Political System* (New York: Knopf).

Fischer, F. (1980) *Politics, Values, and Public Policy* (Boulder, CO: Westview Press).

Greenberger, M. (1977) Closing the circuit between modelers and decision makers. *EPRI Journal* 2:6–13.

Greenberger, M. (1979) Getting to know policy models, in *The Interface between Model Builder and Decision Maker*, Symposium Papers, Energy Modeling II, Institute of Gas Technology, Chicago.

Greenberger, M., Crenson, M., and Crissey, B. (1976) *Models in the Policy Process* (New York: Russel Sage Foundation).

Greenberger, M. and Richels, R. (1979) Assessing energy policy models. *Annual Review of Energy* 4:467–500.

Gregg, P.M. (Ed) (1976) *Problems of Theory in Policy Analysis* (Lexington: Heath-Lexington).

Häfele, W. and Kirchmayer, L.K. (Eds) (1981) *Modeling of Large-Scale Energy Systems*, Proceedings of an IIASA/IFAC Symposium. IIASA Proceedings Series Vol. 12 (Oxford: Pergamon).

Hogan, W. (1978) *Energy Modeling: Building Understanding for Better Use.* Paper presented at the Lawrence Symposium on Systems and Decision Sciences, Berkeley, CA, October 1978.

Hoos, I.A. (1972) *Systems Analysis in Public Policy* (Berkeley, CA: University of California Press).

House, P.W. and Williams, T. (1981) Using models for policy analysis. *Energy Systems and Policy* 5:1–24.

Issaev, B., Nijkamp, P., Rietveld, P., and Snickars, F. (Eds) (1982) *Multiregional Economic Modeling: Practice and Prospect* (Amsterdam: North-Holland).

Jenkins, W.I. (1978) *Policy Analysis: A Political and Organizational Perspective* (New York: St. Martin's).

Kash, D.E. (1977) Observations on interdisciplinary studies and government roles, in R. Scribner and R. Chalk (Eds) *Adapting Science to Social Needs* (Washington: American Association for the Advancement of Science).

Kash, D.E. (1982) Impact assessment premises – right and wrong. *Impact Assessment Bulletin* 1:5–14.

Kash, D.E. and Rycroft, R. (1984) *U.S. Energy Policy: Crisis and Complacency* (Norman: University of Oklahoma).

Lakshmanan, T.R. and Nijkamp, P. (Eds) (1980) *Economic–Environmental–Energy Interactions* (Boston, MA: Martinus Nijhoff).

Landsberg, H., *et al.* (1979) *Energy: The Next Twenty Years* (Cambridge, MA: Bal-linger).

Lee, R., Barron, W., Perlack, R., Kerley, C., Peterson, B., Kolstad, C., and Burris, A. (1982) *U.S. Regional Coal Production Forecasts for the Year 1990.* ORNL/TM-8468/VI, V2, V3 (Oak Ridge, TN: Energy Division, Oak Ridge National Laboratory).

Lee, R. and Thomas, C. (1983) *Recommendations for the Analysis of Non-fuel Mineral Supply.* Report for the US Bureau of Mines, contract No. J0113112 (Oak Ridge, TN: Energy Division, Oak Ridge National Laboratory). Available from National Technical Information Service, Springfield, VA.

Lerner, D. and Lasswell, H.D. (1951) *The Policy Sciences: Recent Developments in Scope and Method* (Stanford, CT: Stanford University Press).

Loucks, D.P., *et al.* (1982) Water resources and environmental planning using interactive graphics. *Water Supply and Management* 6:303–20.

Lynn, L.E., Jr. (Ed) (1978) *Knowledge and Policy: The Uncertain Connection* (Washington, DC: National Academy of Sciences).

Majone, G. (1980) *Beware the Pitfalls: A Short Guide to Avoiding Errors in Sys-tems Analysis.* Executive Report ER-80-2 (Laxenburg, Austria: Interna-tional Institute for Applied Systems Analysis).

Majone, G. and Quade, E.S. (1980) *Pitfalls of Analysis* (Chichester, UK: Wiley).

Mayer, R.R. and Greenwood, E. (1980) *The Design of Social Policy Research* (Englewood Cliffs, NJ: Prentice-Hall).

Meadows, D. (1981) A critique of the IIASA energy models. *The Energy Journal* 2:17–28.

Meadows, D., *et al.* (1982) *Groping in the Dark: The First Decade of Global Model-ling* (Chichester, UK: Wiley).

Nagel, S.S. and Neef, M. (1979) *Policy Analysis in Social Science Research* (Bev-erly Hills, CA: Sage).

Olsson, G. (1975) *Birds in Egg.* Michigan Geographical Publication No. 15, Ann Arbor.

Papon, P. (1979) Centres of decision in French science policy. *Research Policy* 8:384–98.

Perez, G. (1978) Simulation, modelling, and decisions in energy systems, in M. Carver and M. Hamza (Eds) *Proc. Int. Symp. on Simulation, Modelling, and Decisions in Energy Systems* (Anaheim, CA: Acta).

Poister, T.H. (1978) *Public Program Analysis* (Baltimore: University Park Press).

Price, D.K. (1954) *Government and Science* (New York: New York University Press).

Rein, M. (1976) *Social Science and Public Policy* (Harmondsworth, UK: Penguin).

Rose, R. (Ed) (1976) *The Dynamics of Public Policy* (Beverly Hills, CA: Sage).

Schlesinger, J.R. (1980) Energy policy: An economist's confessions. *The Energy Journal* 1:218.

Schurr, S., *et al.* (1979) *Energy in America's Future: The Choices Before Us* (Bal-timore, MD: Johns Hopkins University Press).

Scioli, F.P., Jr. and Cook, T.J. (1975) *Methodologies for Analyzing Public Policies* (Lexington: Heath-Lexington).

Snow, C.P. (1959) *The Two Cultures and the Scientific Revolution* (New York: Cambridge University Press).

Sternlight, D. (1978) Making energy policy analysis relevant, in *Energy Modeling and Net Energy Analysis* (Chicago, IL: Institute of Gas Technology).

Stobaugh, R. and Yergin, D. (1979) *Energy Future* (New York: Random House).

Sundquist, J.L. (1978) Research brokerage: The weak link, in L.E. Lynn (Ed) *Knowledge and Policy: The Uncertain Connection* (Washington, DC: National Academy of Sciences) pp 126–44.

Timenes, N., Jr. (1982) Planning and the evolution of energy policy. *Energy Systems and Policy* 6:97–108.

Vogely, W. (1974) Energy modeling and policy making: A review. *Energy Policy,* special publication.

Weinberg, A. (1979) *Energy Policy and Mathematics* (Oak Ridge, TN: Institute for Energy Analysis, Oak Ridge Associated Universities).

Weiss, C.H. (Ed) (1977) *Using Social Research in Public Policy Making* (Lexington: Heath-Lexington).

White, I.L., *et al.* (1979) *Energy from the West: Impact Analysis Report.* 2 vols (Washington, DC: Environmental Protection Agency).

Wilbanks, T.J. (1982a) *Attitudes of Scientists toward Public Servants.* Paper prepared for a Symposium on Science and the Career Public Service, American Association for the Advancement of Science, January 1982.

Wilbanks, T.J. (1982b) Is comprehensive analysis of critical interactions possible?, in G. Daneke (Ed) *Energy, Economics, and the Environment* (Lexington: Heath-Lexington) pp 91–110.

Wilbanks, T.J. (1984) Impact assessment and policy formulation. *Environmental Impact Assessment Review.* (To be published.)

Ziemba, W.T. and Schwartz, S.L. (Eds) (1980) *Energy Policy Modeling: United States and Canadian Experience,* 2 vols (Boston, MA: Martinus Nijhoff).

Large-Scale Energy Projects: Assessment of Regional Consequences
T.R. Lakshmanan and B. Johansson (Editors)
Elsevier Science Publishers B.V. (North-Holland)
© IIASA, 1985

CHAPTER 11

Energy Decisions and Models: Review and Prospects

T.R. Lakshmanan and B. Johansson

Introduction

After the 1973–74 oil crisis one can identify two generations of energy studies. The first addressed three pressing issues: (1) the so-called "tight fit" between energy use and economic growth and the anxiety about economic growth in the context of rising energy prices; (2) the potential for energy conservation in the intermediate term; and (3) the range of technological choices in switching to more abundant fuels, given the demand for environmental quality. One outcome of these studies was a widespread recognition that there is considerable potential for switching among fuels and for conservation, and that the level of energy consumption can be varied without adversely affecting economic growth.

This book focuses on the second generation of energy studies by surveying the experiences with energy policy strategies in two energy-exporting countries (the USSR and Canada) and two energy importers (the US and Sweden) who have combined new production, conservation, and fuel switching strategies with concomitant adjustments in the economic, environmental, and metropolitan structures. The various models and methods used in the four countries to assess and manage the consequences associated with such strategies have been developed in what we would view as a second generation of analytical studies. These studies attempted to develop information pertinent to such strategies.

In this chapter we summarize what we have learned and missed from our comparative study with regard to (1) the context and scope, (2) the treatment of analytical issues, and (3) the interface between analysis and decision making in the various decision and analytical settings covered in the book. Similarities and differences between the cases are summarized in the six tables in this chapter.

The Context and Scope of the Case Studies

The context of the US case study carried out in the late 1970s was the lively energy debate that raged throughout the decade, and which involved basic value conflicts, summarized by Brubaker (1972, 1975) as a conflict between the "expansionist" and "limited" views regarding economic growth, resource use, and environmental protection (see also Schurr *et al.* 1979).[1] Public discussions covered basic questions such as (i) the futures people desired, (ii) distribution of cost, benefits, and risks associated with energy alternatives, and (iii) the legitimacy of economic growth and its effects on the environment as well as on the intra- and international distribution of incomes, and the morality of nuclear power.

The energy debate also focused on the distributional effects of various energy policies with "windfall" gains and losses associated with unstable energy prices, and a corresponding re-evaluation of oil and gas reserves in producing regions. Moreover, many of the solutions proposed during the energy debate involved considerable uncertainty coupled with heavy capital needs and issues of technological feasibility. Finally, the processes by which decisions on energy conservation and new production are made, became in the 1970s more broadly participatory with a wide range of interest groups and governmental agencies pressing their diverse points of view.

Much of this background picture is true also for Sweden, but the policy response in Sweden was different from that in the US. The reason lies in the differences in resource endowments and Sweden's greater dependence on oil imports. In Sweden the political system began quickly to emphasize the desirability of adaption and flexibility (partly based on diversification) in the energy system. There was also a widespread agreement on a policy of greater conservation in a society already far more energy efficient than the US.

The post-1973 increase in energy prices promoted greater energy production in the USSR and Canada, and induced a strong policy support for this change. The major issue in such a context of energy resource development in remote resource frontiers was related to the logistic and investment problems of "getting the gas out", and the environmental implications of extraction. The overriding objective became to facilitate increased production and exports from producing regions.

---

[1] Ehrlich *et al.* (1977) used the terms "cornucopians and neo-Malthusians" to distinguish between technological optimists and conservationists.

Table 11.1. Objectives of the studies and associated interest groups.

Study	Objectives of the study	Categories of clients and interest groups
Synfuels acceleration program (USA)	Assessment of feasible locations of coal and oil shale mining plants, given existing and expected environmental constraints.	Study enabled the DOE to support the President's acceleration program. Three interest groups: (i) national and regional policy makers, (ii) oil and coal industries, (iii) environmentalist groups.
CITF system (Colorado, USA)	Creation of a consensus-based information and model system for generating alternative projections of socioeconomic impacts of oil shale and other large-scale investments.	Interest groups: (i) state authorities, (ii) local authorities at the county and municipal levels, (iii) energy companies.
Alberta tar sands (Canada)	Collection of baseline data; monitoring of environmental consequences. No explicit policy objectives.	The study is a joint federal/provincial research project. No explicit policy interest.
Siberian gas network (USSR)	Planning efforts to manage constraints for establishing gas extraction plants and for constructing associated gas networks.	The study is a part of the normal planning process. The coordination has to balance various sectoral and regional goals, as well as national–regional interface constraints.
Commission on Consequences (Sweden)	The objective was to support a referendum by assessing multidimensional consequences of abolishing nuclear power.	The study was led by a parliamentary commission. The interest group comprised political parties that were all internally divided.
Stockholm study (Sweden)	Evaluating alternative designs of a new energy system for a whole region, including reshaped structures of the urban environment.	Interest groups: (i) national and regional policy makers, (ii) municipalities and associated authorities and companies, (iii) private industry.

The differences between the four countries are revealed in Table 11.1, which summarizes the basic objectives of the case studies, and the more important interest groups associated with each energy project. Behind these objectives one can identify a common tendency in the US and Sweden to initiate and promote investments to reduce the vulnerability to changes in the international energy markets. The same changes constituted export opportunities in the USSR and Canada.

Table 11.2 emphasizes that some of the case studies were strongly integrated with the corresponding policy formulation and decision-making processes. This is particularly true of three of the studies: the Synfuels Acceleration Program, the Commission on Consequences, and one part of the Stockholm study. These studies were surrounded by interest groups with partially conflicting objectives. Results from the studies were used in the political debates in the media and they were used as inputs to decision making. They were all carried through under heavy time constraints, which seems to be a necessary characteristic of a study intended as a conflict-resolving input to actual decision making.

The Cumulative Impacts Task Force (CITF) was initiated in order to create a continuously updated model system that could be used (at short notice) whenever a new investment project had to be evaluated; since the clients are participating in the process, both the time for analysis and the time for communication is reduced. Thus, the CITF system constitutes a mean of managing the time pressures in situations involving decision makers with conflicting objectives. We may also note that the Siberian assessment project made use of a continuous planning process; in this respect it may be compared with the CITF system.

The Treatment of Analytical Issues

A comparison of the studies

Figure 11.1 provides a framework for comparing the national case studies by outlining a multilevel, multidimensional picture of repercussions through the social system. It distinguishes three subsystems — economic, environmental, and local community — in which the impacts of energy projects in one region are registered at three geographical scales.

The scheme outlined in Figure 11.1 aims at identifying the analytical agenda for the case studies. Regarding the choice of impact assessment methods, two factors are relevant. First, the *degree of discontinuity* brought about by a large-scale energy project affects the strength and the type of potential repercussions. Second, the *complexity of the disturbances* or impacts determines the degree to which a change will lead to local and marginal effects (as contrasted with global and non-marginal effects), and effects that occur within limited time intervals or that endure over long periods.

Table 11.2. Interface between assessment results and policy making.

Study	Assessment results	Interface between assessment study and policy making
Synfuels acceleration program (USA)	(i) A ranking of sites into subgroups; (ii) sufficient sites were shown to be feasible according to selected criteria.	The study was carried through by the DOE, together with consultants; study results were inputs to decision processes of the President and Congress.
CITF system (Colorado, USA)	An information and model system was created and a consensus-preserving procedure established.	The whole process is controlled by the client group; actual model work has been carried through by consultants supervised by committees representing private and public clients.
Alberta tar sands (Canada)	Collection of baseline data; *ex post* recording of environmental effects; exercises with socioeconomic models.	The various environmental studies and boom town analyses seem to have had small effects on policy formulation.
Siberian gas network (USSR)	Formation of long-term overall plans and schedules for construction activities as regards gas network and settlements.	Assessment results are integral parts of the planning and decision-making process. The roles of different decision-making bodies unclear.
Commission on Consequences (Sweden)	Assessment of alternatives available in the referendum. Calculation of income per capita reductions caused by abolishing nuclear power.	Results were intensively used in the political debates preceding the referendum. Representatives from the different political parties and opinion groups participated in the committee and subcommittees of the study.
Stockholm study (Sweden)	Evaluation of different investment and design programs related to various alternative energy supply systems to be introduced in the period 1980–2010.	Industries, authorities, and planners participated in the assessment studies. Direct contacts between analysts and decision makers.

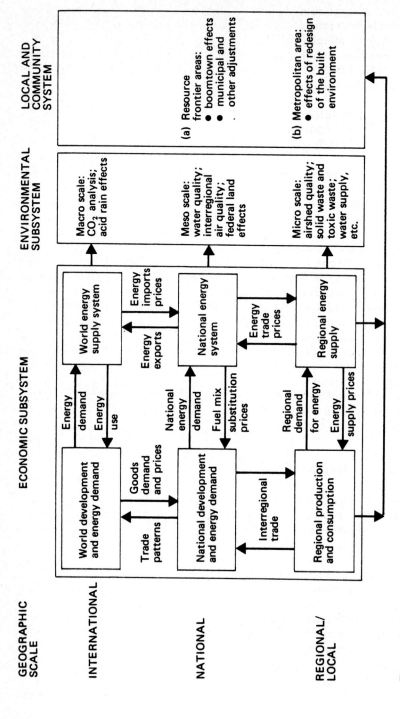

Figure 11.1. A framework for assessing energy impacts.

A system change may be characterized as complex if it involves synergistic effects between changes in several subsystems, time periods, etc. When synergistic effects are small, certain repercussions may be disregarded and the assessment may be decomposed into a series of separate analyses. One may identify at least three such domains of separability across the case studies (see Table 11.3):

- separability of subsystem changes;
- separability of impacts in different time periods;
- separability in different regions or zones.

Table 11.4 summarizes the comparison of the four case studies and sheds more light on the complexity of economic impacts. The Swedish study was clearly the leader in the range of economic impacts considered. The magnitude of the proposed investments in conservation and fuel switching is relatively large in relation to the Swedish economy, and the economic impacts are consequently highly nontrivial. In the US study the focus was on environmental assessment, and even though only a few economic impacts were assessed, the databases and functional relationships from large economic models were used. The Soviet case focused primarily on economic interactions and can in this respect be contrasted with the Canadian study in which economic impacts were not analyzed.

Table 11.5 illustrates how environmental impacts were analyzed in the different studies. Comparing this table with Table 11.4 we can see that economic aspects have been suppressed in those cases in which the assessment concentrates on environmental consequences; to some extent the Soviet and Swedish studies display a reverse tendency. Except for the Stockholm and CITF studies, limited attention is paid to local community effects (Table 11.6).

Future directions for analysis

While a number of analytical issues have been tackled in these studies, there are a few more that should be addressed in future studies of this kind. These include:

- *Distributional issues* related to ownership of resource assets, labor dislocations, and boom town effects.
- *Dynamic adjustment processes* induced by energy changes. The changes themselves may occur both in short, medium, and long terms. Simultaneously, the time profiles of the corresponding responses vary markedly by industrial sector, type of household, and type of public agency.

Table 11.3. Temporal and spatial scales.

Study	Temporal scale	Spatial scale
Synfuels acceleration program (USA)	Mainly static analysis including existing and anticipated environmental restrictions and regulations.	Hierarchical divisions with states as regions and with an interregional subdivision into county and subcounty areas. Limited interregional analysis.
CITF system (Colorado, USA)	The system produces a sequence of annually specified projections of consequences given a prespecified sequence of impact-generating investments.	A fine subdivision of the selected counties into jurisdiction areas. Certain interregional flows analyzed like migration and commuting phenomena.
Alberta tar sands (Canada)	Investigation of existing environmental conditions. Diffusion models showing potential effects over time.	Investigation of local areas around the tar sands plants. No consideration of interprovincial relations.
Siberian gas network (USSR)	1, 5, and 10 years as integral parts of a 20-year planning period with a moving plan horizon.	Primarily top-down approach starting with the investments in an international and national perspective. Multiregional feasibility and interregional allocation of deliveries. Local and intraregional analysis of settlements and networks.
Commission on Consequences (Sweden)	Scenarios of consequences for the period 1980–2000. Only limited analysis of intertemporal adjustment processes.	Primarily top-down approach as regards energy and economy assessments. Regional and local subdivisions. Separate analyses of local areas with special problems. Only limited interregional analysis.
Stockholm study (Sweden)	Time paths for the period 1980–2000. Time divided into intervals with intertemporal dependences. Specific attention paid to the dynamics of gradual introduction of new subsystems (techniques) into the energy supply system.	Economic development based on a top-down structure supplemented by multiregional analyses. Regional sectoral analyses. Zonal specification for the assessment of alternative designs of energy systems and associated restructuring of urban environment, etc.

Table 11.4. The economic impacts and assessment methods.

	USA	Canada	USSR	Sweden
Cost structure and relative prices in the economy			Extraction and transmission costs evaluated against market prices in Europe.	Changes in the unit cost level of major economic sectors in response to world energy prices derived.
Substitution and technology				Interfuel substitution, factor substitution and technological processes in the energy sector captured.
Multiregional, multisectoral allocation			Multiregional allocation of labor and capital investments. Transportation networks.	National consequences of large energy projects allocated to regions in terms of employment, production, investments, energy use, etc.
Mix of energy supply systems	Alternative synfuels technologies and their characteristics.		The investment, labor, and material implications of the new energy technologies estimated.	The essential stages of the metropolitan energy chains ranging from primary energy to final energy consumption identifiable.
Assessment methods	Though specific economic impacts were not estimated in the prior studies, such capability exists from models such as SEAS, PIES, Hudson–Jorgenson–BESOM models, etc. (see Chapter 6).	Though no economic models were used in this study, models for such purposes exist in Helliwell model, Alberta energy planning model, etc.	The Siberian Power Institute model available for description of the energy supply system; also the IIASA model IMPACT.	An integrated set of models used: the Bergman national model, multiregional, multisectoral models (MORSE, PROMISE), and METRO-MESSAGE, a dynamic LP model of the Stockholm energy supply system.

Table 11.5. Resources and natural environment: Impact dimensions and methods.

	USA	Canada	USSR	Sweden
Resource impacts	Water availability, transportation, federal land management.		Seasonal constraints on energy production.	
Media pollution	Micro scale: air quality, solid waste, toxic waste; Meso scale: water quality; Macro scale: CO_2 analysis, acid rain.	Air and water quality assessment.		Pollution consequences of alternative energy technologies, particularly coal processing.
Ecological effects	Intrusions into wildlife habitats.	Absorption capacity of biotic processes.		Ecological impacts of heat pump system in Sweden.
Assessment methods	Aggregate analysis and the use of stylized terrain in environmental quality models in phase I; in phase II, media quality models used at the individual facility and sub-county levels.	Monitoring procedures, air quality diffusion models (CRSTER, LIRAQ); collection of baseline biotic and abiotic information.		Fixed-coefficient models of pollution effects of alternative energy technologies.

Table 11.6. Local and community impacts.

Impacts	USA	Canada	USSR	Sweden
Job creation and workplace location	Production, construction, and service workforce; worker productivity at community and jurisdiction levels.	Simple estimates of construction and production workers.	Project workers and multipliers.	The spatial distribution of future activites and workers in the Stockholm region, given the redesigned regional energy supply system.
Migration and housing	Population and housing demand for the project community.	Population forecasts for the community.	Population and housing requirements.	Future geographic patterns of population, household formation and demand, and housing structures under the new energy supply system.
Public construction and municipal finance	Public expenditures, capital outlays; revenues and fiscal balance.	Infrastructure demands.	Infrastructure demands.	Transport network, land-use planning, and locational decisions.
Assessment methods	CITF model system comprising baseline activity forecasts, county projections, subcounty allocation modules. Fixed-coefficient calculations will not capture nonlinear feedback effects between spatially specified impacts.	BOOM-H model (developed originally by Los Alamos Lab) adapted for Fort McMurray.		An elaborate set of sophisticated models of household location, housing type and land use, e.g., Markov-type multiregional demographic model; logit-type housing demand model; land-use and housing allocation models.

- *Regional, national, and international linkages* should be an important item of future efforts. Moreover, it is important to consider the time profiles of spatial interactions.
- *Interactions between public and private sectors* are especially strong in the area of energy system development. An ideal model should incorporate the behavioral constraints on both sectors.

Energy Analysis and the Decision Interface

The decision environment, styles of decision making, and the institutional frameworks for decision implementation within a society are the outcome of several factors such as the political structure, the constellation of interest groups, the ground rules for the interactions between interest groups, and the avenues for conflict management.

Since energy facility planning is one dimension of regional physical planning, the emphasis in the Soviet case is on the coordination of different levels of decision making as well as of the agencies responsible for sectoral planning. Since the energy projects in the US and Sweden are located in pluralistic settings, the corresponding studies are far more process-oriented. In such settings the key issue is how the analytical results are used, if at all. Further, there is always a tension between scientific policy analysis and the decision-making environment in democratic, pluralistic societies. Policy analysis in such contexts is very much a newcomer.

Future investigations to address the above aspects should, in our view, attempt the following:

- Greenberger *et al.* (1983) questions the role of the expert in energy decision making and the need for institutional support for that role in the US. The analytical tradition of studying energy systems uses the economic paradigm (choice under conditions of scarcity) as a starting point, which abstracts from institutions and organizations that are directly involved in decision making. The appropriate analytical tradition of decision making from an organizational perspective is that of political science, which focuses on choice under conditions of uncertainty. Moreover, the energy decision environment encompasses not only energy decisions but also *implementation*. A comprehensive approach should therefore include three basic aspects: analytical rationality, value conflict and resolution, and bureaucratic maintenance.[2]

---

[2] Various interpretations of the notion of a bureaucratic perspective can be found in Allison (1971), Steinbrunner (1975), and Linstone *et al.* (1981).

- Different approaches to energy decision analysis focus on the substance of the policy, the process of its formulation, and its
  effectiveness in terms of impacts (goal achievements), and ignore
  action or implementation components. A more complete analysis of
  the policy process would need an understanding of the way energy
  policies are modified and reinterpreted during implementation.
- T.S. Eliot suggests that the technique of cooking cabbages is a man-
  ifestation of culture, and there are books blending cuisine and
  anthropology to bear him out. We would argue that energy policy is
  no less a matter of culture. The differences in the nature of energy
  policies can be understood in comparative terms, if they are placed
  firmly in the political, geographic, economic and sociohistorical contexts of each country.

These final reflections suggest an approach that we believe will help clarify a tenable role in affluent societies for modeling and analysis of energy
decisions.

References

Allison, G. (1971) *Essence of Decision: Explaining the Cuban Missile Crisis* (New
    York: Little, Brown, & Co.).
Brubaker, S. (1972) *To Live on Earth: Man and his Environment in Perspective*
    (Baltimore: The John Hopkins University Press).
Brubaker, S. (1975) *In Command of Tomorrow* (Baltimore: The John Hopkins
    University Press).
Ehrlich, P.R., *et al.* (1977) *Ecoscience: Population Resources and Environment*
    (San Francisco: Freeman).
Greenberger, M., Brewer, G.D., Hogan, W.W., and Russell, M. (1983) *Caught
    Unawares: The Energy Decade in Retrospect* (Cambridge, MA: Ballinger).
Linstone, H.A., *et al.* (1981) The multiple perspective concept with applications
    to technological assessment and other decision areas. *Technological Fore-
    casting and Social Change* 20:275–325.
Schurr, S.H., *et al.* (1979) *Energy in America's Future* (Baltimore, MD: Johns
    Hopkins University Press).
Steinbrunner, J.D. (1975) *The Cybernetic Theory of Decision* (Princeton, NJ:
    Princeton University Press).

AUTHOR INDEX

SUBJECT INDEX